ABOUT THIS PUBLICATION

FOR SERVICE ASSISTANCE

Customer Service
1.704.898.0770

North Carolina General Statues is published by The Muliti-Media Group of Greater Charlotte in Charlotte, North Carolina. Copyright 2015 by the Multi-Media Group of Greater Charlotte. This book or parts thereof may not be reproduced in any form, stored in a retrieval system, or transmitted in any form by any means—electronic, mechanical, photocopy, recording or otherwise—without prior written permission of the publisher, except as provided by United States of America copyright law.

The records required by U.S. Code 2257(a) through (c) and the pertinent regulations 28 C.F.R. Cli. 1, Part 75 with respect to this publication and all materials associated with such records are maintained by The Multi-Media Group of Greater Charlotte, Publisher and available for review by Attorney General.

www.visionbooks.org

Copyright © 2015 by MMGGC
All rights reserved!

TID: 5109319
ISBN (10) digit: 150325478X
ISBN (13) digit: 978-1503254787

123-4-56789-01239-Paperback
123-4-56789-01239-Hardback

First Edition

090520140547

Printed in the United States of America

2015 EDITION

North Carolina Criminal Law And Procedure-Pamphlet # 90

Printed In conjunction with the Administration of the Courts

North Carolina Criminal Law and Procedure
Pamphlet Reference Guide

Chapters	Pamphlet
Chapter 1 Civil Procedure	1
Chapter 1 Civil Procedure (Continue)	2
Chapter 1A Rules of Civil Procedure	2
Chapter 1B Contribution.	2
Chapter 1C Enforcement of Judgments.	2
Chapter 1D Punitive Damages.	2
Chapter 1E Eastern Band of Cherokee Indians.	2
Chapter 1F North Carolina Uniform Interstate Depositions and Discovery Act.	2
Chapter 2 - Clerk of Superior Court [Repealed and Transferred.]	3
Chapter 3 - Commissioners of Affidavits and Deeds [Repealed.]	3
Chapter 4 - Common Law	3
Chapter 5 - Contempt [Repealed.]	3
Chapter 5A - Contempt	3
Chapter 6 - Liability for Court Costs	3
Chapter 7 - Courts [Repealed and Transferred.]	3
Chapter 7A – Judicial Department	3
Chapter 7A – Continuation (Judicial Department)	4
Chapter 7A – Continuation (Judicial Department)	5
Chapter 7B - Juvenile Code	5
Chapter 8 - Evidence	6
Chapter 8A - Interpreters for Deaf Persons [Recodified.]	6
Chapter 8B - Interpreters for Deaf Persons	6
Chapter 8C - Evidence Code	6
Chapter 9 - Jurors	6
Chapter 10 - Notaries [Repealed.]	6
Chapter 10A - Notaries [Recodified.]	6
Chapter 10B - Notaries	6
Chapter 11 - Oaths	6
Chapter 12 - Statutory Construction	6
Chapter 13 - Citizenship Restored	6
Chapter 14 - Criminal Law	7
Chapter 14 –Criminal Law (Continuation)	8
Chapter 15 - Criminal Procedure	9
Chapter 15A - Criminal Procedure Act (Continuation)	10
Chapter 15A - Criminal Procedure Act (Continuation)	11
Chapter 15B - Victims Compensation	11
Chapter 15C - Address Confidentiality Program	11
Chapter 16 - Gaming Contracts and Futures	11
Chapter 17 - Habeas Corpus	11

Chapter 17A - Law-Enforcement Officers [Recodified.]	11
Chapter 17B - North Carolina Criminal Justice Education and Training System [Recodified.] Chapter 17C - North Carolina Criminal Justice Education and Training Standards Commission	11 11
Chapter 17D - North Carolina Justice Academy	11
Chapter 17E - North Carolina Sheriffs' Education and Training Standards Commission	11
Chapter 18 - Regulation of Intoxicating Liquors [Repealed.]	12
Chapter 18A - Regulation of Intoxicating Liquors [Repealed.]	12
Chapter 18B - Regulation of Alcoholic Beverages	12
Chapter 18C - North Carolina State Lottery	12
Chapter 19 - Offenses against Public Morals	12
Chapter 19A - Protection of Animals	12
Chapter 20 - Motor Vehicles	13
Chapter 20 - Motor Vehicles (Continuation)	14
Chapter 20 - Motor Vehicles (Continuation)	15
Chapter 20 - Motor Vehicles (Continuation)	16
Chapter 21 - Bills of Lading	17
Chapter 22 - Contracts Requiring Writing	17
Chapter 22A - Signatures	17
Chapter 22B - Contracts Against Public Policy	17
Chapter 22C - Payments to Subcontractors	17
Chapter 23 - Debtor and Creditor	17
Chapter 24 – Interest	17
Chapter 25 – Uniform Commercial Code	18
Chapter 25 – Uniform Commercial Code (Continuation)	19
Chapter 25A – Retail Installment Sales Act	20
Chapter 25B - Credit	20
Chapter 25C - Sales of Artwork	20
Chapter 26 - Suretyship	20
Chapter 27 - Warehouse Receipts [Repealed.]	20
Chapter 28 - Administration [Repealed.]	20
Chapter 28A - Administration of Decedents' Estates	20
Chapter 28B - Estates of Absentees in Military Service	20
Chapter 28C - Estates of Missing Persons	20
Chapter 29 - Intestate Succession	21
Chapter 30 - Surviving Spouses	21
Chapter 31 - Wills	21
Chapter 31A - Acts Barring Property Rights	21
Chapter 31B - Renunciation of Property and Renunciation of Fiduciary Powers Act	21
Chapter 31C - Uniform Disposition of Community Property Rights at Death Act	21
Chapter 32 - Fiduciaries	21
Chapter 32A - Powers of Attorney	21
Chapter 33 - Guardian and Ward [Repealed and Recodified.]	21

Chapter 33A - North Carolina Uniform Transfers to Minors Act	21
Chapter 33B - North Carolina Uniform Custodial Trust Act	21
Chapter 34 - Veterans' Guardianship Act	22
Chapter 35 - Sterilization Procedures	22
Chapter 35A - Incompetency and Guardianship	22
Chapter 36 - Trusts and Trustees [Repealed.]	22
Chapter 36A - Trusts and Trustees	22
Chapter 36B - Uniform Management of Institutional Funds Act [Repealed.]	22
Chapter 36C - North Carolina Uniform Trust Code	22
Chapter 36D - North Carolina Community Third Party Trusts, Pooled Trusts	23
Chapter 36E - Uniform Prudent Management of Institutional Funds Act	23
Chapter 37 - Allocation of Principal and Income [Repealed.]	23
Chapter 37A - Uniform Principal and Income Act	23
Chapter 38 - Boundaries	23
Chapter 38A - Landowner Liability	23
Chapter 39 - Conveyances	23
Chapter 39A - Transfer Fee Covenants Prohibited	23
Chapter 40 - Eminent Domain [Repealed.]	23
Chapter 40A - Eminent Domain	23
Chapter 41 - Estates	23
Chapter 41A - State Fair Housing Act	23
Chapter 42 - Landlord and Tenant	23
Chapter 42A - Vacation Rental Act	23
Chapter 43 - Land Registration	23
Chapter 44 - Liens	24
Chapter 44A - Statutory Liens and Charges	24
Chapter 45 - Mortgages and Deeds of Trust	24
Chapter 45A - Good Funds Settlement Act	24
Chapter 46 - Partition	24
Chapter 47 - Probate and Registration	25
Chapter 47A - Unit Ownership	25
Chapter 47B - Real Property Marketable Title Act	25
Chapter 47C - North Carolina Condominium Act	25
Chapter 47D - Notice of Settlement Act [Expired.]	25
Chapter 47E - Residential Property Disclosure Act	25
Chapter 47F - North Carolina Planned Community Act	25
Chapter 47G - Option to Purchase Contracts	25
Chapter 47H - Contracts for Deed	25
Chapter 48 - Adoptions	26
Chapter 48A - Minors	26
Chapter 49 - Bastardy	26
Chapter 49A - Rights of Children	26
Chapter 50 - Divorce and Alimony	26
Chapter 50A - Uniform Child-Custody Jurisdiction and	

Enforcement Act	26
Chapter 50B - Domestic Violence	26
Chapter 50C - Civil No-Contact Orders	26
Chapter 51 - Marriage	26
Chapter 52 - Powers and Liabilities of Married Persons	27
Chapter 52A - Uniform Reciprocal Enforcement of Support Act [Repealed.]	27
Chapter 52B - Uniform Premarital Agreement Act	27
Chapter 52C - Uniform Interstate Family Support Act	27
Chapter 53 - Banks	27
Chapter 53A - Business Development Corporations and North Carolina Capital Resource Corporations	28
Chapter 53B - Financial Privacy Act	28
Chapter 54 - Cooperative Organizations	28
Chapter 54A - Capital Stock Savings and Loan Associations [Repealed.]	28
Chapter 54B - Savings and Loan Associations	29
Chapter 54C - Savings Banks	29
Chapter 55 - North Carolina Business Corporation Act	30
Chapter 55A - North Carolina Nonprofit Corporation Act	31
Chapter 55B - Professional Corporation Act	31
Chapter 55C - Foreign Trade Zones	31
Chapter 55D - Filings, Names, and Registered Agents for Corporations, Nonprofit Corporations, and Partnerships	31
Chapter 56 - Electric, Telegraph and Power Companies [Repealed.]	31
Chapter 57 - Hospital, Medical and Dental Service Corporations [Recodified.]	31
Chapter 57A - Health Maintenance Organization Act [Recodified.]	31
Chapter 57B Health Maintenance Organization Act [Recodified.]	31
Chapter 57C - North Carolina Limited Liability Company Act.	31
Chapter 58 - Insurance.	32
Chapter 58 - Insurance (Continuation)	33
Chapter 58 - Insurance (Continuation)	34
Chapter 58 - Insurance (Continuation)	35
Chapter 58 - Insurance (Continuation)	36
Chapter 58 - Insurance (Continuation)	37
Chapter 58 - Insurance (Continuation)	38
Chapter 58A - North Carolina Health Insurance Trust Commission [Recodified.]	38
Chapter 59 - Partnership.	39
Chapter 59B - Uniform Unincorporated Nonprofit Association Act.	39
Chapter 60 - Railroads and Other Carriers [Repealed and Transferred.]	39
Chapter 61 - Religious Societies	39
Chapter 62 - Public Utilities	39

Chapter 62 - Public Utilities (Continuation)	40
Chapter 62A - Public Safety Telephone Service And Wireless Telephone Service	40
Chapter 63 - Aeronautics	40
Chapter 63A - North Carolina Global TransPark Authority	40
Chapter 64 - Aliens	40
Chapter 65 – Cemeteries	40
Chapter 66 - Commerce and Business	41
Chapter 67 - Dogs	41
Chapter 68 - Fences and Stock Law	41
Chapter 69 - Fire Protection	41
Chapter 70 - Indian Antiquities, Archaeological Resources and Unmarked Human Skeletal Remains Protection	42
Chapter 71 - Indians [Repealed.]	42
Chapter 71A - Indians	42
Chapter 72 - Inns, Hotels and Restaurants	42
Chapter 73 - Mills	42
Chapter 74 - Mines and Quarries	42
Chapter 74A - Company Police [Repealed.]	42
Chapter 74B - Private Protective Services Act [Repealed.]	42
Chapter 74C - Private Protective Services	42
Chapter 74D - Alarm Systems	42
Chapter 74E - Company Police Act	42
Chapter 74F - Locksmith Licensing Act	42
Chapter 74G - Campus Police Act	42
Chapter 75 - Monopolies, Trusts and Consumer Protection	42
Chapter 75A - Boating and Water Safety	43
Chapter 75B - Discrimination in Business	43
Chapter 75C - Motion Picture Fair Competition Act	43
Chapter 75D - Racketeer Influenced and Corrupt Organizations	43
Chapter 75E - Unlawful Activities in Connection With Certain Corporate Transactions	43
Chapter 76 - Navigation	43
Chapter 76A - Navigation and Pilotage Commissions	43
Chapter 77 - Rivers, Creeks, and Coastal Waters	43
Chapter 78 - Securities Law [Repealed.]	43
Chapter 78A - North Carolina Securities Act	43
Chapter 78B - Tender Offer Disclosure Act [Repealed.]	43
Chapter 78C - Investment Advisers	43
Chapter 78D - Commodities Act	43
Chapter 79 - Strays [Repealed.]	43
Chapter 80 - Trademarks, Brands, etc.	44
Chapter 81 - Weights and Measures [Recodified.]	44
Chapter 81A - Weights and Measures Act of 1975.	44
Chapter 82 - Wrecks [Repealed.]	44
Chapter 83 - Architects [Recodified.]	44

Chapter 83A - Architects	44
Chapter 84 - Attorneys-at-Law	44
Chapter 84A - Foreign Legal Consultants	44
Chapter 85 - Auctions and Auctioneers [Repealed.]	44
Chapter 85A - Bail Bondsmen and Runners [Recodified.]	44
Chapter 85B - Auctions and Auctioneers	44
Chapter 85C - Bail Bondsmen and Runners [Recodified.]	44
Chapter 86 - Barbers [Recodified.]	44
Chapter 86A - Barbers	44
Chapter 87 - Contractors	44
Chapter 88 - Cosmetic Art [Repealed.]	44
Chapter 88A - Electrolysis Practice Act	44
Chapter 88B - Cosmetic Art	45
Chapter 89 - Engineering and Land Surveying [Recodified.]	45
Chapter 89A - Landscape Architects	45
Chapter 89B - Foresters	45
Chapter 89C - Engineering and Land Surveying	45
Chapter 89D - Landscape Contractors	45
Chapter 89E - Geologists Licensing Act	45
Chapter 89F - North Carolina Soil Scientist Licensing Act	45
Chapter 89G - Irrigation Contractors	45
Chapter 90 - Medicine and Allied Occupations	45
Chapter 90 - Medicine and Allied Occupations (Continuation)	46
Chapter 90 - Medicine and Allied Occupations (Continuation)	47
Chapter 90 - Medicine and Allied Occupations (Continuation)	48
Chapter 90A - Sanitarians and Water and Wastewater Treatment Facility Operators	48
Chapter 90B - Social Worker Certification and Licensure Act	48
Chapter 90C - North Carolina Recreational Therapy Licensure Act	48
Chapter 90D - Interpreters and Transliterators	48
Chapter 91 - Pawnbrokers [Repealed.]	48
Chapter 91A - Pawnbrokers Modernization Act of 1989	48
Chapter 92 - Photographers [Deleted.]	48
Chapter 93 - Certified Public Accountants	48
Chapter 93A - Real Estate License Law	49
Chapter 93B - Occupational Licensing Boards	49
Chapter 93C - Watchmakers [Repealed.]	49
Chapter 93D - North Carolina State Hearing Aid Dealers and Fitters Board.	49
Chapter 93E - North Carolina Appraisers Act	49
Chapter 94 - Apprenticeship	49
Chapter 95 - Department of Labor and Labor Regulations	49
Chapter 95 - Department of Labor and Labor Regulations (Continuation)	50
Chapter 96 - Employment Security	50
Chapter 97 - Workers' Compensation Act	50
Chapter 97 - Workers' Compensation Act (Continuation)	51

Chapter 98 - Burnt and Lost Records	51
Chapter 99 - Libel and Slander	51
Chapter 99A - Civil Remedies for Criminal Actions	51
Chapter 99B - Products Liability	51
Chapter 99C - Actions Relating to Winter Sports Safety and Accidents	51
Chapter 99D - Civil Rights	51
Chapter 99E - Special Liability Provisions	51
Chapter 100 - Monuments, Memorials and Parks	51
Chapter 101 - Names of Persons	51
Chapter 102 - Official Survey Base	51
Chapter 103 - Sundays, Holidays and Special Days	51
Chapter 104 - United States Lands	51
Chapter 104A - Degrees of Kinship	51
Chapter 104B - Hurricanes or Other Acts of Nature	51
Chapter 104C - Atomic Energy, Radioactivity and Ionizing Radiation [Repealed and Recodified.]	51
Chapter 104D - Southern States Energy Compact	51
Chapter 104E - North Carolina Radiation Protection Act	51
Chapter 104F - Southeast Interstate Low-Level Radioactive Waste Management Compact [Repealed]	51
Chapter 104G - North Carolina Low-Level Radioactive Waste Management Authority Act of 1987 [Repealed]	51
Chapter 105 - Taxation	51
Chapter 105 - Taxation (Continuation)	52
Chapter 105 - Taxation (Continuation)	53
Chapter 105 - Taxation (Continuation)	54
Chapter 105A - Setoff Debt Collection Act	55
Chapter 105B - Defaulted Student Loan Recovery Act	55
Chapter 106 - Agriculture	55
Chapter 106 - Agriculture (Continue)	56
Chapter 106 - Agriculture (Continue)	57
Chapter 107 - Agricultural Development Districts [Repealed.]	57
Chapter 108 - Social Services [Repealed and Recodified.]	57
Chapter 108A - Social Services	57
Chapter 108B - Community Action Programs	58
Chapter 108C Medicaid and Health Choice Provider Requirements.	58
Chapter 108D Medicaid Managed Care for Behavioral Health Services.	58
Chapter 109 - Bonds [Recodified.]	58
Chapter 110 - Child Welfare	58
Chapter 111 - Aid to the Blind	58
Chapter 112 - Confederate Homes and Pensions [Repealed.]	58
Chapter 113 - Conservation and Development	58
Chapter 113 - Conservation and Development (Continuation)	59

Chapter 113A - Pollution Control and Environment	59
Chapter 113A - Pollution Control and Environment (Continuation)	60
Chapter 113B - North Carolina Energy Policy Act of 1975	60
Chapter 114 - Department of Justice	60
Chapter 115 - Elementary and Secondary Education [Repealed.]	60
Chapter 115A - Community Colleges, Technical Institutes, and Industrial Education Centers [Repealed.]	60
Chapter 115B - Tuition and Fee Waivers	60
Chapter 115C - Elementary and Secondary Education	60
Chapter 115C - Elementary and Secondary Education (Continuation)	61
Chapter 115C - Elementary and Secondary Education (Continuation)	62
Chapter 115C - Elementary and Secondary Education (Continuation)	63
Chapter 115D - Community Colleges	63
Chapter 115E - Private Educational Facilities Finance Act [Recodified]	63
Chapter 116 - Higher Education	63
Chapter 116 - Higher Education (Continuation)	63
Chapter 116A - Escheats and Abandoned Property [Repealed.]	64
Chapter 116B - Escheats and Abandoned Property	64
Chapter 116C - Continuum of Education Programs	64
Chapter 116D - Higher Education Bonds	64
Chapter 116E -Education Longitudinal Data System	64
Chapter 117 - Electrification	64
Chapter 118 - Firemen's and Rescue Squad Workers' Relief and Pension Funds [Recodified.]	64
Chapter 118A - Firemen's Death Benefit Act [Repealed.]	64
Chapter 118B - Members of a Rescue Squad Death Benefit Act [Repealed.]	64
Chapter 119 - Gasoline and Oil Inspection and Regulation	64
Chapter 120 - General Assembly	65
Chapter 120 - General Assembly (Continuation)	66
Chapter 120 - General Assembly (Continuation)	67
Chapter 120C - Lobbying	67
Chapter 121 - Archives and History	67
Chapter 122 - Hospitals for the Mentally Disordered [Repealed.]	67
Chapter 122A - North Carolina Housing Finance Agency	67
Chapter 122B - North Carolina Agricultural Facilities Finance Act [Repealed.]	67
Chapter 122C - Mental Health, Developmental Disabilities, and Substance Abuse Act of 1985	67
Chapter 122C - Mental Health, Developmental Disabilities, and Substance Abuse Act of 1985 (Continuation)	68

Chapter 122D - North Carolina Agricultural Finance Act	68
Chapter 122E - North Carolina Housing Trust and Oil Overcharge Act	68
Chapter 123 - Impeachment	69
Chapter 123A - Industrial Development [Repealed.]	69
Chapter 124 - Internal Improvements	69
Chapter 125 - Libraries	69
Chapter 126 - State Personnel System	69
Chapter 127 - Militia [Repealed.]	69
Chapter 127A - Militia	69
Chapter 127B - Military Affairs	69
Chapter 127C - Advisory Commission on Military Affairs	69
Chapter 128 - Offices and Public Officers	69
Chapter 128 - Offices and Public Officers (Continuation)	70
Chapter 129 - Public Buildings and Grounds	70
Chapter 130 - Public Health [Repealed.]	70
Chapter 130A - Public Health	70
Chapter 130A - Public Health (Continuation)	71
Chapter 130A - Public Health (Continuation)	72
Chapter 130B - Hazardous Waste Management Commission [Repealed.]	72
Chapter 131 - Public Hospitals [Repealed.]	72
Chapter 131A - Health Care Facilities Finance Act	72
Chapter 131B - Licensing of Ambulatory Surgical Facilities [Repealed.]	72
Chapter 131C - Charitable Solicitation Licensure Act [Repealed.]	72
Chapter 131D - Inspection and Licensing of Facilities	72
Chapter 131E - Health Care Facilities and Services	72
Chapter 131E - Health Care Facilities and Services (Continuation)	73
Chapter 131F - Solicitation of Contributions	73
Chapter 132 - Public Records	73
Chapter 133 - Public Works	74
Chapter 134 - Youth Development [Recodified.]	74
Chapter 134A - Youth Services [Repealed.]	74
Chapter 135 - Retirement System for Teachers and State Employees; Social Security; Health Insurance Program for Children	74
Chapter 135 - Retirement System for Teachers and State Employees; Social Security; Health Insurance Program for Children	75
Chapter 136 - Transportation	75
Chapter 136 - Transportation (Continuation)	76
Chapter 137 - Rural Rehabilitation [Repealed.]	76
Chapter 138 - Salaries, Fees and Allowances	76
Chapter 138A - State Government Ethics Act	76

Chapter 139 - Soil and Water Conservation Districts	76
Chapter 140 - State Art Museum; Symphony and Art Societies	76
Chapter 140A - State Awards System	76
Chapter 141 - State Boundaries	76
Chapter 142 - State Debt	76
Chapter 143 - State Departments, Institutions, and Commissions	77
Chapter 143 - State Departments, Institutions, and Commissions (Continuation)	78
Chapter 143 - State Departments, Institutions, and Commissions (Continuation)	79
Chapter 143 - State Departments, Institutions, and Commissions (Continuation)	80
Chapter 143A - State Government Reorganization	80
Chapter 143B - Executive Organization Act of 1973	80
Chapter 143B - Executive Organization Act of 1973 (Continuation)	81
Chapter 143B - Executive Organization Act of 1973 (Continuation)	82
Chapter 143C - State Budget Act	83
Chapter 143D - The State Governmental Accountability and Internal Control Act	83
Chapter 144 - State Flag, Official Governmental Flags, Motto, and Colors	83
Chapter 145 - State Symbols and Other Official Adoptions.	83
Chapter 146 - State Lands	83
Chapter 147 - State Officers	83
Chapter 148 - State Prison System	84
Chapter 149 - State Song and Toast	84
Chapter 150 - Uniform Revocation of Licenses [Repealed.]	84
Chapter 150A - Administrative Procedure Act [Recodified.]	84
Chapter 150B - Administrative Procedure Act	84
Chapter 151 - Constables [Repealed.]	84
Chapter 152 - Coroners	84
Chapter 152A - County Medical Examiner [Repealed.]	84
Chapter 152A - County Medical Examiner [Repealed.] (Continuation)	84
Chapter 153 - Counties and County Commissioners [Repealed.]	84
Chapter 153A - Counties	84
Chapter 153A - Counties (Continue)	85
Chapter 153B - Mountain Resources Planning Act	85
Chapter 153C - Uwharrie Regional Resources Act	85
Chapter 154 - County Surveyor [Repealed.]	85
Chapter 155 - County Treasurer [Repealed.]	85

Chapter 156 - Drainage	85
Chapter 156 – Drainage (Continuation)	86
Chapter 157 - Housing Authorities and Projects	86
Chapter 157A - Historic Properties Commissions [Transferred.]	86
Chapter 158 - Local Development	86
Chapter 159 - Local Government Finance	86
Chapter 159 - Local Government Finance (Continuation)	87
Chapter 159A - Pollution Abatement and Industrial Facilities Financing Act [Unconstitutional.]	87
Chapter 159B - Joint Municipal Electric Power and Energy Act	87
Chapter 159C - Industrial and Pollution Control Facilities Financing Act	87
Chapter 159D - The North Carolina Capital Facilities Financing Act	87
Chapter 159E - Registered Public Obligations Act	87
Chapter 159F - North Carolina Energy Development Authority [Repealed.]	87
Chapter 159G - Water Infrastructure	87
Chapter 159H - [Reserved.]	87
Chapter 159I - Solid Waste Management Loan Program and Local Government Special Obligation Bonds	87
Chapter 160 - Municipal Corporations [Repealed And Transferred.]	87
Chapter 160A - Cities and Towns	88
Chapter 160A - Cities and Towns (Continuation)	89
Chapter 160B - Consolidated City-County Act	89
Chapter 160C - Baseball Park Districts [Repealed.]	90
Chapter 161 - Register of Deeds	90
Chapter 162 - Sheriff	90
Chapter 162A - Water and Sewer Systems	90
Chapter 162B Continuity of Local Government in Emergency.	90
Chapter 163 Elections and Election Laws.	90
Chapter 163 Elections and Election Laws. (Continuation)	91
Chapter 164 Concerning the General Statutes of North Carolina.	92
Chapter 165 Veterans.	92
Chapter 166 Civil Preparedness Agencies [Repealed.]	92
Chapter 166A North Carolina Emergency Management Act.	92
Chapter 167 State Civil Air Patrol [Repealed.]	92
Chapter 168 Persons with Disabilities.	92
Chapter 168A Persons With Disabilities Protection Act.	92

Chapter 160C.

Baseball Park Districts.

§§ 160C-1 through 160C-2: Repealed by Session Laws 2001-414, s. 52.

Chapter 161.

Register of Deeds.

Article 1.

The Office.

§ 161-1. Election and term of office.

In each county there shall be elected biennially by the qualified voters thereof, as provided for the election of members of the General Assembly, a register of deeds. (Const., art. 7, s. 1; Rev., s. 2650; C.S., s. 3543; 1981, c. 504, s. 9.)

§ 161-2. Four-year term for registers of deeds.

A register of deeds shall be elected in each county of the State by the qualified voters of the county. The register of deeds shall serve for a term of four years beginning on the first Monday in December after the election and until a successor register of deeds is elected and qualified. (1935, cc. 362, 392, 462; 1937, c. 271; 1939, cc. 11, 99; 1941, c. 192; 1949, cc. 756, 830; 1957, c. 1022, s. 2; 1973, c. 215, s. 1; 1991, c. 60, s. 2.)

§ 161-3. Oath of office.

The register of deeds shall take the oath of office on the first Monday of December next after his election, before a person authorized to administer oaths as defined in G.S. 11-7.1. (1868, c. 35, s. 2; 1876-7, c. 276, s. 5; Code, s. 3647; Rev., s. 2652; C.S., s. 3544; 1987, c. 620, s. 4.)

§ 161-4. Bond required.

(a) Every register of deeds shall give bond with sufficient surety, to be approved by the board of county commissioners, in a sum of not less than ten thousand dollars ($10,000) nor more than fifty thousand dollars ($50,000), payable to the State, and conditioned for the safekeeping of the books and records, and for the faithful discharge of the duties of his office.

(b) The bond and surety required under subsection (a) shall further be conditioned for the safekeeping of the books and records, and for the faithful discharge of the duties of office of the register of deeds by any incumbent assistant and deputy register of deeds appointed prior to the vacancy pursuant to G.S. 161-6 and holding over after vacancy in the office of register of deeds for the interim, as provided in G.S. 161-5(b). (1868, c. 35, s. 3; 1876-7, c. 276, s. 5; Code, s. 3648; 1899, c. 54, s. 52; Rev., s. 301; C.S., s. 3545; 1963, c. 204; 1965, c. 900; 1969, c. 636.)

§ 161-4.1. Salary in counties where fees formerly allowed.

In any county where during the fiscal year beginning July 1, 1980, and ending June 30, 1981, the register of deeds received fees in addition to salary, and retained them personally as allowed by local act, the salary of the register of deeds in such county in any future fiscal year shall not be less than the sum of the salary plus fees received in the fiscal year beginning July 1, 1980 and ending June 30, 1981. (1981, c. 968, s. 4.)

§ 161-4.2. Liability insurance for register of deeds.

To the same extent that the county provides liability insurance to other county officers or employees, pursuant to G.S. 153A-97 and 160A-167, or 58-32-10, or Article 23 of Chapter 58 of the General Statutes, the county shall provide insurance to the register of deeds. If the county does not provide insurance to any officers or employees, then the county shall notify the register of deeds, in writing, prior to the first Monday in December of each year, of its intent not to provide insurance coverage to the register of deeds. This required notification shall be in the form of a letter signed by the chairman of the board of county commissioners, attested by the clerk of the board of county commissioners. If the county fails to provide the required notice, then the county shall be liable for damages that would have been paid had the county purchased the insurance pursuant to the General Statutes sections cited above. (1991, c. 470, s. 1.)

§ 161-5. Vacancy in office.

(a)   Repealed by Session Laws 1991, c. 60, s. 1.

(a1)   When a vacancy occurs from any cause in the office of register of deeds, the board of county commissioners shall fill such vacancy by the appointment of a successor for the unexpired term, who shall qualify and give bond as required by law. If the register of deeds was elected as the nominee of a political party, the board of county commissioners shall consult the county executive committee of that political party before filling the vacancy and shall appoint the person recommended by that committee, if the party makes a recommendation within 30 days of the occurrence of the vacancy.

(b)   In the interim between a vacancy in the office of register of deeds and the appointment and qualification of a successor register of deeds, under the provisions of subsection (a), any incumbent assistant or deputy register of deeds appointed under G.S. 161-6 prior to the vacancy shall continue to hold office as assistant or deputy registers of deeds until discharged or otherwise lawfully relieved of office by the lawful successor to the office of register of deeds. (1868, c. 35, s. 4; Code, s. 3649; Rev., s. 2651; C.S., s. 3546; 1965, c. 900; 1975, c. 868, ss. 1, 2; 1977, c. 180; 1981, c. 763, ss. 8, 9, 14; c. 830; 1987, c. 196, s. 2; 1989, c. 497, s. 4; 1989 (Reg. Sess., 1990), c. 1056; 1991, c. 14, s. 1, c. 60, ss. 1, 4.)

§ 161-6. Appointment of assistant and deputy registers of deeds; authority to sign in name of register of deeds; holdover assistants and deputies.

(a)   The registers of deeds of the several counties are hereby authorized to appoint one or more assistant registers of deeds and one or more deputy registers of deeds, whose acts as assistants or deputies shall be valid and for which the registers of deeds shall be officially responsible. The certificate of appointment of an assistant or deputy shall be filed by the appointing register of deeds in the office of the clerk of the superior court, who shall record the same.

(b) Each assistant and deputy register of deeds so appointed shall be authorized, in addition to his other powers and duties, to register and sign instruments and documents in the name and under the title of the appointing register of deeds, by himself as assistant or deputy, as appropriate. Such signing shall be substantially as follows:

John Doe, Register of Deeds

by Richard Roe, Assistant (or Deputy, as appropriate).

(c) Such registering and signing, when regular and sufficient in all other respects, shall be valid for all purposes, and of the same force and effect as if the instrument or document had been registered and signed by the register of deeds personally.

(d) Wherever in the General Statutes reference is made to "the register of deeds and (or) his assistant" or "the register of deeds and (or) his deputy" or words substantially to this effect, or reference is made only to "the assistant register of deeds" or "the deputy register of deeds," such reference to either assistant or deputy, unless the contrary intent is specifically stated in the text, shall also include the other, insofar as such reference pertains to the authority, powers, duties, rights, privileges, or qualifications for office of assistant or deputy register of deeds.

(e) Incumbent assistant and deputy registers of deeds holding over after a vacancy in the office of register of deeds, pursuant to the provisions of G.S. 161-5(b), shall continue to have and exercise all lawful power and authority of office until lawfully relieved of office, including, but not restricted to, all power and authority set forth in subsections (a), (b), (c) and (d), and in Chapter 161 generally, and their acts as assistant or deputy registers of deeds shall be official and valid, and the appointing register of deeds, or his estate, and the official bond under G.S. 161-4 shall be responsible for their acts as assistant or deputy registers of deeds, and such assistant or deputy register of deeds shall also be individually, personally and officially responsible for his own acts. (1909, c. 628, s. 1; C.S., s. 3547; 1949, c. 261; 1959, c. 279; 1963, c. 191; 1965, c. 900.)

§ 161-7. Office at courthouse.

The register shall keep his office at the courthouse unless the board of county commissioners shall deem it impracticable. (1868, c. 35, s. 5; Code, s. 3650; Rev., s. 2653; C.S., s. 3548.)

§ 161-8. Attendance at office.

The board of county commissioners may fix by order, to be entered on their records, what days of each week, and at what hours of each day, the register of deeds shall attend at his office in person or by deputy, and he shall give his attendance accordingly. (1868, c. 35, s. 6; Code, s. 3651; Rev., s. 2654; C.S., s. 3549.)

§ 161-9. Official seal.

The office of register of deeds for every county shall have and use an official seal or stamp, which shall be provided by the county commissioners. The official seal or stamp shall be round, and the size shall not exceed one and five-eighths inches in diameter. Contained thereon shall be the name of the register of deeds, the county and letters "N.C.," and the words "Register of Deeds." The ink used for the official stamp shall be of the reproducible type; provided, that any register of deeds using a nonconforming seal or stamp prior to July 1, 1969 may continue to use such seal or stamp. (1893, c. 119, s. 1; Rev., s. 2649; C.S., s. 3550; 1969, c. 1028.)

§ 161-10. Uniform fees of registers of deeds.

(a) Except as otherwise provided in this Article, all fees collected under this section shall be deposited into the county general fund. While performing the duties of the office, the register of deeds shall collect the following fees which shall be uniform throughout the State:

(1) Instruments in General. - For registering or filing any instrument for which no other provision is made by this section, the fee shall be twenty-six dollars ($26.00) for the first 15 pages plus four dollars ($4.00) for each additional page or fraction thereof.

For any instrument that assigns more than one security instrument as defined in G.S. 45-36.4(18) by reference to previously recorded instrument recording data that are required to be indexed pursuant to G.S. 161-14.1(b), the fee shall be an additional ten dollars ($10.00) for each additional reference.

When a document is presented for registration that consists of multiple instruments, the fee shall be an additional ten dollars ($10.00) for each additional instrument. A document consists of multiple instruments when it contains two or more instruments with different legal consequences or intent, each of which is separately executed and acknowledged and could be recorded alone.

(1a) Deeds of Trust, Mortgages, and Cancellation of Deeds of Trust and Mortgages. - For registering or filing any deed of trust or mortgage, whether written, printed, or typewritten, the fee shall be fifty-six dollars ($56.00) for the first 15 pages plus four dollars ($4.00) for each additional page or fraction thereof.

When a deed of trust or mortgage is presented for registration that contains one or more additional instruments, the fee shall be ten dollars ($10.00) for each additional instrument. A deed of trust or mortgage contains one or more additional instruments if such additional instrument or instruments has or have different legal consequences or intent, each of which is separately executed and acknowledged and could be recorded alone.

For recording records of satisfaction, or the cancellation of record by any other means, of deeds of trust or mortgages, there shall be no fee.

(2) Marriage Licenses. - For issuing a license sixty dollars ($60.00); for issuing a delayed certificate with one certified copy twenty dollars ($20.00); and for a proceeding for correction of an application, license or certificate, with one certified copy ten dollars ($10.00).

(3) Plats. - For each original or revised plat recorded twenty-one dollars ($21.00) per sheet or page; for furnishing a certified copy of a plat five dollars ($5.00).

(4) Right-of-Way Plans. - For each original or amended plan and profile sheet recorded twenty-one dollars ($21.00) for the first page and five dollars ($5.00) per page for each additional page. This fee is to be collected from the Board of Transportation.

(5) Registration of Birth Certificate One Year or More after Birth. - For preparation of necessary papers when birth to be registered in another county ten dollars ($10.00); for registration when necessary papers prepared in another county, with one certified copy ten dollars ($10.00); for preparation of necessary papers and registration in the same county, with one certified copy twenty dollars ($20.00).

(6) Amendment of Birth or Death Record. - For preparation of amendment and affecting correction ten dollars ($10.00).

(7) Legitimations. - For preparation of all documents concerned with legitimations ten dollars ($10.00).

(8) Certified Copies of Birth and Death Certificates and Marriage Licenses. - For furnishing a certified copy of a death or birth certificate or marriage license ten dollars ($10.00). Provided however, a register of deeds, in accordance with G.S. 130A-93, may issue without charge a certified birth certificate to any person over the age of 62 years. Provided, however, upon verification of voter registration, a register of deeds, in accordance with G.S. 130A-93, shall issue without charge a certified copy of a birth certificate or a certified copy of a marriage license to any registered voter who declares the registered voter is registered to vote in this State and does not have a certified copy of that registered voter's birth certificate or marriage license necessary to obtain photo identification acceptable under G.S. 163-166.13. Any declaration shall prominently include the penalty under G.S. 163-275(13) for falsely or fraudulently making the declaration.

(8a) Repealed by Session Laws 2012-18, s. 2.2, as amended by Session Laws 2012-194, s. 54, effective July 1, 2012.

(9) Certified Copies. - For furnishing a certified copy of an instrument for which no other provision is made by this section five dollars ($5.00) for the first page, plus two dollars ($2.00) for each additional page or fraction thereof.

(10) Comparing Copy for Certification. - For comparing and certifying a copy of any instrument filed for registration, when the copy is furnished by the party filing the instrument for registration and at the time of filing thereof five dollars ($5.00).

(11) Uncertified Copies. - A register of deeds who supplies uncertified copies of instruments, or index pages, as a convenience to the public, may charge fees

that the register of deeds determines bear a reasonable relation to the quality of copies supplied and the cost of purchasing and maintaining copying and/or computer equipment. These fees may be changed from time to time, but the amount of these fees shall at all times be uniform and prominently posted in the office of the register of deeds.

(12) Notarial Acts. - For taking an acknowledgment, oath, or affirmation or performing any other notarial act the maximum fee set in G.S. 10B-31 or G.S. 10B-118 for electronic notarial acts. This fee shall not be charged if the act is performed as a part of one of the services for which a fee is provided by this subsection; except that this fee shall be charged in addition to the fees for registering, filing, or recording instruments or plats as provided by subdivisions (1) and (3) of this subsection.

(13) Uniform Commercial Code. - Such fees as are provided for in Chapter 25, Article 9, Part 5, of the General Statutes.

(14) Torrens Registration. - Such fees as are provided in G.S. 43-5.

(15) Master Forms. - Such fees as are provided for instruments in general.

(16) Repealed by Session Laws 2011-296, s. 1, effective October 1, 2011.

(17) Qualification of Notary Public. - For administering the oaths of office to a notary public and making the appropriate record entries as provided in G.S. 10B-10 ten dollars ($10.00).

(18) Reinstatement of Articles of Incorporation. - For filing reinstatements of Articles of Incorporation prepared pursuant to G.S. 105-232; such fees as provided for instruments in general. The fee shall be paid by the corporation affected.

(18a) Nonstandard Document. - For registering or filing any document not in compliance with the recording standards adopted under G.S. 161-14(b), the fee shall be twenty-five dollars ($25.00) in addition to all other applicable recording fees.

(19) Miscellaneous Services. - For performing miscellaneous services such as faxing documents, providing laminated copies of documents, expedited delivery of documents, and similar services, the cost of the service.

(b)   The uniform fees set forth in this section are complete and exclusive and no other fees shall be charged by the register of deeds.

(c)   These fees shall be collected in every case prior to filing, registration, recordation, certification or other service rendered by the register of deeds unless by law it is provided that the service shall be rendered without charge. (Code, ss. 710, 3109, 3751; 1887, c. 283; 1891, c. 324; 1897, cc. 27, 68; 1899, c. 17, s. 2; c. 247, s. 3; cc. 261, 302, 578, 723; 1901, c. 294; 1903, c. 792; 1905, cc. 226, 292, 319; Rev., s. 2776; 1911, c. 55, s. 3; C.S., s. 3906; 1967, c. 639, s. 4; c. 823, s. 33; 1969, c. 80, s. 1; c. 912, s. 3; 1973, c. 507, s. 5; c. 1317; 1975, c. 428; 1977, 2nd Sess., c. 1132; 1981, c. 968, ss. 1, 2; 1983, c. 894, ss. 2, 3; 1987, c. 792, ss. 2-5; 1989, c. 523, s. 1; 1991, c. 636, s. 18; c. 683, s. 3; c. 693, s. 1; 1991 (Reg. Sess., 1992), c. 1030, s. 49; 1993, c. 425, s. 1; 1997-309, s. 9; 2000-167, s. 1; 2000-169, s. 44; 2001-390, s. 1; 2005-123, s. 7; 2005-391, s. 8; 2008-107, s. 29.7(a); 2009-451, ss. 17.8(a), 20A.4(a); 2011-296, s. 1; 2012-18, s. 2.2; 2012-79, s. 2.16; 2012-194, s. 54; 2013-225, s. 7(a), (b); 2013-381, s. 3.3.)

§ 161-10.1. Exemption of Armed Forces discharge documents and certain other records needed in support of claims for veterans' benefits.

Any schedule of fees which is now or may be prescribed in Chapter 161 of the General Statutes or in G.S. 161-10 shall not apply to nor shall the same repeal any of the provisions of Article 5 of Chapter 47 of the General Statutes. Any schedule of fees which is now or may be hereafter prescribed in Chapter 161 of the General Statutes or as may appear in G.S. 161-10 shall not apply to nor shall the same repeal any of the provisions of G.S. 165-11. (1971, c. 679; 2011-183, s. 109.)

§ 161-10.2. Repealed by Session Laws 1969, c. 80, s. 6.

§ 161-11. Repealed by Session Laws 1973, c. 1027.

§ 161-11.1. Fees for Children's Trust Fund.

(a)   Five dollars ($5.00) of each fee collected by a register of deeds on or after October 1, 1983, for issuance of a marriage license pursuant to G.S. 161-10(a)(2) shall be forwarded, as soon as practical but no later than 60 days after collection by the register of deeds, to the county finance officer, who shall forward same to the Department of Health and Human Services, Division of Social Services, for deposit in the Children's Trust Fund.

(b)   Repealed by Session Laws 1997-136, s. 1, effective June 4, 1997. (1983, c. 894, s. 4; 1989 (Reg. Sess., 1990), c. 1039, s. 8; 1997-136, s. 1; 2010-31, s. 10.20A(b).)

§ 161-11.2. Fees for domestic violence centers.

Thirty dollars ($30.00) of each fee collected by a register of deeds for issuance of a marriage license pursuant to G.S. 161-10(a)(2) shall be forwarded by the register of deeds to the county finance officer, who shall forward the funds to the Department of Administration to be credited to the Domestic Violence Center Fund established under G.S. 50B-9. The register of deeds shall forward the fees to the county finance officer as soon as practical. The county finance officer shall forward the fees to the Department of Administration within 60 days after receiving the fees. The Register of Deeds shall inform the applicants that thirty dollars ($30.00) of the fee for a marriage license shall be used for Domestic Violence programs. (1991, c. 693, s. 2; 2009-451, s. 20A.4(b).)

§ 161-11.3. Automation Enhancement and Preservation Fund.

Ten percent (10%) of the fees collected pursuant to G.S. 161-10 and retained by the county, or six dollars and twenty cents ($6.20) in the case of a fee collected pursuant to G.S. 161-10(a)(1a) for the first page of a deed of trust or mortgage, shall be set aside annually and placed in a nonreverting Automation Enhancement and Preservation Fund, the proceeds of which shall be expended on computer or imaging technology and needs associated with the preservation and storage of public records in the office of the register of deeds. Nothing in this section shall be construed to affect the duty of the board of county commissioners to furnish supplies and equipment to the office of the register of deeds. (2001-390, s. 2; 2007-353, s. 5; 2009-451, s. 17.8(c); 2011-296, s. 2; 2013-225, s. 7(a).)

§ 161-11.4: Repealed by Session Laws 2013-225, s. 7(c), effective July 1, 2013.

§ 161-11.5. Fees to be remitted to State Treasurer.

Six dollars and twenty cents ($6.20) of each fee collected by the register of deeds under G.S. 161-10(a)(1) and (a)(1a) shall be remitted by the register of deeds to the county finance officer, who shall remit the funds to the State Treasurer on a monthly basis to be credited as follows:

(1)   Fifty-five percent (55%) to the Floodplain Mapping Fund established under G.S. 143-215.56A.

(2)   Twenty percent (20%) to the General Fund as nontax revenue.

(3)   Twenty-five percent (25%) to the Department of Cultural Resources to be used as provided in G.S. 121-5(e). (2009-451, s. 17.8(b); 2011-296, s. 3; 2013-225, s. 7(a).)

§ 161-11.6: Repealed by Session Laws 2013-225, s. 7(c), effective July 1, 2013.

Article 2.

The Duties.

§§ 161-12 through 161-13: Repealed by Session Laws 1973, c. 1027.

§ 161-14. Registration of instruments.

(a)   After the register of deeds has determined that all statutory and locally adopted prerequisites for recording have been met, the register of deeds shall immediately register all written instruments presented to him for registration. When an instrument is presented for registration, the register of deeds shall endorse upon it the day and hour on which it was presented. This endorsement forms a part of the registration of the instrument. All instruments shall be registered in the precise order in which they were presented for registration. Immediately after endorsing the day and hour of presentation upon an instrument, the register of deeds shall index and cross-index it in its proper sequence. The register of deeds shall then proceed to register it on the day that it is presented unless a temporary index has been established.

The register of deeds may establish a temporary index in which all instruments presented for registration shall be indexed until they are registered and entered in the permanent indexes. A temporary index shall operate in all respects as the permanent index. All instruments presented for registration shall be registered and indexed and cross-indexed on the permanent indexes not later than 30 days after the date of presentation.

(b) All instruments, except instruments conforming to the provisions of G.S. 25-9-521, presented for registration on paper shall meet all of the following requirements:

(1) Be eight and one-half inches by eleven inches or eight and one-half inches by fourteen inches.

(2) Have a blank margin of three inches at the top of the first page and blank margins of at least one-quarter inches on the remaining sides of the first page and on all sides of subsequent pages.

(3) Be typed or printed in black on white paper in a legible font. A font size no smaller than 9 points shall be considered legible. Blanks in an instrument may be completed in pen and corrections to an instrument may be made in pen.

(4) Have text typed or printed on one side of a page only.

(5) State the type of instrument at the top of the first page.

If an instrument does not meet these requirements, the register of deeds shall register the instrument after collecting the fee for nonstandard documents as required by G.S. 161-10(a)(18a) in addition to all other applicable recording fees. However, if an instrument fails to meet the requirements because it contains print in a font size smaller than 9 points, the register of deeds may register the instrument without collecting the fee for nonstandard documents if, in the discretion of the register of deeds, the instrument is legible.

(c) Transportation corridor official maps authorized under Article 2E of Chapter 136 shall be registered and indexed by the end of the third business day after the business day the map is presented to the register of deeds.

(d) For the purposes of this section, the term "instrument" means all of the following for which a fee is collected under G.S. 161-10(a):

(1) Instruments in General.

(2) Deeds of Trust, Mortgages, and Cancellation of Deeds of Trust and Mortgages.

(3) Uniform Commercial Code filings.

(4) Torrens Registrations.

(5) Master Forms.

(e) Notwithstanding subsection (a) of this section, the register of deeds shall immediately register a written instrument presented to him or her for registration that meets the following requirements: (i) the instrument is a portion of a map of a cemetery that was divided into sections based upon race, (ii) the other portion of the map of a cemetery was properly registered in the office of the register of deeds, and (iii) the unregistered portion of the map does not have the surveyor's stamp or seal and original signature affixed. (R.C., c. 37, s. 23; 1868, c. 35, s. 9; Code, s. 3654; Rev., s. 2658; C.S., s. 3553; 1921, c. 114; 1971, c. 657; 1998-184, s. 5; 2001-390, s. 5; 2001-464, ss. 2, 3; 2002-159, s. 53; 2011-75, s. 1; 2011-296, s. 6.)

§ 161-14.01. Registration of instruments for business and other purposes.

(a) The register of deeds is hereby authorized to record and file documents relating to persons, partnerships, and corporations for business and other purposes, including but not limited to certificates of partnerships, assumed business names, incorporations, dissolutions, or amendments thereto, in a consolidated book or record, including books or records used for the filing of deeds, deeds of trust, leases, and similar documents. It is the intent of this section that the register of deeds may file and record some or all of the above instruments and documents and those of a similar nature in one book or record or in a series of books or records consolidated for recording purposes; provided, said instruments and documents shall be indexed as required by law.

(b) All other laws providing for the filing of documents provided for herein shall not be applicable to the county upon adoption by the register of deeds of a consolidated recording and filing system as authorized herein. (1973, c. 1013, ss. 1, 2.)

§ 161-14.1. Recording subsequent entries as separate instruments.

(a) As used in this section, the following terms mean:

(1) Original instrument. - The previously recorded instrument that is modified, amended, supplemented, assigned, satisfied, terminated, revoked, or cancelled by a subsequent instrument.

(2) Recording data. - The book and page number or document number that indicates where an instrument is recorded in the office of the register of deeds.

(3) Subsequent instrument. - Any instrument presented for registration that indicates in its title or within the first two pages of its text that it is intended or purports to modify, amend, supplement, assign, satisfy, terminate, revoke, or cancel a previously registered instrument. Examples of subsequent instruments include the following:

a. The appointment or designation of a substitute trustee in a deed of trust.

b. A corrective affidavit registered pursuant to G.S. 45-36.1.

c. A lien maturity extension agreement or notice of maturity date registered pursuant to G.S. 45-36.1.

d. A document of rescission registered pursuant to G.S. 45-36.6.

e. The cancellation of a Notice of Inactive Hazardous Substance or Waste Disposal Site registered pursuant to G.S. 130A-310.8(f).

f. A record of satisfaction or other instrument purporting to satisfy a security instrument registered pursuant to G.S. 45-37 or G.S. 45-37.2.

g. A notice of foreclosure registered pursuant to G.S. 45-38.

h. An assignment of a security instrument or lease.

i. An amendment or modification agreement.

j. A release or partial release of property from the lien of a security instrument, including a partial release registered pursuant to G.S. 45-36.22 or a deed of release or reconveyance.

k. An obligation release registered pursuant to G.S. 45-36.23.

l. An assumption agreement.

m. A subordination agreement.

n. An instrument terminating future optional advances registered pursuant to G.S. 45-72.

o. A certificate of extension extending the period for advances under an equity line of credit registered pursuant to G.S. 45-82.1.

p. A notice of extension relating to after-acquired property registered pursuant to G.S. 47-20.5.

q. The revocation of a power of attorney.

r. Any instrument authorized or directed by law to be indexed under the provisions of this section.

s. Any instrument for which the register of deeds is authorized or directed by law to make a subsequent entry upon the margin of the record of an original instrument.

(b) The register of deeds shall register each subsequent instrument as a separate instrument and do all of the following:

(1) Index the parties to the subsequent instrument.

(2) If the subsequent instrument names one or more of the original parties to the original instrument, index the original parties to the original instrument as they are named in the subsequent instrument.

(3) If the subsequent instrument states the recording data for the original instrument, reference the recording data of the original instrument as that recording data is stated in the subsequent instrument to each name so indexed.

(c) The register of deeds shall not be required to (i) read or examine any page of an instrument, other than the first two pages, to determine whether it is a subsequent instrument within the meaning of this section, or (ii) verify or make inquiry concerning the accuracy, sufficiency, or completeness of information about an original instrument contained in any subsequent instrument. The register of deeds is expressly authorized to rely solely on the information contained in the subsequent instrument, including, but not limited to, the names of the original parties to the original instrument and the recording data for the original instrument. (1963, c. 1021, s. 3; 1991, c. 114, s. 1; 2005-123, s. 8; 2011-312, s. 28.)

§ 161-14.2. Indexing procedures for instruments and documents filed in the office of the register of deeds.

The following procedure shall be used in making index entries:

(1)   When each word of the signature is legible and it gives the complete name of the party, the signature shall govern.

(2)   When the signature is legible but initials or abbreviations are used, any additional information given by the printed or typed name and not in conflict with the signature shall govern.

(3)   When none of the words in the signature are legible, the printed or typed name shall govern.

(4)   When one or more of the words in the signature are legible, then the words that are legible shall govern; the words that appear in the printed or typed name shall govern over the words of the signature that are not legible.

(5)   When the spelling of any word in a legible signature and the spelling of the corresponding word in the typed or printed name is at variance, and the variance would cause the entries to be made at different places in the index, then the instrument shall be indexed under both spellings.

(6)   When a reasonable interpretation of an illegible word in a signature is at variance with the corresponding word in a typed or printed name, and the variance would cause the entries to be made at different places in the index, then the instrument shall be indexed in both places. (1969, c. 694, s. 1.)

§ 161-15. Certify and register copies.

When a deed, mortgage, or other conveyance conveying real estate situate in two or more counties is presented for registration duly probated and a copy thereof is presented with the same, the register shall compare the copy with the original, and if it be a true copy thereof he shall certify the same, and thereupon the register shall endorse the original deed or conveyance as duly registered in his county, designating the book in which the same is registered, and deliver the original deed to the party entitled thereto and register the same from the certified copy thereof to be retained by him for that purpose. (1899, c. 302; Rev., s. 2657; C.S., s. 3554.)

§ 161-16. Liability for failure to register.

In case of his failure to register any deed or other instrument within the time and in the manner required by G.S. 161-15, the register shall be liable, in an action on his official bond, to the party injured by such delay. (1868, c. 35, s. 10; Code, s. 3660; Rev., s. 2659; C.S., s. 3555.)

§ 161-17. Papers filed alphabetically.

The register shall keep in files alphabetically labeled all original instruments delivered to him for registration, and on application for such originals by any person entitled to their custody, he shall deliver the same. (1868, c. 35, s. 11; Code, s. 3661; Rev., s. 2660; C.S., s. 3556.)

§ 161-18. Transcribe and index books.

The board of county commissioners, when they deem it necessary, may direct the register of deeds to transcribe and index such of the books in the register's office as from decay or other cause may require to be transcribed and indexed. They may allow him such compensation at the expense of the county for this work as they think just. The books when so transcribed and approved by the board shall be public records as the original books, and copies therefrom may be certified accordingly. (1868, c. 35, s. 12; Code, s. 3662; Rev., s. 2661; C.S., s. 3557.)

§ 161-19. Number of survey in grants registered.

The register of deeds in each county in this State, when grants have been registered without the number of tract or survey, shall place in the registration of the grants the number of the tract or survey, when the same shall be furnished him by the grantee or other person; and in registering any grant he shall register the number of the tract or survey. (1889, c. 522, s. 2; Rev., s. 2662; C.S., s. 3558.)

§ 161-20. Certificate of survey registered.

It shall be the duty of the register of deeds in each county, when any grant is presented for registration with a certificate of survey attached, to register such certificate of survey, together with all endorsements thereon, together with said grant, and a record of any certificate of survey so made shall be read in evidence in any action or proceeding: Provided, the failure to register such certificate of survey shall not invalidate the registration of the grant. (1905, c. 243; Rev., s. 2663; C.S., s. 3559.)

§ 161-21. General index kept.

The board of county commissioners shall, at the expense of the county, maintain a consolidated index of all the deeds and other documents affecting real property in the register's office. (1868, c. 35, s. 13; Code, s. 3663; Rev., s. 2664; C.S., s. 3560; 1929, c. 327, s. 1; 1987, c. 620, s. 5; 2008-194, s. 7(d).)

§ 161-22. Index of registered instruments.

(a) Except as otherwise provided by statute, the register of deeds shall provide and keep in the register's office full and complete alphabetical indexes of the names of the parties to all liens, grants, deeds, mortgages, bonds, and other instruments required or authorized to be registered, and the indexes shall state in full the names of all parties, whether grantors, grantees, vendors, vendees, obligors, or obligees. The full names of parties shall be entered in the indexes in accordance with the minimum indexing standards adopted pursuant to G.S. 147-54.3(b) and (b1). Reference shall be made, opposite each name, to the book and page or other location where the instrument is registered. All instruments shall be indexed on either the temporary or permanent index within 24 hours of registration. The register of deeds is not required to index an instrument that is part of a document containing multiple instruments, as defined in G.S. 161-10(a)(1), unless the title of that instrument is shown on the first page of the document and the additional registration fee is paid as required by G.S. 161-10(a)(1).

(b) Repealed by Session Laws 2008-194, s. 7(e), effective August 8, 2008.

(c) Repealed by Session Laws 2008-194, s. 7(e), effective July 1, 2008.

(d) Deeds of trust may be indexed in the names of the grantor and beneficiary only.

(e) Certificates filed for recording pursuant to G.S. 59-2, the Uniform Limited Partnership Act, shall be indexed only under the names of the partnership and each of the general partners. The register of deeds shall cause a statement to be affixed or printed on the index page of the book or books in which limited partnership agreements are filed that the documents are indexed only in the names of the partnership and of each of the general partners.

(f) The alphabetical indexes required by this section may be maintained in index books, on index cards, on film, or in computers or other automated data-processing machines. If the index is maintained in a computer or other automated data processing machine, the register of deeds shall, at least once each month, obtain from the computer or other automated data-processing machine a printed copy on paper or film, or a tape or disk, of all index entries made since the previous printed or filmed copy, or tape or disk, was obtained. These printed or filmed copies, tapes or disks, shall be retained as security copies and may not be altered or destroyed until a subsequent security copy is made containing the index entries from all previous security copies.

(g) The register of deeds may adopt rules establishing indexing procedures and the format of the indexes. The rules shall conform with the requirements of this section and of other applicable statutes. The rules may address such subjects, by way of example and not limitation, as the indexing of business firms, the indexing of names containing numerals, and the indexing of government agencies. The rules shall be posted in at least two prominent places in the office of register of deeds and shall also be placed near the index books or in user manuals in offices using automated indexing systems.

(h) No instrument shall be deemed registered until it has been indexed in a manner to put a reasonably careful and prudent examiner on notice upon inquiry, and, if upon inquiry, the instrument would have been found.

(i) Repealed by Session Laws 2008-194, s. 7(e), effective August 8, 2008. (1876-7, c. 93, s. 1; Code, s. 3664; 1899, c. 501; Rev., ss. 2665, 3600; C.S., s. 3561; 1929, c. 327, s. 2; 1967, cc. 443, 1262; 1973, c. 1136, ss. 1, 2; 1983, c. 127; c. 699, ss. 1, 3; 1989, c. 523, s. 2; 1993, c. 178, ss. 1, 2, 4, 5; c. 539, s. 1096; 1994, Ex. Sess., c. 24, s. 14(c); 2005-123, s. 9; 2008-194, s. 7(e).)

§ 161-22.1. Index and cross-index of immediate prior owners of land.

Whenever, any deed or other instrument conveying real property by a trustee, mortgagee, commissioner, or other officer appointed by the court, or by the sheriff under execution, is filed with the register of deeds for the purpose of being recorded, it shall be the duty of the register of deeds to index and cross-index as grantors the names of all persons recited in said instrument to be the persons whose interest in such real estate is being conveyed or from whom the title of such real estate was acquired by the grantor in such instrument. (1947, c. 211, ss. 1, 2; 1969, c. 80, s. 5.)

§ 161-22.2. Parcel identifier number indexes.

(a) In lieu of the alphabetical indexes required by G.S. 161-21, 161-22 and 161-22.1, the register of deeds of any county in which unique parcel identifier numbers have been assigned to all parcels of real property may install an index by land parcel identifier numbers. For each instrument filed of record, the entry in a land parcel identifier number index must contain the following information:

(1) The parcel identifier number of the parcel or parcels affected;

(2) A brief description of the parcel or parcels, including subdivision block and lot number, if any;

(3) A description of the type of instrument recorded and the date the instrument was filed;

(4) The names of the parties to the instrument to the same extent as required by G.S. 161-22 and the legal status of the parties indexed;

(5) The book and page number, or film reel and frame number, or other file number where the instrument is recorded.

(b) Every instrument affecting real property filed for recording in the office of such register of deeds shall be indexed under the parcel identifier number of the land parcel or parcels affected.

(c) The parcel identifier number index may be maintained in index books, on index cards, on film, or in computers or other automated data-processing machines. If the parcel identifier number index is maintained in a computer or other automated data-processing machine, the register of deeds shall, at least once each month, obtain from the computer or other data-processing machine a printed copy on paper or film of all index entries made since the previous printed copy was obtained. The printed copies shall be retained as security copies and shall not be altered or destroyed.

(d) Before a register of deeds may install a parcel identifier number index in lieu of the alphabetical indexes required by G.S. 161-22, the proposed index must be approved by the Secretary of State. Before approving a parcel identifier number index, the Secretary must find that:

(1) The requirements of this section, G.S. 161-22, and all other applicable indexing requirements of the North Carolina General Statutes and applicable judicial decisions will be met by the index;

(2) Measures for the protection of the indexed information are such that computer or other machine failure will not cause an irremediable loss of the information;

(3) Printed forms and index sheets used in the index permit a display of all information required by law and are otherwise adequate;

(4) Any computer or other data-processing machine used and the program for the use of such machines are adequate to perform the tasks assigned to them;

(5) Access to the information contained in the index can be obtained by the use of both a parcel identifier number and the name of any party to an instrument filed of record;

(6) Any parcel identifier number either reflects the State plane coordinates of some point in the parcel, or is keyed to a map of the parcel that shows the location of the parcel within the county;

(7) The parcel identifier numbering system is designed so that no parcel will be assigned the same number as any other parcel within the county;

(8) The parcel identifier numbering system shows for parcels of land created by subdivision, the number of the parcel of land subdivided in addition to the numbers of the newly-created parcels;

(9) The parcel identifier numbering system shows for parcels of land created by the combining of separate parcels, the numbers of the land parcels that were combined in addition to the number of the newly-created parcel;

(10) The parcel identifier numbering system is capable of identifying condominium units and other separate legal interests that may be created in a single parcel of land;

(11) The parcel identifier numbering system will meet the needs of the users as well as or better than the alphabetical indexes required by G.S. 161-21, 161-22 and 161-22.1.

The Secretary may require a register of deeds seeking approval of a parcel identifier number index to furnish him with any information concerning the index that is pertinent to the findings required for approval.

(e) (1) An approved parcel identifier number index shall become effective as the official real property index of the county as of the first day of July or the first day of January, as the board of commissioners directs, following approval by the Secretary of State.

(2) In any county in which a parcel identifier index is the official index, the register of deeds shall post notices in the alphabetical index books and at other appropriate places in his office stating that the parcel identifier number index is the official index and the date when the change became effective. (1977, c. 589; 1979, c. 700, s. 2; 1983, c. 49; 1985, c. 757, s. 161(a), (b); 1989, c. 727, s. 218(163); 1989 (Reg. Sess., 1990), c. 1004, s. 19(b); 1997-443, s. 11A.119(a); 1999-119, s. 3.)

§ 161-22.3. Minimum standards for land records management.

In addition to the recording and indexing procedures set forth in this Article, the register of deeds shall follow the rules specifying minimum standards and procedures in land records management adopted by the Department of Secretary of State pursuant to G.S. 143-345.6(b1). (1991, c. 697, s. 2; 1993, c. 178, s. 3.)

§ 161-23. Clerk to board of commissioners.

The register of deeds, or such other county officer or employee as the board of county commissioners shall designate in accordance with the provisions of G.S. 153-40, shall be ex officio clerk of the board of county commissioners, and as such shall perform the duties imposed by law or by order of said board. (Const., art. 7, s. 2; 1868, c. 35, s. 15; Code, s. 3656; Rev., s. 2666; C.S., s. 3562; 1955, c. 247, s. 2.)

§ 161-24. Repealed by Session Laws 1973, c. 108, s. 99.

§ 161-25. Repealed by Session Laws 1973, c. 803, s. 36.

§ 161-26. Duties unperformed at expiration of term.

Whenever, upon the termination for any cause of the term of office of the register of deeds, it appears that he has failed to perform any of the duties of his office, the board of commissioners shall cause the same to be performed by another person or the successor of any such defaulting register. Such person or successor shall receive for his compensation the fees allowed for such services, and if any portion of the compensation has been paid to such defaulting register, the same may be recovered by the board of county commissioners, by suit on his official bond, for the benefit of the county or person injured thereby. (1868, c. 35, s. 14; Code, s. 3655; Rev., s. 2669; C.S., s. 3566.)

§ 161-27. Register of deeds failing to discharge duties; penalty.

If any register of deeds fails to perform any of the duties imposed or authorized by law, he shall be guilty of a Class 1 misdemeanor, and he shall be removed from office. (1868, c. 35, s. 18; Code, s. 3659; Rev., s. 3599; C.S., s. 3567; 1993, c. 539, s. 1097; 1994, Ex. Sess., c. 24, s. 14(c).)

§ 161-28. Validation of acts of assistant and deputy registers of deeds performed pending filling of vacancy in office of register of deeds.

Any and all acts and duties performed by any and all assistant or deputy registers of deeds appointed and acting under the provisions of G.S. 161-6 or any other provisions of law, general, local, or special, after a vacancy may have occurred from any cause in the office of register of deeds, including, but not restricted to, a vacancy occurring as a result of the death in office of any incumbent register of deeds, and before the board of county commissioners shall have filled such vacancy by the appointment of a successor and his qualification for office as required by law, under and pursuant to the provisions of G.S. 161-5 and any other applicable provisions of law, shall be and the same are hereby validated, ratified and confirmed to all intents and purposes as if performed by an incumbent in the office of register of deeds and to all intents and purposes as if performed under and pursuant to specific provisions of law authorizing and empowering the register of deeds, or any assistant or deputy registers of deeds, to perform all such acts and duties. The provisions of this validating act shall include, but not be restricted to, all acts and duties of the office of register of deeds, or of the office of assistant or deputy register of deeds, as enumerated and set forth under the specific provisions of this Chapter, or under the provisions of any other general laws as set forth in the General Statutes of North Carolina, or in any other provisions of law, private, local or special. (1965, c. 835, s. 1.)

§ 161-29. Validating acts of assistant and deputy registers of deeds in failing to execute instruments in the name of the register of deeds.

(a)   Any and all acts and duties performed by any and all assistant or deputy registers of deeds in executing any instrument, while acting under the provisions of G.S. 161-6 or any other provisions of law, general, local or special, which failed to substantially comply with G.S. 161-6(b), shall be and the same are hereby validated, ratified and confirmed to all intents and purposes as if executed in full compliance with G.S. 161-6(b).

(b)   The provisions of this validating act shall include all acts and duties of the office of assistant or deputy register of deeds, as enumerated and set forth under the specific provisions of this Chapter, or under the provisions of any general laws as set forth in the General Statutes of North Carolina, or in any other provisions of law, private, local or special. (1973, c. 166, ss. 1, 2.)

§ 161-29.1. Validating acts of assistant and deputy registers of deeds performed before they were sworn into office.

All acts and duties heretofore performed by any and all assistant or deputy registers of deeds, who were appointed but who were not sworn into office or who were sworn into office after their duties commenced, shall be and the same are hereby validated, ratified, and confirmed to all intents and purposes as if performed by assistant or deputy registers of deeds who were theretofore formally appointed and sworn into office, as required by G.S. 161-6, or as required by any other provision of law. (1977, c. 124, s. 1.)

§ 161-30. Modernization of land records.

(a) The county commissioners of any county may require that the register of deeds shall not accept for registration any map or instrument affecting real property unless the following requirements are satisfied:

(1) The name and address of the person to whom the map or instrument is to be returned is affixed on the face thereof.

(2) The grantee's or owner's permanent mailing address is affixed on the face thereof.

(b) In any county in which parcel identifiers have been assigned to any of the real property situated within the county, the county commissioners may require that the register of deeds shall not accept for registration any map, deed, deed of trust or other instrument affecting real property unless the parcel identifier for all of the property described and affected is affixed and verified by the county on the face of the map or instrument or affixed and verified by the county as a part of the legal description contained in any instrument.

(c) Failure to comply with the provisions of subsections (a) and (b) above shall not affect the validity of any map or other instrument that is duly recorded. (1973, c. 992.)

§ 161-31. Tax certification.

(a) Tax Certification. - The board of commissioners of a county may, by resolution, require the register of deeds not to accept any deed transferring real property for registration unless the county tax collector has certified that no delinquent ad valorem county taxes, ad valorem municipal taxes, or other taxes with which the collector is charged are a lien on the property described in the deed. The county commissioners may describe the form the certification must take in its resolution.

(a1) Exception to Tax Certification. - If a board of county commissioners adopts a resolution pursuant to subsection (a) of this section, notwithstanding the resolution, the register of deeds shall accept without certification a deed submitted for registration under the supervision of a closing attorney and containing this statement on the deed: "This instrument prepared by: _____, a licensed North Carolina attorney. Delinquent taxes, if any, to be paid by the closing attorney to the county tax collector upon disbursement of closing proceeds.

(b) Applicability. - This section applies only to Alamance, Alexander, Anson, Beaufort, Bertie, Brunswick, Buncombe, Burke, Cabarrus, Camden, Carteret, Caswell, Catawba, Cherokee, Chowan, Clay, Cleveland, Currituck, Dare, Davidson, Davie, Duplin, Durham, Edgecombe, Forsyth, Gaston, Gates, Graham, Granville, Greene, Halifax, Harnett, Haywood, Henderson, Hertford, Hyde, Iredell, Jackson, Johnston, Jones, Lee, Lenoir, Lincoln, Macon, Madison, Martin, McDowell, Montgomery, Nash, Northampton, Onslow, Pasquotank, Pender, Perquimans, Person, Pitt, Polk, Robeson, Rockingham, Rowan, Rutherford, Sampson, Stanly, Stokes, Surry, Swain, Transylvania, Tyrrell, Vance, Warren, Washington, Wayne, Wilson, Yadkin, and Yancey Counties. (2001-464, s. 1; 2001-513, s. 14; 2002-51, s. 1; 2003-72, s. 1; 2003-189, s. 6; 2003-354, s. 3; 2004-65, s. 1; 2005-109, s. 1; 2005-433, s. 2(a); 2006-16, s. 1; 2006-150, s. 1; 2007-221, s. 1; 2009-290, s. 1; 2010-44, s. 1; 2011-33, s. 1; 2011-45, s. 1; 2012-23, s. 3; 2012-114, s. 1.)

§§ 161-32 through 161-49. Reserved for future codification purposes.

Article 3.

Register of Deeds' Supplemental Pension Fund Act of 1987.

§ 161-50. Short title and purpose.

(a) This Article shall be known and may be cited as the "Registers of Deeds' Supplemental Pension Fund Act of 1987."

(b) The purpose of this Article is to create a pension fund to supplement local government retirement benefits which will attract the most highly qualified talent available within the State to the position of register of deeds. (1987, c. 792, s. 1.)

§ 161-50.1. Scope.

(a) This Article provides supplemental pension benefits for all county registers of deeds who are retired from the Local Governmental Employees' Retirement System or an equivalent locally sponsored plan as herein described.

(b) The Board of Trustees of the Local Governmental Employees' Retirement System shall administer the provisions of this Article.

(c) The provisions of this Article shall be subject to future legislative change or revision, and no person is deemed to have acquired any vested right to a pension payment provided by this Article. (1987, c. 792, s. 1; 2013-287, s. 2.)

§ 161-50.2. Assets.

(a) On and after October 1, 1987, each County Commission shall remit monthly to the Department of State Treasurer an amount equal to one and one-half percent (1.5%) of the monthly receipts collected pursuant to Article 1 of Chapter 161 of the General Statutes, to be deposited to the credit of the Registers of Deeds' Supplemental Pension Fund, hereinafter referred to as the Fund, to be used in making monthly pension payments to eligible retired registers of deeds under the provisions of this Article and to pay the cost of administering the provisions of this Article.

(b) The State Treasurer shall be the custodian of the Registers of Deeds' Supplemental Pension Fund and shall invest its assets in accordance with the provisions of G.S. 147-69.2 and G.S. 147-69.3. (1987, c. 792, s. 1; 2007-245, s. 1.)

§ 161-50.3. Disbursements.

(a)   Immediately following July 1, 1988, the Department of State Treasurer shall divide an amount equal to forty-five percent (45%) of the assets of the Fund at the end of the preceding fiscal year into equal shares and disburse the same as monthly pension payments to all eligible retired registers of deeds as of July 1, 1988, payable in accordance with the method described in G.S. 161-50.5, except that such pension benefit shall be computed for a six-months basis beginning with the month of July, 1988.

(b)   Immediately following January 1, 1996, and the first of January of each succeeding calendar year thereafter, the Department of State Treasurer shall divide an amount equal to ninety-three percent (93%) of the assets of the Fund at the end of the preceding calendar year into equal shares and disburse the same as monthly payments in accordance with the provisions of this Article.

(c)   The remaining seven percent (7%) of the Fund's assets as of December 31, 1995, and at the end of each calendar year thereafter, may be used by the Department of State Treasurer in administering the provisions of this Article.

(d)   All the Fund's disbursements shall be conducted in the same manner as disbursements are conducted for other special funds of the State.

(e)   If, for any reason, the Fund shall be insufficient to pay any pension benefits or other charges, then all benefits or payments shall be reduced pro rata for as long as the deficiency in amount exists. No claim shall accrue with respect to any amount by which a pension payment shall have been reduced. (1987, c. 792, s. 1; 1995, c. 259, s. 2.)

§ 161-50.4. Eligibility.

(a)   Each county register of deeds who has retired with at least 12 years eligible service as register of deeds from the Local Governmental Employees' Retirement System or an equivalent locally sponsored plan before June 30, 1988, and those who retire on or after June 30, 1988, but before July 1, 1991, and who have completed at least 12 years of eligible service as register of deeds is entitled to receive a monthly pension under this Article, beginning July 1, 1988. Effective July 1, 1991, each county register of deeds who retires with at least 10 years of eligible service as register of deeds is entitled to receive a monthly pension under this Article.

(a1)   Notwithstanding the provisions of subsection (a) of this section, effective January 1, 1996, any county register of deeds who separates from service as register of deeds after completing at least 10 years of eligible service as register of deeds, but who does not commence retirement with the Local Governmental Employees' Retirement System, shall have the right to receive a monthly pension under this Article payable upon retirement with the Local Governmental Employees' Retirement System.

(a2)   Each county register of deeds who is not eligible to retire with the Local Governmental Employees' Retirement System solely because the county has not elected to participate as an employer with the Local Governmental Employees' Retirement System and who has either (i) attained the age of 65, (ii) attained 30 years of creditable service regardless of age, or (iii) attained the age of 60 with not less than 25 years of creditable service, and who has completed at least 10 years of creditable service as a register of deeds is entitled to receive a monthly pension under this Article, provided that register of deeds is not eligible to receive any retirement benefits from any State or locally sponsored plan.

(b)   Each eligible retired register of deeds as defined in subsection (a), (a1), or (a2) of this section relating to service and retirement status shall be entitled to receive a monthly pension under this Article beginning with the month of retirement. (1987, c. 792, s. 1; 1991, c. 443, s. 1; 1995, c. 259, s. 1; 1998-147, s. 1; 2007-245, s. 2.)

§ 161-50.5. Benefits.

(a)   An eligible retired register of deeds shall be entitled to receive an annual pension benefit, payable in equal monthly installments, equal to one share for each full year of eligible service as register of deeds multiplied by his total number of years of eligible service. The amount of each share shall be determined by dividing the total number of years of eligible service for all eligible retired registers of deeds on December 31 of each calendar year into the amount to be disbursed as monthly pension payments in accordance with the provisions of G.S. 161-50.3. In no event, however, shall a monthly pension under this Article exceed an amount which, when added to a retirement allowance under the maximum allowance at retirement from the Local Governmental Employees' Retirement System or an equivalent locally sponsored plan, is greater than seventy-five percent (75%) of a register of deed's equivalent annual salary immediately preceding retirement computed on the latest monthly rate, including any and all supplements, to a maximum amount of one thousand five hundred dollars ($1,500).

(a1) A register of deeds eligible under G.S. 161-50.4(a2) shall be entitled to receive an annual pension benefit, payable in equal monthly installments as determined under the provisions of subsection (a) of this section, but reduced by an amount equal to the benefit that would be payable from the Local Governmental Employees' Retirement System if the register of deeds had been a member of the Local Governmental Employees' Retirement System and all of the years of local service were creditable to that System.

(b) All monthly pensions payable under this Article shall be paid on the same business day of each month that benefits are paid from the Local Governmental Employees' Retirement System.

(c) Monthly pensions payable under this Article shall cease at the death of the pensioner and no payment will be made to any beneficiaries or to the decedent's estate.

(d) Monthly pensions payable under this Article will cease upon the full-time reemployment of a pensioner with an employer participating in the Local Governmental Employees' Retirement System for as long as the pensioner is so reemployed.

(e) Repealed by Session Laws 1989, c. 792, s. 2.11, effective for taxable years beginning on or after January 1, 1989.

(f) Nothing contained in this Article shall preclude or in any way affect the benefits that a pensioner may be entitled to from any state, federal or private pension, retirement or other deferred compensation plan. (1987, c. 792, s. 1; 1989, c. 792, s. 2.11; 1991, c. 50, s. 1; c. 443, s. 2; 1998-147, s. 2; 2007-245, s. 3; 2009-576, s. 1.)

Chapter 162.

Sheriff.

Article 1.

The Office.

§ 162-1. Election and term of office.

In each county a sheriff shall be elected by the qualified voters thereof, as is prescribed for members of the General Assembly, and shall hold his office for four years. (Const., art. 4, s. 24; Rev., s. 2808; C.S., s. 3925.)

§ 162-2. Disqualifications for the office.

No person shall be eligible for the office of sheriff who is not of the age of 21 years, or has not resided in the county in which he is chosen for one year immediately preceding his election. No person shall engage in the practice of law or serve as a member of the General Assembly while serving as sheriff. (1777, c. 118, ss. 2, 4, P.R.; 1806, c. 699, s. 2, P.R.; 1829, c. 5, s. 6; 1830, c. 25, ss. 2, 3; R.C., c. 105, ss. 5, 6, 7; Code, ss. 2067, 2068, 2069; Rev., s. 2809; C.S., s. 3926; 1971, c. 1231, s. 1; 1983, c. 670, s. 1.)

§ 162-3. Sheriff may resign.

Every sheriff may vacate his office by resigning the same to the board of county commissioners of his county; and thereupon the board may proceed to elect another sheriff. (1777, c. 118, s. 1, P.R.; 1808, c. 752, P.R.; R.C., c. 105, s. 15; Code, s. 2077; Rev., s. 2810; C.S., s. 3927.)

§ 162-4. Repealed by Session Laws 1979, c. 518.

§ 162-5. Vacancy filled; duties performed by coroner or chief deputy.

If any vacancy occurs in the office of sheriff, the coroner of the county shall execute all process directed to the sheriff until the first meeting of the county commissioners next succeeding such vacancy, when the board shall elect a sheriff to supply the vacancy for the residue of the term, who shall possess the same qualifications, enter into the same bond, and be subject to removal, as the sheriff regularly elected. If the board should fail to fill such vacancy, the coroner shall continue to discharge the duties of sheriff until it shall be filled.

In those counties where the office of coroner has been abolished, the chief deputy sheriff, or if there is no chief deputy, then the senior deputy in years of service, shall perform all the duties of the sheriff until the county commissioners appoint some person to fill the unexpired term. In all counties the regular deputy sheriffs shall, during the interim of the vacancy, continue to perform their duties with full authority. (1829, c. 5, s. 8; R.S., c. 109, s. 11; R.C., c. 105, s. 11; Code, s. 2071; Rev., s. 2811; C.S., s. 3929; 1973, c. 74; 1983, c. 670, s. 2.)

§ 162-5.1. Vacancy filled in certain counties; duties performed by coroner or chief deputy.

If any vacancy occurs in the office of sheriff, the coroner of the county shall execute all process directed to the sheriff until the board shall elect a sheriff to supply the vacancy for the residue of the term, who shall possess the same qualifications, enter into the same bond, and be subject to removal, as the sheriff regularly elected. If the sheriff were elected as a nominee of a political party, the board of commissioners shall consult the county executive committee of that political party before filling the vacancy, and shall elect the person recommended by the county executive committee of that party, if the party makes a recommendation within 30 days of the occurrence of the vacancy. If the board should fail to fill such vacancy, the coroner shall continue to discharge the duties of sheriff until it shall be filled.

In those counties where the office of coroner has been abolished, the chief deputy sheriff, or if there is no chief deputy, then the senior deputy in years of service, shall perform all the duties of the sheriff until the county commissioners appoint some person to fill the unexpired term. In all counties the regular deputy sheriffs shall, during the interim of the vacancy, continue to perform their duties with full authority.

This section shall apply only in the following counties: Alamance, Alexander, Alleghany, Avery, Beaufort, Brunswick, Buncombe, Burke, Cabarrus, Caldwell, Carteret, Cherokee, Clay, Cleveland, Davidson, Davie, Edgecombe, Forsyth, Gaston, Graham, Guilford, Haywood, Henderson, Hyde, Jackson, Lee, Lincoln, Madison, McDowell, Mecklenburg, Moore, New Hanover, Onslow, Pender, Polk, Randolph, Richmond, Rockingham, Rutherford, Sampson, Stokes, Surry, Transylvania, Wake, Wayne, and Yancey. (1981, c. 763, ss. 10, 14; c. 830; 1983, c. 670, s. 2; 1987, c. 196, s. 3; 1989, c. 83; c. 497, s. 1; 1991, c. 15, s. 1; c. 558, s. 2; 2001-257, s. 2; 2003-39, s. 1; 2003-90, s. 1; 2009-32, s. 2; 2011-175, s. 4(a); 2012-25, s. 1.)

§§ 162-6 through 162-7. Repealed by Session Laws 1973, c. 108, s. 99.

Article 2.

Sheriff's Bond.

§ 162-8. Bond required.

The sheriff shall furnish a bond payable to the State of North Carolina for the due execution and return of process, the payment of fees and moneys collected, and the faithful execution of his office as sheriff, which shall be conditioned as follows:

The condition of the above obligation is such that, whereas the above bounden _____ is elected and appointed sheriff of _____ County; if therefore, he shall well and truly execute and due return make of all process and precepts to him directed, and pay and satisfy all fees and sums of money by him received or levied by virtue of any process into the proper office into which the same, by the tenor thereof, ought to be paid, or to the person to whom the same shall be due, his executors, administrators, attorneys, or agents; and in all other things well and truly and faithfully execute the said office of sheriff during his continuance therein, then above obligation to be void; otherwise to remain in full force and effect.

The amount of the bond shall be determined by the board of county commissioners, but shall not exceed twenty-five thousand dollars ($25,000). (1777, c. 118, s. 1, P.R.; 1823, c. 1223, P.R.; R.C., c. 105, s. 13; 1879, c. 109; Code, s. 2073; 1895, c. 270, ss. 1, 2; 1899, c. 54, s. 52; c. 207, s. 2; 1903, c. 12; Rev., s. 298; C.S., s. 3930; 1943, c. 543; 1983, c. 670, s. 4.)

§ 162-9. County commissioners to take and approve bonds.

The board of county commissioners in every county shall take and approve the official bond of the sheriffs, which they shall cause to be registered and the original deposited with the clerk of superior court for safekeeping. The bond shall be taken on the first Monday of December next after the election. (1806, c. 699, s. 2, P.R.; 1830, c. 5, s. 5; R.C., c. 105, s. 6; 1868, c. 20, s. 32; 1876-7, c. 276, s. 5; Code, ss. 2066, 2068; Rev., s. 2812; C.S., s. 3931; 1983, c. 670, s. 5.)

§ 162-10. Duty of commissioners when bond insufficient.

Whenever the board of county commissioners finds that the sheriff has been unable to provide the bond prescribed by the board, the board shall give written notice to the sheriff to appear before the board within 10 days and provide a sufficient bond. If the sheriff fails to appear or provide a sufficient bond, the sheriff shall forfeit his office, and the commissioners shall elect a suitable person in the county as sheriff for the unexpired term, pursuant to G.S. 162-5 or G.S. 162-5.1, as appropriate. (1879, c. 109, s. 2; Code, s. 2074; Rev., s. 2813; C.S., s. 3932; 1983, c. 670, s. 6.)

§ 162-11: Repealed by Session Laws 1983, c. 670, s. 7.

§ 162-12. Liability of sureties.

The sureties to a sheriff's bond shall be liable for all fines and amercements imposed on him, in the same manner as they are liable for other defaults in his official duty. (1829, c. 33; R.C., c. 105, s. 14; Code, s. 2076; Rev., s. 2815; C.S., s. 3934.)

Article 3.

Duties of Sheriff.

§ 162-13. To receipt for process.

Every sheriff or coroner shall, when requested, give his receipt for all original and mesne process placed in his hands for execution, to the party suing out the same, his agent or attorney; and such receipt shall be admissible as evidence of the facts therein stated, against such officer and his sureties, in any suit between the party taking the receipt and such officer and his sureties. (1848, c. 97; R.C., c. 105, s. 18; Code, s. 2081; Rev., s. 2816; C.S., s. 3935; 1995, c. 379, s. 14(d).)

§ 162-14. Duty to execute process.

Every sheriff, by himself or his lawful deputies, shall execute and make due return of all writs and other process to him legally issued and directed, within his county or upon any river, bay or creek adjoining thereto, or in any other place where he may lawfully execute the same. (1777, c. 218, s. 5, P.R.; 1821, c. 1110, P.R.; R.C., c. 105, s. 17; 1874, c. 33; Code, s. 2079; 1899, c. 25; Rev., s. 2817; C.S., s. 3936; 1973, c. 108, s. 98; 1983, c. 670, s. 8.)

§ 162-15. Imposition of penalty; procedure.

In any case in which a person aggrieved seeks the imposition of penalties against a sheriff for failure or neglect to perform any duty of office or for any default in office as provided in G.S. 162-12, he may proceed by motion in the cause, supported by an affidavit, in a pending action. Upon the filing of a motion in the cause the clerk shall deliver a copy of the motion and affidavit and an order to show cause to the sheriff. (1871-2, c. 74, s. 4; Code, s. 446; Rev., s. 2818; C.S., s. 3937; 1983, c. 670, s. 9.)

§ 162-16. Execute summons, order or judgment.

Whenever the sheriff may be required to serve or execute any summons, order or judgment, or to do any other act, he shall be bound to do so in like manner as upon process issued to him, and shall be equally liable in all respects for neglect of duty; and if the sheriff be a party, the coroner shall be bound to perform the service, as he is now bound to execute process where the sheriff is a party; and this Chapter relating to sheriffs shall apply to coroners when the sheriff is a party. Sheriffs and coroners may return process by mail. Their liabilities in respect to the execution of process shall be as prescribed by law.

In those counties where the office of coroner has been abolished, or is vacant, and in which process is required to be served or executed on the sheriff, the authority to serve or execute such process shall be vested in the clerk of court; however, the clerk of court is hereby empowered to designate and direct by appropriate order some person to act in his stead to serve or execute the same. (C.C.P., s. 354; Code, s. 598; Rev., s. 2819; C.S., s. 3938; 1971, c. 653, s. 1.)

§ 162-17. Duties of outgoing sheriff for unexecuted process.

It shall be the duty of any sheriff who shall have received a precept, and shall go out of office before the return day thereof, without having executed the same, to deliver same to the succeeding sheriff with sufficient time allowed for it to be executed by him. (R.C., c. 105, s. 25; Code, s. 2088; Rev., s. 2820; C.S., s. 3939; 1983, c. 670, s. 10.)

§ 162-18. Payment of money collected on execution.

In all cases where a sheriff has collected money upon an execution placed in his hands, if there be no bona fide contest over the application thereof, he shall immediately pay the same to the plaintiff, or into the office of the clerk of the court from which the execution issued. (Code, s. 2080; Rev., s. 2821; C.S., s. 3940; 1983, c. 670, s. 11.)

§ 162-19. Repealed by Session Laws 1953, c. 973, s. 3.

§§ 162-20 through 162-21: Repealed by Session Laws 1983, c. 670, ss. 12, 13.

§ 162-22. Custody of jail.

The sheriff shall have the care and custody of the jail in his county; and shall be, or appoint, the keeper thereof.

No law-enforcement officer or jailer who shall have the care and custody of any jail shall receive any portion of any jail fee or charge paid by or for any person confined in such jail, nor shall the compensation or remuneration of such officer be affected to any extent by the costs of goods or services furnished to any person confined in such jail. (R.C., c. 105, s. 22; Code, s. 2085; Rev., s. 2824; C.S., s. 3944; 1967, c. 581, s. 3; 1969, c. 1090; 1983, c. 670, s. 14.)

§ 162-23. Prevent entering jail for lynching; county liable.

When the sheriff of any county has good reason to believe that the jail of his county is in danger of being broken or entered for the purpose of killing or injuring a prisoner placed by the law in his custody, it shall be his duty at once to call on the commissioners of the county, or some one of them, for a sufficient guard for the jail, and in such case, if the commissioner or commissioners fail to authorize the employment of necessary guards to protect the jail, and by reason of such failure the jail is entered and a prisoner killed, the county in whose jail the prisoner is confined shall be responsible in damages, to be recovered by the personal representatives of the prisoner thus killed, by action begun and prosecuted before the superior court of any county in this State. (1893, c. 461, s. 7; Rev., s. 2825; C.S., s. 3945.)

§ 162-24. Delegation of official duties.

The sheriff may not delegate to another person the final responsibility for discharging his official duties, but he may appoint a deputy or employ others to assist him in performing his official duties. (23 Hen. VI, c. 10; R.C., c. 105, s. 21; Code, s. 2084; Rev., s. 2828; C.S., s. 3946; 1983, c. 670, s. 15.)

§ 162-25. Obligations taken by sheriff payable to himself.

The sheriff or his deputy shall take no obligation of or from any person in his custody for or concerning any matter or thing relating to his office otherwise payable than to himself as sheriff and dischargeable upon the prisoner's appearance and rendering himself at the day and place required in the writ (whereupon he was or shall be taken or arrested), and his sureties discharging themselves therefrom as special bail of such prisoner or such person keeping within the limits and rules of any prison; and every other obligation taken by any sheriff in any other manner or form, by color of his office, shall be void, except in any special case and other obligation shall be, by law, particularly and expressly directed; and no sheriff shall demand, exact, take or receive any greater fee or reward whatsoever, nor shall have any allowance, reward or satisfaction from the public, for any service by him done, other than such sum as the court shall allow for ex officio services and the allowance given and provided by law. (1777, c. 118, s. 8, P.R.; R.C., c. 105, s. 19; Code, s. 2082; Rev., s. 2829; C.S., s. 3947.)

§ 162-26. Sheriff may establish volunteer school safety resource officer program.

(a) The sheriff may establish a volunteer school safety resource officer program to provide nonsalaried special deputies to serve as school safety resource officers in public schools. To be a volunteer in the program, a person must have prior experience as either (i) a sworn law enforcement officer or (ii) a military police officer with a minimum of two years' service. If a person with experience as a military police officer is no longer in the armed services, the person must also have an honorable discharge. A program volunteer must receive training on research into the social and cognitive development of elementary, middle, and high school children and must also meet the selection standards and any additional criteria established by the sheriff.

(b)   Each volunteer shall report to the sheriff and shall work under the direction and supervision of the sheriff or the sheriff's designee when carrying out the volunteer's duties as a school safety resource officer. No volunteer may be assigned to a school as a school safety resource officer until the volunteer has updated or renewed the volunteer's law enforcement training and has been certified by the North Carolina Sheriff's Education and Training Standards Commission as meeting the educational and firearms proficiency standards required of persons serving as special deputy sheriffs. A volunteer is not required to meet the physical standards required by the North Carolina Sheriff's Education and Training Standards Commission but must have a standard medical exam to ensure the volunteer is in good health. A person selected by the sheriff to serve as a volunteer under this section shall have the power of arrest while performing official duties as a volunteer school safety resource officer.

(c)   The sheriff may enter into an agreement with the local board of education to provide volunteer school safety resource officers who meet both the criteria established by this section and the selection and training requirements set by the sheriff of the county for the schools. The sheriff shall be responsible for the assignment of any volunteer school safety resource officer assigned to a public school and for the supervision of the officer.

(d)   There shall be no liability on the part of and no cause of action shall arise against a volunteer school safety resource officer, the Sheriff or employees of the sheriff supervising a volunteer school safety officer, or the public school system or its employees for any good-faith action taken by them in the performance of their duties with regard to the volunteer school safety resource officer program established pursuant to this section. (2013-360, s. 8.45(e).)

§ 162-27: Reserved for future codification purposes.

§ 162-28: Reserved for future codification purposes.

§ 162-29: Reserved for future codification purposes.

§ 162-30: Reserved for future codification purposes.

Article 4.

County Prisoners.

§ 162-31. Repealed by Session Laws 1975, c. 166, s. 26.

§ 162-32. Bond of prisoner committed on capias in civil action.

Every bond given by any person committed in arrest and bail, or in custody after final judgment, shall be assigned by the sheriff to the party at whose instance such person was committed to jail, and shall be returned to the office of the clerk of the court where the judgment was rendered, and shall have the force of a judgment. If any person who obtains the rules of any prison, as aforesaid, escapes out of the same before he has paid the debt or damages and costs according to the condition of his bond, the court where the bond is filed, upon motion of the assignee thereof, shall award execution against such person and his sureties for the debt or damages and costs, with interest from the time of escape till payment, and no person committed to jail on such execution shall be allowed the rules of prison: Provided, the obligors have ten days' previous notice of such motion, in writing; but they shall not be admitted to deny the making of the bond in their answer, unless by affidavit they prove the truth of the plea. (1759, c. 65, ss. 2, 3, P.R.; R.C., c. 87, s. 14; Code, s. 3469; Rev., s. 1341; C.S., s. 1345; 1973, c. 822, s. 3.)

§ 162-33. Prisoner may furnish necessaries.

With the sheriff's approval, prisoners shall be allowed to purchase and procure such necessaries, in addition to the diet furnished by the jailer, as they may think proper. (1795, c. 433, s. 6, P.R.; R.C., c. 87, s. 8; Code, s. 3463; Rev., s. 1344; C.S., s. 1348; 1973, c. 822, s. 3; 2001-487, s. 95.)

§ 162-34. United States prisoners.

When a prisoner is delivered to the keeper of the county jail by the authority of the United States, such keeper shall receive and commit such prisoner if the jail has adequate and available housing space. The keeper of the county jail shall not be subject to any pains or penalties for refusal to receive and commit a federal prisoner. The United States shall reimburse the county for the incarceration of any federal prisoner at such rate as may be agreed upon between the county and the United States. (1790, c. 322, ss. 1, 2, P.R.; R.C., c. 87, s. 1; Code, s. 3456; Rev., s. 1342; C.S., s. 1349; 1973, c. 822, s. 3; 1983, c. 219.)

§ 162-35. Arrest of escaped persons from penal institutions.

Upon information received from the superintendent of any correctional or any penal institution, established by the laws of the State, that any person confined in such institution or assigned thereto by juvenile or other court under authority of law, has escaped therefrom and is still at large, it shall be the duty of sheriffs of the respective counties of the State, and of any peace officer in whose jurisdiction such person may be found, to take into his custody such escaped person, if to be found in his county, and to cause his return to the custody of the proper officer of the institution from which he has escaped. (1933, c. 105, s. 1; 1973, c. 822, s. 3.)

§ 162-36. Transfer of prisoners to succeeding sheriff.

The delivery of prisoners, by indenture between the late and present sheriff, or the entering on record in court the names of the several prisoners, and the causes of their commitment, delivered over to the present sheriff, shall be sufficient to discharge the late sheriff from all liability for any escape that shall happen. (1777, c. 118, s. 12, P.R.; R.C., c. 87, s. 15; Code, s. 3470; Rev., s. 1348; C.S., s. 1352; 1973, c. 822, s. 3.)

§ 162-37: Repealed by Session Laws 1983, c. 670, s. 16.

§ 162-38. Where jail unfit or insecure, courts may commit to jail of adjoining county.

Whenever there is an unfit or insecure jail in any county, the judicial officers of such county may commit any persons brought before them, whether in a criminal or civil proceeding, to the jail of any adjoining county, for the same causes and under the like regulations that they might have ordered commitments to the usual jail; and the sheriffs and other officers of such county in which there is an unfit or insecure jail, and the sheriffs or keepers of the jails of the adjoining counties, shall obey any order of commitment so made. (1835, c. 2, s. 2; R.C., c. 87, s. 3; Code, s. 3458; Rev., s. 1350; C.S., s. 1354; 1973, c. 57, s. 2; c. 822, s. 3; 1983, c. 670, s. 17.)

§ 162-39. Transfer of prisoners when necessary for safety and security; application of section to municipalities.

(a)   Whenever necessary for the safety of a prisoner held in any county jail or to avoid a breach of the peace in any county or whenever prisoners are arrested in such numbers that county jail facilities are insufficient and inadequate for the housing of such prisoners, the resident judge of the superior court or any judge holding superior court in the district or any district court judge may order the prisoner transferred to a fit and secure jail in some other county where the prisoner shall be held for such length of time as the judge may direct.

(b)   Whenever necessary to avoid a security risk in any county jail, or whenever prisoners are arrested in such numbers that county jail facilities are insufficient and inadequate for the housing of such prisoners, the resident judge of the superior court or any judge holding superior court in the district or any district court judge may order the prisoner transferred to a unit of the State prison system designated by the Secretary of Public Safety or his authorized representative. For purposes of this subsection, a prisoner poses a security risk if the prisoner:

(1)   Poses a serious escape risk;

(2)   Exhibits violently aggressive behavior that cannot be contained and warrants a higher level of supervision;

(3)   Needs to be protected from other inmates, and the county jail facility cannot provide such protection;

(4) Is a female or a person 18 years of age or younger, and the county jail facility does not have adequate housing for such prisoners;

(5) Is in custody at a time when a fire or other catastrophic event has caused the county jail facility to cease or curtail operations; or

(6) Otherwise poses an imminent danger to the staff of the county jail facility or to other prisoners in the facility.

(c) The sheriff of the county from which the prisoner is removed shall be responsible for conveying the prisoner to the jail or prison unit where he is to be held, and for returning him to the common jail of the county from which he was transferred. The return shall be made at the expiration of the time designated in the court order directing the transfer unless the judge, by appropriate order, shall direct otherwise. The sheriff or keeper of the jail of the county designated in the court order, or the officer in charge of the prison unit designated by the Secretary of Public Safety, shall receive and release custody of the prisoner in accordance with the terms of the court order. If a prisoner is transferred to a unit of the State prison system, the county from which the prisoner is transferred shall pay the Division of Adult Correction of the Department of Public Safety for maintaining the prisoner for the time designated by the court at the per day, per inmate rate at which the Division of Adult Correction of the Department of Public Safety pays a local jail for maintaining a prisoner. The county shall also pay the Division of Adult Correction of the Department of Public Safety for the costs of extraordinary medical care incurred while the prisoner was in the custody of the Division of Adult Correction of the Department of Public Safety, defined as follows:

(1) Medical expenses incurred as a result of providing health care to a prisoner as an inpatient (hospitalized);

(2) Other medical expenses when the total cost exceeds thirty-five dollars ($35.00) per occurrence or illness as a result of providing health care to a prisoner as an outpatient (nonhospitalized); and

(3) Cost of replacement of eyeglasses and dental prosthetic devices if those eyeglasses or devices are broken while the prisoner is incarcerated, provided the prisoner was using the eyeglasses or devices at the time of his commitment and then only if prior written consent of the county is obtained by the Division.

If the prisoner is transferred to a jail in some other county, the county from which the prisoner is transferred shall pay to the county receiving the prisoner in its jail the actual cost of maintaining the prisoner for the time designated by the court. Counties are hereby authorized to enter into contractual agreements with other counties to provide jail facilities to which prisoners may be transferred as deemed necessary under this section.

Whenever prisoners are arrested in such numbers that county jail facilities are insufficient and inadequate for the safekeeping of such prisoners, the resident judge of the superior court or any superior or district court judge holding court in the district may order the prisoners transferred to a unit of the Division of Adult Correction of the Department of Public Safety designated by the Secretary of Public Safety or his authorized representative, where the prisoners may be held for such length of time as the judge may direct, such detention to be in cell separate from that used for imprisonment of persons already convicted of crimes, except when admission to an inpatient prison medical or mental health unit is required to provide services deemed necessary by a prison health care clinician. The sheriff of the county from which the prisoners are removed shall be responsible for conveying the prisoners to the prison unit or units where they are to be held, and for returning them to the common jail of the county from which they were transferred. However, if due to the number of prisoners to be conveyed the sheriff is unable to provide adequate transportation, he may request the assistance of the Division of Adult Correction of the Department of Public Safety, and the Division of Adult Correction of the Department of Public Safety is hereby authorized and directed to cooperate with the sheriff and provide whatever assistance is available, both in vehicles and manpower, to accomplish the conveying of the prisoners to and from the county to the designated prison unit or units. The officer in charge of the prison unit designated by the Secretary of Public Safety or his authorized representative shall receive and release the custody of the prisoners in accordance with the terms of the court order. The county from which the prisoners are transferred shall pay to the Division of Adult Correction of the Department of Public Safety the actual cost of transporting the prisoners and the cost of maintaining the prisoners at the per day, per inmate rate at which the Division of Adult Correction of the Department of Public Safety pays a local jail for maintaining a prisoner, provided, however, that a county is not required to reimburse the State for transporting or maintaining a prisoner who was a resident of another state or county at the time he was arrested. However, if the county commissioners shall certify to the Governor that the county is unable to pay the bill submitted by the Division of Adult Correction of the Department of Public Safety to the county for the services rendered, either in whole or in part, the Governor may recommend to the Council of State that the State of North Carolina assume and pay, in whole or in part, the obligation of the county to the Division of Adult Correction of the Department of Public Safety, and upon approval of the Council of State the amount so approved shall be paid from Contingency and Emergency Fund to the Division of Adult Correction of the Department of Public Safety.

When, due to an emergency, it is not feasible to obtain from a judge of the superior or district court a prior order of transfer, the sheriff of the county and the Division of Adult Correction of the Department of Public Safety may exercise the authority hereinafter conferred; provided, however, that the sheriff shall, as soon as possible after the emergency, obtain an order from the judge authorizing the prisoners to be held in the designated place of confinement for such period as the judge may direct. All provisions of this subsection shall be applicable to municipalities whenever prisoners are arrested in such numbers that the municipal jail facilities and the county jail facilities are insufficient and inadequate for the safekeeping of the prisoners. The chief of police is hereby authorized to exercise the authority herein conferred upon the sheriff, and the municipality shall be liable for the cost of transporting and maintaining the prisoners to the same extent as a county would be unless action is taken by the Governor and Council of State as herein provided for counties which are unable to pay such costs.

(d) Whenever a prisoner held in a county jail requires medical or mental health treatment that the county decides can best be provided by the Division of Adult Correction of the Department of Public Safety, the resident judge of the superior court or any judge holding superior court in the district or any district court judge may order the prisoner transferred to a unit of the State prison system designated by the Secretary of Public Safety or his authorized representative. The sheriff of the county from which the prisoner is removed shall be responsible for conveying the prisoner to the prison unit where he is to be held, and for returning him to the jail of the county from which he was transferred. The prisoner shall be returned when the attending medical or mental health professional determines that the prisoner may be returned safely. The officer in charge of the prison unit designated by the Secretary of Public Safety shall receive custody of the prisoner in accordance with the terms of the order and shall release custody of the prisoner in accordance with the instructions of the attending medical or mental health professional. The county from which the prisoner is transferred shall pay the Division of Adult Correction of the Department of Public Safety for maintaining the prisoner for the period of treatment at the per day, per inmate rate at which the Division of Adult Correction of the Department of Public Safety pays a local jail for maintaining a prisoner, and for extraordinary medical expenses as set forth in subsection (c) of this section.

(e) The number of county prisoners incarcerated in the State prison system pursuant to safekeeping orders from the various counties pursuant to subsection (b) of this section or for medical or mental health treatment pursuant to subsection (d) of this section may not exceed 200 at any given time unless authorized by the Secretary of Public Safety. The Secretary may refuse to accept any safekeeper and may return any safekeeper transferred under a safekeeping order when this capacity limit is reached. (1957, c. 1265; 1967, c. 996, ss. 13, 15; 1969, cc. 462, 1130; 1973, c. 822, s. 3; c. 1262, s. 10; 1983, c. 165, ss. 1-4; 1985 (Reg. Sess., 1986), c. 1014, s. 198(a)-(c); 1989, c. 1, s. 7; 1991, c. 535, s. 1; 1991 (Reg. Sess., 1992), c. 983, s. 1; 2002-126, s. 17.1; 2011-145, s. 19.1(h), (i); 2012-83, s. 60.)

§ 162-40. When jail destroyed, transfer of prisoners provided for.

When the jail of any county is destroyed by fire or other accident, any judicial officer of such county may cause all prisoners then confined therein to be brought before him. Upon the production of the process under which any prisoner was confined, such judicial officer shall order his commitment to the jail of any adjacent county. The sheriff or other officer of the county deputized for that purpose shall obey the order; and the sheriff or keeper of the common jail of such adjacent county shall receive such prisoners consistent with those provisions of G.S. 162-38. (1835, c. 2, s. 1; R.C., c. 87, s. 2; Code, s. 3457; Rev., s. 1351; C.S., s. 1355; 1973, c. 57, s. 3; c. 822, s. 3; 1983, c. 670, s. 18.)

§ 162-40.1. Reimbursement for transfer of prisoners.

The county receiving prisoners pursuant to G.S. 162-38, 162-39 and 162-40 shall be reimbursed at the usual jail fee rate for each 24 hours of confinement or part thereof by the county from which the prisoner is transferred. (1983, c. 670, s. 19.)

§ 162-41. Repealed by Session Laws 1977, c. 711, s. 33.

§§ 162-42 through 162-44: Repealed by Session Laws 1983, c. 670, s. 20.

§ 162-45. Repealed by Session Laws 1977, c. 711, s. 33.

§ 162-46: Repealed by Session Laws 1979, c. 760, s. 4.

§ 162-47. Repealed by Session Laws 1977, c. 711, s. 33.

§ 162-48: Repealed by Session Laws 1983, c. 670, s. 20.

§ 162-49. Repealed by Session Laws 1977, c. 711, s. 33.

§ 162-50. Penalties.

Upon a finding that the sheriff, personally or through his lawful deputies, has willfully failed or neglected to perform any duty imposed by this Chapter, or has made any false return, he shall be subject to damages of not more than five hundred dollars ($500.00), and such damages recovered shall be paid to the person aggrieved. Nothing in this section bars an independent action for damages by the person aggrieved. (1983, c. 670, s. 21.)

§§ 162-51 through 162-54. Reserved for future codification purposes.

§ 162-55. Injury to prisoner by jailer.

If the keeper of a jail shall do, or cause to be done, any wrong or injury to the prisoners committed to his custody, contrary to law, he shall not only pay treble damages to the person injured, but shall be guilty of a Class 1 misdemeanor. (1795, c. 433, s. 6, P.R.; R.C., c. 87, s. 8; Code, s. 3463; Rev., s. 3661; C.S., s. 4407; 1983, c. 631, s. 1; 1993, c. 539, s. 1098; 1994, Ex. Sess., c. 24, s. 14(c).)

§ 162-56. Place of confinement.

Persons committed to the custody of a sheriff shall be confined in the facilities designated by law for such confinement, and shall not be confined in any other place. Nothing herein shall be construed to prohibit or limit the authority of a sheriff to house prisoners committed to his custody in quarters, approved by the Department of Health and Human Services, other than the county jail. (1795, c.

433, s. 4; R.C., c. 87, s. 16; Code, s. 3471; Rev., s. 3660; C.S., s. 4408; 1983, c. 631, s. 2; 1997-443, s. 11A.118(a).)

§ 162-57. Record to be kept; items of record.

The superintendent or other person having charge of prisoners shall keep a record showing, the name, age, date of sentence, length of sentence, crime for which convicted, home address, next of kin, and the conduct of each prisoner received. (1927, c. 178, s. 2; 1983, c. 631, s. 3.)

§ 162-58. Counties may work prisoners.

The board of commissioners of the several counties may enact by resolution all necessary rules and regulations for work on projects to benefit units of State or local government by persons convicted of misdemeanors or felonies and imprisoned in the local confinement facilities or satellite jail/work release units of their respective counties. The sheriff shall approve rules and regulations enacted by the board. Prisoners working under this section shall be supervised by county employees or by the sheriff. The rules enacted by the board of county commissioners and approved by the sheriff shall specify a procedure for ensuring that county employees supervising prisoners pursuant to this section be provided with notice that the persons placed under their supervision are inmates from a local confinement facility or a satellite jail/work release unit. (1991 (Reg. Sess., 1992), c. 841, s. 1; 2002-159, s. 54.)

§ 162-59. Person having custody to approve prisoners for work.

No prisoner shall perform work pursuant to G.S. 162-58 unless the prisoner has been approved for the work by the person having custody of the prisoner. The decision to approve a prisoner for work shall be based on the prisoner's history of violence, if any, past criminal convictions, and current sentence. For purposes of this section, the person having custody of the prisoner is the sheriff, except that when the prisoner is confined in a district confinement facility the person having custody of the prisoner is the jail administrator. The person having custody of the prisoner may use his discretion to revoke his approval at any time and to return the prisoner to the local confinement facility or satellite jail/work release unit. Neither the person having custody of the prisoner nor any jailer may be held liable for the actions of any prisoner, including those actions committed during and after the escape of a prisoner, while the prisoner is outside their supervision pursuant to this section. (1991 (Reg. Sess., 1992), c. 841, s. 1.)

§ 162-59.1. Person having custody to approve prisoners for participation in education and other programs.

The person having custody of a prisoner convicted of a misdemeanor offense may approve that prisoner's participation in a general education development diploma program (GED program) or in any other education, rehabilitation, or training program. The person having custody of the prisoner may revoke this approval at any time. For purposes of this section, the person having custody of the prisoner is the sheriff, except that when the prisoner is confined in a district confinement facility the person having custody of the prisoner is the jail administrator. (2001-200, s. 1.)

§ 162-60. Reduction in sentence allowed for work, education, and other programs.

(a) A prisoner who has faithfully performed the duties assigned to the prisoner under G.S. 162-58 is entitled to a reduction in the prisoner's sentence of four days for each 30 days of work performed.

(b) A prisoner who is convicted of a misdemeanor offense and housed in a local confinement facility and who faithfully participates in a general education development diploma program (GED program) or in any other education, rehabilitation, or training program is entitled to a reduction in the prisoner's sentence of four days for each 30 days of classes attended, up to the maximum credit allowed under G.S. 15A-1340.20(d).

(c) The person having custody of the prisoner, as defined in G.S. 162-59, is the sole judge as to whether the prisoner has faithfully performed the assigned duties under G.S. 162-58 or has faithfully participated in a GED program or other education, rehabilitation, or training program under subsection (b) of this section. A prisoner who escapes or attempts to escape while performing work pursuant to G.S. 162-58 or while participating in a GED program or other education, rehabilitation, or training program shall forfeit any reduction in sentence that the prisoner would have been entitled to under this section. (1991

(Reg. Sess., 1992), c. 841, s. 1; 1993, c. 538, s. 36; 1994, Ex. Sess., c. 24, s. 14(b); 1993 (Reg. Sess., 1994), c. 767, s. 2; 2001-200, s. 2.)

§ 162-61. Liability of county.

The county working prisoners pursuant to G.S. 162-58 shall remain liable for emergency medical services for those prisoners pursuant to G.S. 153A-224 while the prisoners are working. The county working the prisoners shall be liable to third parties for injuries incurred by the third parties through the negligence of the working prisoners to the same extent as the county is liable for the actions of its employees. Chapters 96 and 97 of the General Statutes shall have no application to prisoners working pursuant to G.S. 162-58. (1991 (Reg. Sess., 1992), c. 841, s. 1.)

§ 162-62. Legal status of prisoners.

(a) When any person charged with a felony or an impaired driving offense is confined for any period in a county jail, local confinement facility, district confinement facility, or satellite jail/work release unit, the administrator or other person in charge of the facility shall attempt to determine if the prisoner is a legal resident of the United States by an inquiry of the prisoner, or by examination of any relevant documents, or both.

(b) If the administrator or other person in charge of the facility is unable to determine if that prisoner is a legal resident or citizen of the United States or its territories, the administrator or other person in charge of the facility holding the prisoner, where possible, shall make a query of Immigration and Customs Enforcement of the United States Department of Homeland Security. If the prisoner has not been lawfully admitted to the United States, the United States Department of Homeland Security will have been notified of the prisoner's status and confinement at the facility by its receipt of the query from the facility.

(c) Nothing in this section shall be construed to deny bond to a prisoner or to prevent a prisoner from being released from confinement when that prisoner is otherwise eligible for release.

(d) Repealed by Session Laws 2010-97, s. 12, effective July 20, 2010. (2007-494, s. 1; 2010-97, s. 12.)

Chapter 162A.

Water and Sewer Systems.

Article 1.

Water and Sewer Authorities.

§ 162A-1. Title.

This Article shall be known and may be cited as the "North Carolina Water and Sewer Authorities Act." (1955, c. 1195, s. 1; 1971, c. 892, s. 1.)

§ 162A-2. Definitions.

As used in this Article the following words and terms shall have the following meanings, unless the context shall indicate another or different meaning or intent:

(1) The word "authority" shall mean an authority created under the provisions of this Article or, if such authority shall be abolished, the board, body or commission succeeding to the principal functions thereof or to whom the powers given by this Article to the authority shall be given by law.

(2) The word "Commission" shall mean the Environmental Management Commission.

(3) The word "cost" as applied to a water system or a sewer system shall include the purchase price of any such system, the cost of construction, the cost of all labor and materials, machinery and equipment, the cost of improvements, the cost of all lands, property, rights, easements and franchises acquired, financing charges, interest prior to and during construction and, if deemed advisable by the authority, for one year after completion of construction, cost of plans and specifications, surveys and estimates of cost and of revenues, cost of engineering and legal services, and all other expenses necessary or incident to determining the feasibility or practicability of such construction, administrative expense and such other expenses, including reasonable provision for working capital, as may be necessary or incident to the financing herein authorized. Any obligation or expense incurred by the authority or by any political subdivision

prior to the issuance of bonds under the provisions of this Article in connection with any of the foregoing items or cost may be regarded as a part of such cost.

(4) The term "governing body" shall mean the board, commission, council or other body, by whatever name it may be known, in which the general legislative powers of the political subdivision are vested.

(5) The word "improvements" shall mean such repairs, replacements, additions, extensions and betterments of and to a water system or a sewer system as are deemed necessary by the authority to place or to maintain such system in proper condition for its safe, efficient and economic operation or to meet requirements for service in areas which may be served by the authority and for which no existing service is being rendered.

(6) The word "person" shall mean any and all persons, including individuals, firms, partnerships, associations, public or private institutions, municipalities, or political subdivisions, governmental agencies, or private or public corporations organized and existing under the laws of this State or any other state or country.

(7) The term "political subdivision" shall mean any county, city, town, incorporated village, sanitary district or other political subdivision or public corporation of this State now or hereafter incorporated.

(7a) The word "revenues" shall mean all moneys received by an authority from or in connection with any sewer system or water system including, without limitation, any moneys received as interest grants.

(8) The word "sewage" shall mean the water-carried wastes created in and carried or to be carried away from residences, hotels, schools, hospitals, industrial establishments, commercial establishments or any other private or public building together with such surface or groundwater or household and industrial wastes as may be present.

(9) The term "sewage disposal system" shall mean and shall include any plant, system, facility, or property used or useful or having the present capacity for future use in connection with the collection, treatment, purification or disposal of sewage (including industrial wastes resulting from any processes of industry, manufacture, trade or business or from the development of any natural resources), or any integral part thereof, including but not limited to septic tank systems or other on-site collection or disposal facilities or systems, treatment plants, pumping stations, intercepting sewers, trunk sewers, pressure lines,

mains and all necessary appurtenances and equipment, and all property, rights, easements and franchises relating thereto and deemed necessary or convenient by the authority for the operation thereof.

(10)   The word "sewers" shall include mains, pipes and laterals for the reception of sewage and carrying such sewage to an outfall or some part of a sewage disposal system, including pumping stations where deemed necessary by the authority.

(11)   The term "sewer system" shall embrace both sewers and sewage disposal systems and all property, rights, easements and franchises relating thereto.

(12)   The term "water system" shall mean and include all plants, systems, facilities or properties used or useful or having the present capacity for future use in connection with the supply or distribution of water or the control and drainage of stormwater runoff and any integral part thereof, including but not limited to water supply systems, water distribution systems, stormwater management programs designed to protect water quality by controlling the level of pollutants in, and the quantity and flow of, stormwater and structural and natural stormwater and drainage systems of all types, sources of water supply including lakes, reservoirs and wells, intakes, mains, laterals, aqueducts, pumping stations, standpipes, filtration plants, purification plants, hydrants, meters, valves, and all necessary appurtenances and equipment and all properties, rights, easements and franchises relating thereto and deemed necessary or convenient by the authority for the operation thereof. (1955, c. 1195, s. 2; 1969, c. 850; 1971, c. 892, s. 1; 1979, c. 619, s. 8; 1989 (Reg. Sess., 1990), c. 1004, s. 43; 1991, c. 591, s. 3; 2000-70, s. 5.)

§ 162A-3. Procedure for creation; certificate of incorporation; certification of principal office and officers.

(a)   The governing body of a single county or the governing bodies of any two or more political subdivisions may by resolution signify their determination to organize an authority under the provisions of this Article. Each of such resolutions shall be adopted after a public hearing thereon, notice of which hearing shall be given by publication at least once, not less than 10 days prior to the date fixed for such hearing, in a newspaper having a general circulation in the political subdivision. Such notice shall contain a brief statement of the substance of the proposed resolution, shall set forth the proposed articles of incorporation of the authority and shall state the time and place of the public hearing to be held thereof. No such political subdivision shall be required to make any other publication of such resolution under the provisions of any other law.

(a1)   If an authority is organized by three or more political subdivisions, it may include in its organization nonprofit water corporations. The board of directors of a nonprofit water corporation must signify the corporation's determination to participate in the organization of the authority by adopting a resolution that meets the requirements of subsection (b) of this section. The nonprofit water corporation is not subject to the notice and public hearing requirements of subsection (a) of this section. For all other purposes of this Article, the nonprofit water corporation shall be considered to be a political subdivision.

(a2)   If an authority is organized by three or more political subdivisions, it may include in its organization the State of North Carolina. The State of North Carolina is not subject to the notice and public hearing requirements of subsection (a) of this section. For purposes of this Article, the State of North Carolina shall be a political subdivision and its governing body shall be the Council of State.

(b)   Each such resolution shall include articles of incorporation which shall set forth:

(1)   The name of the authority;

(2)   A statement that such authority is organized under this Article;

(3)   The names of the organizing political subdivisions; and

(4)   The names and addresses of the first members of the authority appointed by the organizing political subdivisions.

(c)   A certified copy of each of such resolutions signifying the determination to organize an authority under the provisions of this Article shall be filed with the Secretary of State of North Carolina, together with proof of publication of the notice of hearing on each of such resolutions. If the Secretary of State finds that the resolutions, including the articles of incorporation, conform to the provisions of this Article and that the notices of hearing were properly published, he shall file such resolutions and proofs of publication in his office and shall issue a certificate of incorporation under the seal of the State and shall record the same in an appropriate book of record in his office. The issuance of such certificate of incorporation by the Secretary of State shall constitute the authority a public body and body politic and corporate of the State of North Carolina. Said certificate of incorporation shall be conclusive evidence of the fact that such authority has been duly created and established under the provisions of this Article.

(d) When the authority has been duly organized and its officers elected as herein provided the secretary of the authority shall certify to the Secretary of State the names and addresses of such officers as well as the address of the principal office of the authority. (1955, c. 1195, s. 3; 1971, c. 892, s. 1; 1991, c. 516, s. 1; 2001-224, s. 1; 2002-76, s. 1.)

§ 162A-3.1. Alternative procedure for creation.

(a) As an alternative to the procedure set forth in G.S. 162A-3, the governing body of a single county or the governing bodies of any two or more political subdivisions may by resolution signify their determination to organize an authority under the provisions of this section of this Article. Each of such resolutions shall be adopted after a public hearing thereon, notice of which hearing shall be given by publication at least once, not less than 10 days prior to the date fixed for such hearing, in a newspaper having a general circulation in the political subdivision. Such notice shall contain a brief statement of the substance of the proposed resolution, shall set forth the proposed articles of incorporation of the authority and shall state the time and place of the public hearing. No such political subdivision shall be required to make any other publication of such resolution under the provisions of any other law.

(a1) If an authority is organized by three or more political subdivisions, it may include in its organization nonprofit water corporations. The board of directors of a nonprofit water corporation must signify the corporation's determination to participate in the organization of the authority by adopting a resolution that meets the requirements of subsection (b) of this section. The nonprofit water corporation is not subject to the notice and public hearing requirements of subsection (a) of this section. For all other purposes of this Article, the nonprofit water corporation shall be considered to be a political subdivision.

(a2) If an authority is organized by three or more political subdivisions, it may include in its organization the State of North Carolina. The State of North

Carolina is not subject to the notice and public hearing requirements of subsection (a) of this section. For purposes of this Article, the State of North Carolina shall be a political subdivision and its governing body shall be the Council of State.

(b)   Each such resolution shall include articles of incorporation which shall set forth:

(1)   The name of the authority;

(2)   A statement that such authority is organized under this section of this Article;

(3)   The names of the organizing political subdivisions;

(4)   The names and addresses of the members of the authority appointed by the organizing political subdivisions; and

(5)   A statement that members of the authority will be limited to such members as may be appointed from time to time by the organizing political subdivisions.

(c)   A certified copy of each of such resolutions signifying the determination to organize an authority under the provisions of this section of this Article shall be filed with the Secretary of State of North Carolina, together with proof of publication of the notice of hearing on each of such resolutions. If the Secretary of State finds that the resolutions, including the articles of incorporation, conform to the provisions of this section of this Article and that the notices of hearing were properly published, he shall file such resolutions and proofs of publication in his office and shall issue a certificate of incorporation under the seal of the State and shall record the same in an appropriate book of record in his office. The issuance of such certificate of incorporation by the Secretary of State shall constitute the authority a public body and body politic and corporate of the State of North Carolina. Said certificate of incorporation shall be conclusive evidence of the fact that such authority has been duly created and established under the provisions of this section of this Article.

(d)   When the authority has been duly organized and its officers elected as herein provided the secretary of the authority shall certify to the Secretary of State the names and addresses of such officers as well as the address of the principal office of the authority. (1975, c. 224, s. 1; 1991, c. 516, s. 2; 2001-224, s. 2; 2002-76, s. 2.)

§ 162A-4. Withdrawal from authority; joinder of new subdivision.

(a) Whenever an authority has been organized under the provisions of this Chapter, any political subdivision may withdraw therefrom at any time prior to the creation of any obligations by the authority, and any political subdivision not having joined in the original organization may, with the consent of the authority, join the authority; provided, that any political subdivision not having joined the original organization shall have the right upon reasonable terms and conditions, whether the authority shall consent thereto or not, to join the authority if the authority's water system or sewer system, or any part thereof is situated within the boundaries of the political subdivision or of the county within which the political subdivision is located; provided, further, that any political subdivision authorized to join the authority by G.S. 162A-5.1 may do so without the consent of the authority.

(b) Any political subdivision desiring to withdraw from or to join an existing authority shall signify its desire by resolution adopted after a public hearing thereon, notice of which hearing shall be given in the manner and at the time provided in G.S. 162A-3 or 162A-3.1, as appropriate. Such notice shall contain a brief statement of the substance of said resolution and shall state the time and place of the public hearing to be held thereon. In the case of a political subdivision desiring to join the authority, the resolution shall set forth all of the information required under G.S. 162A-3 or 162A-3.1, as appropriate, in connection with the original organization of the authority, including the name and address of the first member of the authority from the joining political subdivision if the authority was organized under G.S. 162A-3.

(c) A certified copy of each such resolution signifying the desire of a political subdivision to withdraw from or to join an existing authority, together with proof of publication of the notice of hearing on each such resolution and, in cases where such resolution provides for the political subdivision joining the authority, certified copies of the resolution of the governing bodies creating the authority consenting to such joining shall be filed with the Secretary of State of North Carolina. If the Secretary of State finds that the resolutions conform to the provisions of this Article and that the notices of hearing were properly published, he shall file such resolutions and proofs of publication in his office and shall issue a certificate of withdrawal, or a certificate of joinder, as the case may be, and shall record the same in an appropriate book of record in his office. The withdrawal or joining shall become effective upon the issuance of such certificate, and such certificate shall be conclusive evidence thereof. (1955, c. 1195, s. 4; 1969, c. 850; 1971, c. 892, s. 1; c. 1093, s. 6; 1975, c. 224, s. 2; 1995, c. 207, s. 2; c. 509, s. 135.2(c).)

§ 162A-5. Members of authority; organization; quorum.

(a) Each authority organized under this Article shall consist of the number of members as may be agreed upon by the participating political subdivisions, such members to be selected by the respective political subdivision. A proportionate number (as nearly as can be) of members of the authority first appointed shall have terms expiring one year, two years and three years respectively from the date on which the creation of the authority becomes effective. Successor members and members appointed by a political subdivision subsequently joining the authority shall each be appointed for a term of three years, but any person appointed to fill the vacancy shall be appointed to serve only for the unexpired term and any member may be reappointed; provided, however, that a political subdivision subsequently joining an authority created under G.S. 162A-3.1, or under the provisions of G.S. 162A-3 other than subsection (a1), shall not have the right to appoint any members to such authority. Appointments of successor members shall, in each instance, be made by the governing body of the political subdivision appointing the member whose successor is to be appointed. Any member of the authority may be removed, with or without cause, by the governing body appointing said member. This subsection does not apply in the case of an authority that a city joins under G.S. 162A-5.1.

(b) Each authority organized under this Article that a city has joined under G.S. 162A-5.1 shall consist of the number of members provided by that section, such members to be selected as provided by that section. Two each of the members of the authority first appointed after a city has joined under G.S. 162A-5.1 shall have terms expiring one year and two years respectively from the date on which the certificate of joinder was issued, and three of the members of the authority first appointed after a city has joined under G.S. 162A-5.1 shall have terms expiring three years from the date on which the certificate of joinder was issued. Such designation shall be made by the authority by lot at the meeting where members take their oaths of office. Successor members shall each be appointed for a term of three years to commence on the day that the terms of the prior members' terms expire, but any person appointed to fill a vacancy shall be appointed to serve only for the unexpired term and any member may be reappointed. Appointments of successor members shall, in each instance, be made by the governing body of the political subdivision appointing the member whose successor is to be appointed. Any member of the authority may be removed, with or without cause, by the governing body appointing said member.

(c)   Each member of the authority before entering upon his duties shall take and subscribe an oath or affirmation to support the Constitution of the United States and of this State and to discharge faithfully the duties of his office, and a record of each such oath shall be filed with the secretary of the authority.

The authority shall select one of its members as chairman and another as vice-chairman and shall also select a secretary and a treasurer who may but need not be members of the authority. The offices of secretary and treasurer may be combined. The terms of office of the chairman, vice-chairman, secretary and treasurer shall be as provided in the bylaws of the authority.

A majority of the members of the authority shall constitute a quorum and the affirmative vote of a majority of all of the members of the authority shall be necessary for any action taken by the authority. No vacancy in the membership of the authority shall impair the right of a quorum to exercise all the rights and perform all of the duties of the authority. The members of the authority may be paid a per diem compensation set by the authority which per diem may not exceed the total amount of four thousand dollars ($4,000) annually, and shall be reimbursed for the amount of actual expenses incurred by them in the performance of their duties. (1955, c. 1195, s. 5; 1969, c. 850; 1971, c. 892, s. 1; 1975, c. 224, ss. 3, 4; 1995, c. 207, s. 3; 1999-456, s. 43; 2001-224, s. 2.1; 2005-127, s. 2; 2006-226, s. 29.)

§ 162A-5.1. Political subdivision allowed to join certain authorities.

(a)   As used in this section, "city" means a city, town, or incorporated village.

(b)   When an authority was organized under G.S. 162A-3.1 by one county and one city, and the majority of the authority's water customers are located within a city which is not the city that was one of the two original organizers, then that city may join the authority and appoint members as provided by this section.

(c) A city joining the authority under this section shall do so in accordance with the procedures of G.S. 162A-4. The resolution shall become effective upon the issuance of a certificate of joinder under G.S. 162A-4(c).

(d) When a city joins an authority under this section, then effective on a date set in the resolution, but not earlier than the first day of the second calendar month after the issuance of the certificate of joinder under G.S. 162A-4(c), the terms of office of all the members of the authority are terminated, and the authority shall consist of members appointed as follows:

(1) Two members appointed by the governing board of the city joining the authority under this section. These members must be residents of that city.

(2) One member appointed by the governing board of the city that was one of the two original organizers. That member must be a resident of that city.

(3) One member appointed by the board of commissioners of the county that was one of the two original organizers. This member must be a resident of a household served by the authority's water system.

(4) One member appointed by the board of commissioners of the county that was one of the two original organizers. This member must be a resident of a household served by a sewer system operated by the authority, but may not be a resident of a household served by the authority's water system.

(5) One member appointed by the board of commissioners of the county that was one of the two original organizers. This member must be a resident of a household served by the authority's water system which is located outside the corporate limits of any municipality.

(6) One member appointed by the board of commissioners of the county that was one of the two original organizers. That member must be a resident of the city that has the second highest number of residential water customers served by the authority. (1995, c. 207, s. 1.)

§ 162A-6. Powers of authority generally.

(a) Each authority created hereunder shall be deemed to be a public instrumentality exercising public and essential governmental functions to provide for the public health and welfare, and each authority is authorized and empowered:

(1) To adopt bylaws for the regulation of its affairs and the conduct of its business;

(2) To adopt an official seal and alter the same at pleasure;

(3) To maintain an office at such place or places as it may designate;

(4) To sue and be sued in its own name, plead and be impleaded;

(5) To acquire, lease as lessee or lessor, construct, reconstruct, improve, extend, enlarge, equip, repair, maintain and operate any water system or part thereof or any sewer system or part thereof or any combination thereof within or without the participating political subdivisions or any thereof;

(6) To issue revenue bonds of the authority as hereinafter provided to pay the cost of such acquisition, construction, reconstruction, improvement, extension, enlargement or equipment;

(7) To issue revenue refunding bonds of the authority as hereinafter provided;

(8) To combine any water system and any sewer system as a single system for the purpose of operation and financing;

(9) To fix and revise from time to time and to collect rates, fees and other charges for the use of or for the services and facilities furnished by any system operated by the authority, including rates for water stored by the authority through programs to store and protect water resources in the region served by the authority. Schedules of rates, fees, and other charges may vary according to classes of service for programs to store and protect water resources. For purposes of this subdivision, "programs to store and protect water resources" includes aquifer or surficial storage.

(10) To acquire in the name of the authority by gift, grant, purchase, devise, exchange, lease, acceptance of offers of dedication by plat, or any other lawful method, to the same extent and in the same manner as provided for cities and towns under the provisions of G.S. 160A-240.1 and G.S. 160A-374, or the exercise of the right of eminent domain in accordance with the General Statutes

of North Carolina which may be applicable to the exercise of such powers by municipalities or counties, any lands or rights in land or water rights in connection therewith, and to acquire such personal property, as it may deem necessary in connection with the acquisition, construction, reconstruction, improvement, extension, enlargement or operation of any water system or sewer system, and to hold and dispose of all real and personal property under its control; provided, that the taking of water from any stream or reservoir by any authority created under the provisions of this Article shall not vest in the taker any rights by prescription; provided, further, that nothing in this section shall affect rights by prescription, if any, now held by any municipality and which may be later transferred to any authority of which such municipality may become a member;

(11) To make and enter into all contracts and agreements necessary or incidental to the performance of its duties and the execution of its powers under this Article, including a trust agreement or trust agreements securing any revenue bonds issued hereunder, and to employ such consulting and other engineers, superintendents, managers, construction and financial experts, accountants and attorneys, and such employees and agents as may, in the judgment of the authority be deemed necessary, and to fix their compensation; provided, however, that all such expenses shall be payable solely from funds made available under the provisions of this Article;

(12) To enter into contracts with the government of the United States or any agency or instrumentality thereof, or with any political subdivision, private corporation, copartnership, association or individual providing for the acquisition, construction, reconstruction, improvement, extension, enlargement, operation or maintenance of any water system or sewer system or providing for or relating to the treatment and disposal of sewage or providing for or relating to any water system or the purchase or sale of water;

(13) To receive and accept from any federal, State or other public agency and any private agency, person or other entity, donations, loans, grants, aid or contributions of any money, property, labor or other things of value for any sewer system or water system, and to agree to apply and use the same in accordance with the terms and conditions under which the same are provided;

(14) To enter into contract with any political subdivision by which the authority shall assume the payment of the principal of and interest on indebtedness of such subdivision; and

(14a) To make special assessments against benefited property within the area served or to be served by the authority for the purpose of constructing, reconstructing, extending, or otherwise improving water systems or sanitary collection, treatment, and sewage disposal systems, in the same manner that a county may make special assessments under authority of Chapter 153A, Article 9, except that the language appearing in G.S. 153A-185 reading as follows: "A county may not assess property within a city pursuant to subdivision (1) or (2) of this section unless the governing board of the city has by resolution approved the project," shall not apply to assessments levied by Water and Sewer Authorities established pursuant to Chapter 162A, Article 1, of the General Statutes. For the purposes of this paragraph, references in Chapter 153A, Article 9, to the "county," the "board of county commissioners," "the board" or a specific county official or employee are deemed to refer, respectively, to the authority and to the official or employee of the authority who performs most nearly the same duties performed by the specified county official or employee.

Assessment rolls after being confirmed shall be filed for registration in the office of the Register of Deeds of the county in which the property being assessed is located, and the term "county tax collector" wherever used in G.S. 153A-195 and G.S. 153A-196, shall mean the Executive Director or other administrative officer designated by the authority to perform the functions described in said sections of the statute.

(14b) To provide for the defense of civil and criminal actions and payment of civil judgments against employees and officers or former employees and officers and members or former members of the governing body as authorized by G.S. 160A-167, as amended.

(14c) To adopt ordinances to regulate and control the discharge of sewage or stormwater into any sewerage system owned or operated by the authority, to adopt ordinances concerning stormwater management programs designed to protect water quality by controlling the level of pollutants in and the quantity and flow of stormwater, and to adopt ordinances to regulate and control structural and natural stormwater and drainage systems of all types. Prior to the adoption of any such ordinance or any amendment to any such ordinance, the authority shall first pass a declaration of intent to adopt such ordinance or amendment. The declaration of intent shall describe the ordinance which it is proposed that the authority adopt. The declaration of intent shall be submitted to each governing body for review and comment. The authority shall consider any comment or suggestions offered by any governing body with respect to the proposed ordinance or amendment. Thereafter, the authority shall be authorized to adopt such ordinance or amendment to it at any time after 60 days following the submission of the declaration of intent to each governing body.

(14d) To require the owners of developed property on which there are situated one or more residential dwelling units or commercial establishments located within the jurisdiction of the authority and within a reasonable distance of any waterline or sewer collection line owned, leased as lessee, or operated by the authority to connect the property with the waterline, sewer connection line, or both and fix charges for the connections. The power granted by this subdivision may be exercised by an authority only to the extent that the service, whether water, sewer, or a combination thereof, to be provided by the authority is not then being provided to the improved property by any other political subdivision or by a public utility regulated by the North Carolina Utilities Commission pursuant to Chapter 62 of the General Statutes. In the case of improved property that would qualify for the issuance of a building permit for the construction of one or more residential dwelling units or commercial establishments and where the authority has installed water or sewer lines or a combination thereof directly available to the property, the authority may require payment of a periodic availability charge, not to exceed the minimum periodic service charge for properties that are connected. This subdivision applies only to a water and sewer authority whose membership includes part or all of a county that has a population of at least 40,000 according to the most recent annual population estimates certified by the State Budget Officer.

(15) To do all acts and things necessary or convenient to carry out the powers granted by this Article.

(16) To purchase real or personal property as provided by G.S. 160A-20, in addition to any other method allowed under this Article.

(b) In addition to the powers given under subsection (a) of this section, an authority created under G.S. 162A-3.1 and its participating political subdivisions may enter into agreements obligating these subdivisions to make payments to the authority for treated water delivered or made available or expected to be delivered or made available by the authority, regardless of whether treated water is actually delivered or made available. Such payments may be designed to cover the authority's operating costs (including debt service and related amounts) by allocating those costs among the participating political subdivisions and by requiring these subdivisions to pay additional amounts to make up for the nonpayment of defaulting subdivisions. The participating political subdivisions may agree to budget for and appropriate such payments. Such payment obligations may be made absolute, unconditional, and irrevocable and required to be performed strictly in accordance with the terms of such agreements and without abatement or reduction under all circumstances whatsoever, including whether or not any facility of the authority is completed, operable or operating and, notwithstanding the suspension, interruption, interference, reduction or curtailment of the output of any such facility or the treated water contracted for, and such obligations may be made subject to no reduction, whether by offset or otherwise, and not conditioned upon the performance or nonperformance of the authority or any participating political subdivision under any agreement. Such payment obligations are in consideration of any output or capacity that may at any time be available from facilities of the authority. The participating political subdivisions may agree to make such payments from limited or specified sources. To the extent such payments relate to debt service of the authority and related amounts, they may not be made from any moneys derived from exercise by the participating political subdivisions of their taxing power, and such payment obligations shall not constitute a pledge of such taxing power. The participating political subdivisions may agree (i) not to pledge or encumber any source of payment and (ii) to operate (including fixing rates and charges) in a manner that enables them to make such payments from such sources. The participating political subdivisions may also secure such payment obligations with a pledge of or lien upon any such sources of payment. Notwithstanding the provisions of G.S. 162A-9 or any other law to the contrary, an authority entering into any such agreement need not fix rates, fees and other charges for its services except as provided herein, and such rates, fees and charges need not be uniform through the authority's service areas. Notwithstanding the provisions of G.S. 160A-322 or any other law to the contrary, agreements described herein may have a term not exceeding 50 years. Notwithstanding any law to the contrary, the execution and effectiveness of any agreement authorized hereby shall not be subject to any authorizations or approvals by any entity except the parties thereto. Each authority and its participating political subdivisions shall have the power to do all acts and things necessary or convenient to carry out the powers granted by this subsection.

(c)   In addition to the powers given under subsection (a) of this section, an authority that holds a certificate issued after December 1, 1991, by the Environmental Management Commission under G.S. 162A-7 (repealed) may acquire property by the power of eminent domain or by gift, purchase, grant, exchange, lease, or any other lawful method for one or more of the following purposes:

(1) To relocate a road or to construct a road necessitated by construction of water supply project.

(2) To establish, extend, enlarge, or improve storm sewer and drainage systems and works, or sewer and septic tank lines and systems.

(3) To establish drainage programs and programs to prevent obstructions to the natural flow of streams, creeks and natural water channels or to improve drainage facilities. The authority contained in this subdivision is in addition to any authority contained in Chapter 156 of the General Statutes.

(4) To acquire property for wetlands mitigation. (1955, c. 1195, s. 6; 1969, c. 850; 1971, c. 892, s. 1; 1979, c. 804; 1983, c. 525, s. 5; c. 820, s. 1; 1987 (Reg. Sess., 1988), c. 981, s. 2; 1989, c. 517; 1993 (Reg. Sess., 1994), c. 696, s. 8.1; 1995, c. 509, s. 113; c. 511, s. 1; 1997-436, s. 1; 2000-70, s. 6; 2004-203, s. 5(n); 2013-107, s. 1.)

§ 162A-6.1. Privacy of employee personnel records.

(a) Notwithstanding the provisions of G.S. 132-6 or any other law concerning access to public records, personnel files of employees, former employees, or applicants for employment maintained by an authority are subject to inspection and may be disclosed only as provided by this section. For purposes of this section, an employee's personnel file consists of any information in any form gathered by the authority with respect to that employee and, by way of illustration but not limitation, relating to his application, selection or nonselection, performance, promotions, demotions, transfers, suspension and other disciplinary actions, evaluation forms, leave, salary, and termination of employment. As used in this section, "employee" includes former employees of the authority.

(b) The following information with respect to each authority employee is a matter of public record:

(1) Name.

(2) Age.

(3) Date of original employment or appointment to the service.

(4) The terms of any contract by which the employee is employed whether written or oral, past and current, to the extent that the authority has the written contract or a record of the oral contract in its possession.

(5) Current position.

(6) Title.

(7) Current salary.

(8) Date and amount of each increase or decrease in salary with that authority.

(9) Date and type of each promotion, demotion, transfer, suspension, separation, or other change in position classification with that authority.

(10) Date and general description of the reasons for each promotion with that authority.

(11) Date and type of each dismissal, suspension, or demotion for disciplinary reasons taken by the authority. If the disciplinary action was a dismissal, a copy of the written notice of the final decision of the authority setting forth the specific acts or omissions that are the basis of the dismissal.

(12) The office to which the employee is currently assigned.

(b1) For the purposes of this subsection, the term "salary" includes pay, benefits, incentives, bonuses, and deferred and all other forms of compensation paid by the employing entity.

(b2) The authority shall determine in what form and by whom this information will be maintained. Any person may have access to this information for the purpose of inspection, examination, and copying, during regular business hours, subject only to such rules and regulations for the safekeeping of public records as the authority may have adopted. Any person denied access to this information may apply to the appropriate division of the General Court of Justice for an order compelling disclosure, and the court shall have jurisdiction to issue such orders.

(c) All information contained in an authority employee's personnel file, other than the information made public by subsection (b) of this section, is confidential and shall be open to inspection only in the following instances:

(1) The employee or his duly authorized agent may examine all portions of his personnel file except (i) letters of reference solicited prior to employment, and (ii) information concerning a medical disability, mental or physical, that a prudent physician would not divulge to his patient.

(2) A licensed physician designated in writing by the employee may examine the employee's medical record.

(3) An authority employee having supervisory authority over the employee may examine all material in the employee's personnel file.

(4) By order of a court of competent jurisdiction, any person may examine such portion of an employee's personnel file as may be ordered by the court.

(5) An official of an agency of the State or federal government, or any political subdivision of the State, may inspect any portion of a personnel file when such inspection is deemed by the official having custody of such records to be inspected to be necessary and essential to the pursuance of a proper function of the inspecting agency, but no information shall be divulged for the purpose of assisting in a criminal prosecution (of the employee), or for the purpose of assisting in an investigation of (the employee's) tax liability. However, the official having custody of such records may release the name, address, and telephone number from a personnel file for the purpose of assisting in a criminal investigation.

(6) An employee may sign a written release, to be placed with his personnel file, that permits the person with custody of the file to provide, either in person, by telephone, or by mail, information specified in the release to prospective employers, educational institutions, or other persons specified in the release.

(7) The chief administrative officer, with concurrence of the authority, may inform any person of the employment or nonemployment, promotion, demotion, suspension or other disciplinary action, reinstatement, transfer, or termination of an authority employee and the reasons for that personnel action. Before releasing the information, the chief administrative officer or authority shall determine in writing that the release is essential to maintaining public confidence in the administration of authority services or to maintaining the level

and quality of authority services. This written determination shall be retained in the office of the chief administrative officer or the secretary of the authority, and is a record available for public inspection and shall become part of the employee's personnel file.

(d)   Even if considered part of an employee's personnel file, the following information need not be disclosed to an employee nor to any other person:

(1)   Testing or examination material used solely to determine individual qualifications for appointment, employment, or promotion in the authority's service, when disclosure would compromise the objectivity or the fairness of the testing or examination process.

(2)   Investigative reports or memoranda and other information concerning the investigation of possible criminal actions of an employee, until the investigation is completed and no criminal action taken, or until the criminal action is concluded.

(3)   Information that might identify an undercover law enforcement officer or a law enforcement informer.

(4)   Notes, preliminary drafts, and internal communications concerning an employee. In the event such materials are used for any official personnel decision, then the employee or his duly authorized agent shall have a right to inspect such materials.

(e)   The authority may permit access, subject to limitations it may impose, to selected personnel files by a professional representative of a training, research, or academic institution if that person certifies that that person will not release information identifying the employees whose files are opened and that the information will be used solely for statistical, research, or teaching purposes. This certification shall be retained by the authority as long as each personnel file examined is retained.

(f)   An authority that maintains personnel files containing information other than the information mentioned in subsection (b) of this section shall establish procedures whereby an employee, who objects to material in his file on grounds that it is inaccurate or misleading, may seek to have the material removed from the file or may place in the file a statement relating to the material.

(g) A public official or employee who knowingly, willfully, and with malice permits any person to have access to information contained in a personnel file, except as is permitted by this section, is guilty of a Class 2 misdemeanor and is punishable only by a fine not to exceed five hundred dollars ($500.00).

(h) Any person not specifically authorized by this section to have access to a personnel file designated as confidential, who shall:

(1) Knowingly and willfully examine in its official filing place; or

(2) Remove or copy

any portion of a confidential personnel file shall be guilty of a Class 2 misdemeanor and is punishable only by a fine not to exceed five hundred dollars ($500.00). (1993, c. 505, s. 1; 1994, Ex. Sess., c. 14, ss. 69, 70; 2007-508, s. 8; 2010-169, s. 18(g).)

§ 162A-7: Repealed by Session Laws 1993, c. 348, s. 6.

§ 162A-8. Revenue bonds.

A water and sewer authority shall have power from time to time to issue revenue bonds under the Local Government Revenue Bond Act. (1955, c. 1195, s. 7; 1969, c. 850; 1971, c. 780, s. 32; c. 892, s. 1.)

§ 162A-9. Rates and charges; notice; contracts for water or services; deposits; delinquent charges.

(a) An authority may establish and revise a schedule of rates, fees, and other charges for the use of and for the services furnished or to be furnished by any water system or sewer system or parts thereof owned or operated by the authority. The rates, fees, and charges established under this subsection are not subject to supervision or regulation by any bureau, board, commission, or other agency of the State or of any political subdivision.

Before an authority sets or revises rates, fees, or other charges for stormwater management programs and structural or natural stormwater and drainage system service, the authority shall hold a public hearing on the matter. At least seven days before the hearing, the authority shall publish notice of the public hearing in a newspaper having general circulation in the area. An authority may impose rates, fees, or other charges for stormwater management programs and stormwater and drainage system service on a person even though the person has not entered into a contract to receive the service.

Rates, fees, and charges shall be fixed and revised so that the revenues of the authority, together with any other available funds, will be sufficient at all times:

(1)   To pay the cost of maintaining, repairing, and operating the systems or parts thereof owned or operated by the authority, including reserves for such purposes, and including provision for the payment of principal of and interest on indebtedness of a political subdivision or of political subdivisions which payment shall have been assumed by the authority, and

(2)   To pay the principal of and the interest on all bonds issued by the authority under the provisions of this Article as the same shall become due and payable and to provide reserves therefor.

The fees established under this subsection must be made applicable throughout the service area. Schedules of rates, fees, charges, and penalties for providing stormwater management programs and structural and natural stormwater and drainage system service may vary according to whether the property served is residential, commercial, or industrial property, the property's use, the size of the property, the area of impervious surfaces on the property, the quantity and quality of the runoff from the property, the characteristics of the watershed into which stormwater from the property drains, and other factors that affect the stormwater drainage system. Rates, fees, and charges imposed under this subsection for stormwater management programs and stormwater and drainage system service may not exceed the authority's cost of providing a stormwater management program and a structural and natural stormwater and drainage system. The authority's cost of providing a stormwater management program and a structural and natural stormwater and drainage system includes any costs necessary to assure that all aspects of stormwater quality and quantity are managed in accordance with federal and State laws, regulations, and rules.

No stormwater utility fee may be levied under this subsection whenever two or more units of local government operate separate stormwater management programs or separate structural and natural stormwater and drainage system services in the same area within a county. However, two or more units of local government may allocate among themselves the functions, duties, powers, and responsibilities for jointly operating a stormwater management program and structural and natural stormwater and drainage system service in the same area within a county, provided that only one unit may levy a fee for the service within the joint service area. For purposes of this subsection, a unit of local government shall include a regional authority providing stormwater management programs and structural and natural stormwater and drainage system services.

(a1) An authority shall provide notice to interested parties of the imposition of or increase in rates, fees, and charges under subsection (a) of this section applicable solely to the construction of development subject to Part 2 of Article 19 of Chapter 160A or Part 2 of Article 18 of Chapter 153A of the General Statutes at least seven days prior to the first meeting where the imposition of or increase in the rates, fees, and charges is on the agenda for consideration. The authority shall employ at least two of the following means of communication in order to provide the notice required by this subsection:

(1) Notice of the meeting in a prominent location on a Web site managed or maintained by the authority.

(2) Notice of the meeting in a prominent physical location, including, but not limited to, the authority's headquarters or any government building, library, or courthouse located within the authority's service area.

(3) Notice of the meeting by electronic mail to a list of interested parties that is created by the authority for the purpose of notification as required by this section.

(4) Notice of the meeting by facsimile to a list of interested parties that is created by the authority for the purpose of notification as required by this section.

(a2) If an authority does not maintain its own Web site, it may employ the notice option provided by subdivision (1) of subsection (a1) of this section by submitting a request to a county or counties in which the authority is located to post such notice in a prominent location on a Web site that is maintained by the county or counties. Any authority that elects to provide such notice shall make its request to the county or counties at least 15 days prior to the date of the first meeting where the imposition of or increase in the fees or charges is on the agenda for consideration.

(a3) During the consideration of the imposition of or increase in rates, fees, or charges under this subsection, the authority shall permit a period of public comment.

(a4) The notice requirements in subsection (a1) of this section shall not apply if the imposition of or increase in rates, fees, and charges is contained in a budget filed in accordance with the requirements of G.S. 159-12.

(b) Notwithstanding any of the foregoing provisions of this section, the authority may enter into contracts relating to the collection, treatment or disposal of sewage or the purchase or sale of water which shall not be subject to revision except in accordance with their terms.

(c) In order to insure the payment of such rates, fees and charges as the same shall become due and payable, the authority may do the following in addition to exercising any other remedies which it may have:

(1) Require reasonable advance deposits to be made with it to be subject to application to the payment of delinquent rates, fees and charges.

(2) At the expiration of 30 days after any rates, fees and charges become delinquent, discontinue supplying water or the services and facilities of any water system or sewer system of the authority.

(3) Specify the order in which partial payments are to be applied when a bill covers more than one service. (1955, c. 1195, s. 8; 1971, c. 892, s. 1; 1989 (Reg. Sess., 1990), c. 1004, s. 45; 1991, c. 591, s. 4; 1991 (Reg. Sess., 1992), c. 1007, s. 47; 2000-70, s. 7; 2009-436, s. 4; 2010-180, s. 11(d).)

§ 162A-9.1. Adoption and enforcement of ordinances.

(a) An authority shall have the same power as a city under G.S. 160A-175 to assess civil fines and penalties for violation of its ordinances; and, an authority may seek and recover injunctive relief to insure compliance with its ordinances as provided by this section.

(b) An ordinance may provide that its violation shall subject the offender to a civil penalty of not more than one thousand dollars ($1,000) per violation, to be recovered by the authority in a civil action in the nature of debt if the offender does not pay the penalty within a prescribed period of time after he has been cited for violation of the ordinance. Any person assessed a civil penalty by the authority shall be notified of the assessment by registered or certified mail, and the notice shall specify the reasons for the assessment of the civil penalty. If the person assessed fails to pay the amount of the assessment to the authority within 30 days after receipt of such notice, or such longer period, not to exceed 180 days, as the authority may specify, the authority may institute a civil action in the General Court of Justice of the county in which the violation occurred, or, in the discretion of the authority, in the General Court of Justice of the county in which the person has his or its principal place of business, to recover the amount of the assessment. The validity of the authority's action in assessing the violator may be appealed directly to the General Court of Justice in the county in which the violation occurred, or may be raised at any time in the action to recover the assessment. No failure to contest directly the validity of the authority's action in levying the assessment shall preclude the person assessed from later raising the issue of validity in any action to collect the assessment.

(c) An ordinance may provide that it may be enforced, and it may be enforced, by any appropriate equitable remedy issuing from a court of competent jurisdiction. In such cases, the General Court of Justice shall have jurisdiction and authority to issue such orders as may be appropriate to enforce the ordinances of the authority, and it shall not be a defense to the application made by the authority therefor that there is an adequate remedy at law.

(d) Subject to the express terms of any ordinance, an ordinance adopted by the authority may be enforced by any one, all or a combination of the remedies authorized and prescribed by this section.

(e) An ordinance may provide, when appropriate, that each day's continuing violation thereof shall constitute and be a separate and distinct offense. (1983, c. 820, s. 2.)

§ 162A-10: Repealed by Session Laws 1971, c. 780, s. 33.

§ 162A-11. Moneys received deemed trust funds.

All moneys received pursuant to the authority of this Article shall be deemed to be trust funds, to be held and applied solely as provided in this Article. The resolution authorizing the issuance of bonds or the trust agreement securing such bonds shall provide that any officer to whom, or bank, trust company or fiscal agent to which, such moneys shall be paid shall act as trustee of such moneys and shall hold and apply the same for the purposes hereof, subject to such regulations as this Article and such resolution or trust agreement may provide. (1955, c. 1195, s. 10; 1971, c. 892, s. 1.)

§ 162A-12. Bondholder's remedies.

Any holder of revenue bonds issued under the provisions of this Article or of any of the coupons appertaining thereto, and the trustee under any trust agreement, except to the extent the rights herein given may be restricted by the resolution authorizing the issuance of such bonds or such trust agreement, may, either at law or in equity, by suit, action, mandamus or other proceeding, protect and enforce any and all rights under the laws of the State or granted hereunder or under such resolution or trust agreement, and may enforce and compel the performance of all duties required by this Article or by such resolution or trust agreement to be performed by the authority or by any officer thereof, including the fixing, charging and collecting of rates, fees and charges for the use of or for the services and facilities furnished by a water system or sewer system. (1955, c. 1195, s. 11; 1971, c. 892, s. 1.)

§ 162A-13. Refunding bonds.

Each authority is hereby authorized to issue from time to time revenue refunding bonds for the purpose of refunding any revenue bonds of the authority then outstanding, including the payment of any redemption premium thereon and any interest accrued or to accrue to the date of redemption of such bonds. The authority is further authorized to issue from time to time revenue bonds of the authority for the combined purpose of

(1) Refunding any revenue bonds or revenue refunding bonds of the authority then outstanding, including the payment of any redemption premium thereon and any interest accrued or to accrue to the date of redemption of such bonds, and

(2) Paying all or any part of the cost of acquiring or constructing any additional water system or sewer system or part thereof, or any improvements, extensions or enlargements of any water system or sewer system.

The issuance of such bonds, the maturities and other details thereof, the rights and remedies of the holders thereof, and the rights, powers, privileges, duties and obligations of the authority with respect to the same, shall be governed by the foregoing provisions of this Article insofar as the same may be applicable. (1955, c. 1195, s. 12; 1971, c. 892, s. 1.)

§ 162A-14. Conveyances and contracts between political subdivisions and authority.

The governing body of any political subdivision is hereby authorized and empowered:

(1) Pursuant to the provisions of G.S. 160A-274 and subject to the approval of the Local Government Commission, except for action taken hereunder by any State agency, to transfer jurisdiction over, and to lease, lend, grant or convey to an authority upon the request of the authority, upon such terms and conditions as the governing body of such political subdivision may agree with the authority as reasonable and fair, the whole or any part of any existing water system or sewer system or such real or personal property as may be necessary or desirable in connection with the acquisition, construction, reconstruction, improvement, extension, enlargement, equipment, repair, maintenance or operation of any water system or sewer system or part thereof by the authority, including public roads and other property already devoted to public use;

(2) To make and enter into contracts or agreements with an authority, upon such terms and conditions and for such periods as are agreed to by the governing body of such political subdivision and the authority;

a. For the collection, treatment or disposal of sewage by the authority or for the purchase of a supply of water from the authority;

b. For the collecting by such political subdivision or by the authority of fees, rates or charges for water furnished to such political subdivision or to its inhabitants and for the services and facilities rendered to such political subdivision or to its inhabitants by any water system or sewer system of the authority, and for the enforcement of delinquent charges for such water, services and facilities;

c. For shutting off the supply of water furnished by any water system owned or operated by such political subdivision in the event that the owner, tenant or occupant of any premises utilizing such water shall fail to pay any rates, fees or charges for the use of or for the services furnished by any sewer system of the authority, within the time or times specified in such contract; and

d. For requiring the owners of developed property on which there are situated one or more residential dwelling units or commercial establishments located within the corporate limits of the political subdivision and located within a reasonable distance of any waterline or sewer connection line owned, leased as lessee, or operated by the authority to connect to the line and collecting, on behalf of the authority, charges for the connections and requiring, as a condition to the issuance of any development permit or building permit by the political subdivision, evidence that any impact fee by the authority has been paid by or on behalf of the applicant for the permit.

(3) To fix, and revise from time to time, rates, fees and other charges for water and for the services furnished or to be furnished by any water system or sewer system of the authority, or parts thereof, under any contract between the authority and such political subdivision, and to pledge all or any part of the proceeds of such rates, fees and charges to the payment of any obligation of such political subdivision under such contract; and

(4) In its discretion, to submit to the qualified electors under the election laws applicable to such political subdivision any contract or agreement which such governing body is authorized to make and enter into with the authority under the provisions of this Article. (1955, c. 1195, s. 13; 1971, c. 892, s. 1; 1975, c. 224, ss. 5, 6; 1995, c. 511, s. 2.)

§ 162A-15. Services to authority by private water companies; records of water taken by authority; reports to the Commission.

Each private water company which is supplying water to the owners, lessees or tenants of real property which is or will be served by any sewer system of an authority is authorized to act as the billing and collecting agent of the authority for any rates, fees or charges imposed by the authority for the services rendered by such sewer system. Any such company shall, if requested by an authority furnish to the authority copies of its regular periodic meter reading and water consumption records and other pertinent data as may be required for the authority to act as its own billing and collecting agent. The authority shall pay to such water company the reasonable additional cost of clerical services and other expenses incurred by the water company in rendering such services to the authority. The authority shall by means of suitable measuring and recording devices and facilities record the quantity of water taken daily by it from any stream or reservoir and make monthly reports of such daily recordings to the Commission. (1955, c. 1195, s. 14; 1989 (Reg. Sess., 1990), c. 1004, s. 46.)

§ 162A-16. Contributions or advances to authority by political subdivisions.

Any political subdivision is hereby authorized to make contributions or advances to an authority, from any moneys which may be available for such purpose, to provide for the preliminary expenses of such authority in carrying out the provisions of this Article. Any such advances may be repaid to such political subdivisions from the proceeds of bonds issued by such authority under this Article. (1955, c. 1195, s. 15; 1971, c. 892, s. 1.)

§ 162A-17. Article regarded as supplemental.

This Article shall be deemed to provide an additional and alternative method for the doing of the things authorized hereby and shall be regarded as supplemental and additional to powers conferred by other laws, and shall not be regarded as in derogation of or as repealing any powers now existing under any other law, either general, special or local; provided, however, that the issuance of revenue bonds or revenue refunding bonds under the provisions of this Article need not comply with the requirements of any other law applicable to the issuance of bonds. (1955, c. 1195, s. 16; 1971, c. 892, s. 1.)

§ 162A-18. Actions against authority by riparian owners.

Any riparian owner alleging an injury as a result of any act of an authority created under this Article may maintain an action for relief against the acts of the authority either in the county where the lands of such riparian owner lie or in the county in which the principal office of the authority is maintained. (1955, c. 1195, s. 16 1/2; 1971, c. 892, s. 1.)

§ 162A-19. Inconsistent laws declared inapplicable.

All general, special or local laws, or parts thereof, inconsistent herewith are hereby declared to be inapplicable to the provisions of this Article. (1955, c. 1195, s. 17; 1971, c. 892, s. 1.)

Article 2.

Regional Water Supply Planning.

§ 162A-20. Title.

This Article shall be known and may be cited as the "Regional Water Supply Planning Act of 1971." (1971, c. 892, s. 1.)

§ 162A-21. Preamble.

The Legislative Research Commission was directed by Senate Resolution 875 of the 1969 General Assembly to study and report to the 1971 General Assembly on the need for legislation "concerning local and regional water supplies (including sources of water, and organization and administration of water systems)." Pursuant to said Resolution a report was prepared and adopted by the Legislative Research Commission in 1970 concerning local and regional water supplies. In this report the Legislative Research Commission made the following findings concerning the need for planning and developing regional water supply systems in order to provide adequate supplies of high quality water to the citizens of North Carolina, of which the General Assembly hereby takes cognizance:

(1)   The existing pattern of public water supply development in North Carolina is dominated by many small systems serving few customers. Of the 1,782 public water systems of record on July 1, 1970, according to Department of Health and Human Services statistics, over eighty percent (80%) were serving less than 1,000 people each. These small systems are often underfinanced, inadequately designed and maintained, difficult to coordinate with nearby regional systems, and generally inferior to systems serving larger communities as regards adequacy of source, facilities and quality. The situation which has developed reflects a need for better planning at both State and local levels.

(2) The State's population balance is steadily changing. Sparsely populated counties are losing residents to the more densely populated counties, while the State's total population is increasing. As this trend continues, small towns and communities will find it increasingly difficult to build and maintain public water supply systems. Also, as urban centers expand, and embrace relatively large geographical areas, economic factors will dictate that regional water systems be developed to serve these centers and to meet the demands of commercial and industrial development. It is estimated that countywide or regional water systems are needed now by 50 counties.

(3) If the future public water supply needs of the State are to be met, a change in the existing pattern of public water supply development and management must be undertaken. Regional planning and development is an immediate need. The creation of countywide or regional water supplies, with adequate interconnections, is necessary in order to provide an adequate supply of high quality water to the State's citizens, to make supplies less vulnerable to recurring drought conditions, and to have systems large enough to justify the costs of adequate facilities and of proper operation and maintenance.

(4) The State should provide a framework for comprehensive planning of regional water supply systems, and for the orderly coordination of local actions, so as to make the most efficient use of available water resources and economies of scale for construction, operation and maintenance. The State should also provide financial assistance to local governments and regional authorities in order to assist with the cost of developing comprehensive regional plans, and countywide plans compatible with a regional system. (1971, c. 892, s. 1; 1973, c. 476, s. 128; 1997-443, s. 11A.118(a).)

§ 162A-22. Definition of regional water supply system.

For the purposes of this Article "a regional water supply system" is defined as a public water supply system of a municipality, county, sanitary district, or other political subdivision of the State, or combination thereof, which provides, is intended to provide, or is capable of providing an adequate and safe supply of water to a substantial portion of the population within a county, or to a substantial water service area in a region composed of all or parts of two or more counties, or to a metropolitan area in two or more counties. (1971, c. 892, s. 1.)

§ 162A-23. State role and functions relating to local and regional water supply planning.

(a)   It should be the role of State government to provide a framework for comprehensive planning of regional water supply systems, and for the orderly coordination of local actions relating to water supply, so as to make possible the most efficient use of water resources and to help realize economies of scale in water supply systems. To these ends, it shall be the function of State government to:

(1)   Identify major sources of raw water supply for regional systems, and raw water interconnections as may be desirable and feasible.

(2)   Identify areas suitable for the development of regional systems.

(3)   Establish priorities for regionalization.

(4)   Develop plans for connecting proposed regional systems to major sources of supply, and for such finished water interconnections as may be desirable and feasible.

(5)   Review and approve plans for proposed regional systems, and for proposed municipal and countywide systems which are compatible with a regional plan.

(6)   Administer a State program of financial assistance to local governments and regional planning agencies for the development of comprehensive plans for regional water systems, or county systems compatible with regional plans.

(7)   Provide technical assistance to local and regional planning agencies, and to consulting engineering firms.

(b)   Responsibility for carrying out the role of State government in regional water supply planning shall be assigned to the Department of Environment and Natural Resources. (1971, c. 892, s. 1; 1973, c. 476, s. 128; 1989, c. 727, s. 212; 1997-443, s. 11A.123.)

§ 162A-24. Regional Water Supply Planning Revolving Fund established; conditions and procedures.

(a) There is established under the control and direction of the Department of Administration a Regional Water Supply Planning Revolving Fund, to consist of any moneys that may be appropriated for use through the fund by the General Assembly or that may be made available to it from any other source. The Department may make advances from the fund to any county, municipality, sanitary district, or to counties and municipalities acting collectively or jointly as a regional water authority, for the purpose of meeting the cost of advance planning and engineering work necessary or desirable for the development of a comprehensive plan for a regional water supply system as defined in this Article. Such advances shall be subject to repayment by the recipient to the Department from the proceeds of bonds or other obligations for the regional water supply system, or from other funds available to the recipient including grants, except when, in the judgment of the Department of Environment and Natural Resources, a proposed plan for development and construction of a countywide or other regional water system is not feasible because of design and construction factors or because available sources of raw water supply are inadequate or because construction of a proposed system is not economically feasible, (but not if the applicant decides not to proceed with construction that has been planned and which the Department of Environment and Natural Resources have declared to be feasible).

(b) The Department of Administration shall not make any advance pursuant to this section without first referring the application and proposal to the Department of Environment and Natural Resources for determination as to whether the following conditions have been met:

(1) The proposed area is suitable for development of a regional water supply system from the standpoint of present and projected populations, industrial growth potential, and present and future sources of raw water.

(2) The applicant proposes to undertake long-range comprehensive planning to meet present and projected needs for high quality water service through the construction of a regional water supply system as defined in this Article. The determination by the Department of Environment and Natural Resources that the proposed system would be a "regional system," as defined by this Article, shall be conclusive.

(3) The applicant proposes to coordinate planning of the regional water supply with land-use planning in the area, in order that both planning efforts will be compatible.

(4) The applicant proposes to employ an engineer licensed to practice in the State of North Carolina to prepare a comprehensive regional water supply plan, which plan will provide detailed information on source or sources of water to meet projected domestic and industrial water demands; proposed system, including raw water intake(s), treatment plant, storage facilities, distribution system, and other waterworks appurtenances; proposed interconnections with existing systems, and provisions for interconnections with other county, municipal and regional systems; phased development of systems to achieve ultimate objectives if economic feasibility is in question; projected water service areas; proposed equipment; estimates of cost and projected revenues; and methods of financing.

(c) In addition to the above conditions, the Department of Administration shall not make any advance to any applicant until the following conditions have also been met:

(1) The Department has determined that there is a reasonable prospect of federal (or State) aid in the financing of the projected work if the undertaking is one that will be dependent upon federal (or State) aid.

(2) The Department has received firm assurances from the applicant that the works or project, if feasible, will be undertaken.

(d) All advances made pursuant to this section shall be repaid in full, within one year of the start of construction on the projected system, or within six months after the issuance of bonds for the financing of construction of the system, or within six years from the date of the making of the advance, whichever comes first. The Department may, in its discretion, require the repayment of any advance in installments.

(e) The Department of Administration may adopt such rules and regulations with respect to the making of applications or the receipt of advances as are consistent with the terms and purpose of this section.

(f) The provisions of Chapter 159 of the General Statutes of North Carolina (Local Government Acts) shall not apply to advances made from the Regional Water Supply Planning Revolving Fund as authorized in this Article. (1971, c. 892, s. 1; 1973, c. 476, s. 128; 1989, c. 727, ss. 213, 214; 1997-443, s. 11A.123.)

§ 162A-25. Construction of Article.

This Article shall be construed as providing supplemental authority in addition to the powers of the Department of Environment and Natural Resources under Chapter 130A and Articles 21 and 38 of Chapter 143 of the General Statutes, the powers of the North Carolina Utilities Commission under Chapter 62 of the General Statutes, and any other provisions of law concerning local and regional water supplies. (1971, c. 892, s. 1; 1973, c. 476, s. 128; 1989, c. 727, s. 215; 1997-443, s. 11A.123.)

Article 3.

Regional Sewage Disposal Planning.

§ 162A-26. Title.

This Article shall be known and may be cited as the "Regional Sewage Disposal Planning Act of 1971." (1971, c. 870, s. 1.)

§ 162A-27. Definitions of "regional sewage disposal system" and "comprehensive planning."

For the purposes of this Article "regional sewage disposal system" is defined as a public sewage disposal system of a municipality, county, sanitary district, or other political subdivision of the State, or combination thereof, which provides, is intended to provide, or is capable of providing adequate collection, treatment, purification and disposal of sewage to a substantial portion of the population within a county, or a region composed of all or parts of two or more counties, or to a metropolitan area in two or more counties. "Comprehensive planning" is defined as that planning which is a prerequisite for qualifying for receipt of federal and/or State grant funds for preparation of plans and specifications and for actual construction of regional sewage disposal systems. (1971, c. 870, s. 1; 1975, c. 251, s. 1.)

§ 162A-28. Role and function of Environmental Management Commission.

The North Carolina Environmental Management Commission, in order to provide a framework for comprehensive planning of regional sewage disposal systems and for orderly coordination of local actions relating to sewage disposal, to make possible the most efficient disposal of sewage and to help realize economies of scale in sewage disposal systems, shall perform the following functions:

(1) Identify major sources of sewage for regional systems and sewer system interconnections as may be desirable and feasible.

(2) Identify geographical areas of the State suitable for the development of regional sewage disposal systems that meet federal and State grant requirements.

(3) Establish priorities for regionalization.

(4) Develop plans for connecting proposed regional sewage disposal systems to major sources of sewage and for such sewer system interconnections as may be desirable and feasible.

(5) Review and approve plans for proposed regional sewage disposal systems and for proposed municipal and countywide systems which are compatible with a regional plan.

(6) Administer a State program of financial assistance to local governments and regional planning agencies for the development of comprehensive plans for regional sewage disposal systems or county systems compatible with regional plans.

(7) Provide technical assistance to local and regional planning agencies and to consulting engineering firms. (1971, c. 870, s. 1; 1973, c. 1262, s. 23; 1975, c. 251, s. 2.)

§ 162A-29. Regional Sewage Disposal Planning Revolving Fund established; conditions and procedures.

(a) There is established under the control and direction of the Department of Administration a Regional Sewage Disposal Planning Revolving Fund, to consist of any moneys that may be appropriated for use through the fund by the

General Assembly or that may be made available to it from any other source. The Department may make advances from the fund to any county, municipality, or sanitary district, or to counties and municipalities acting collectively or jointly as a regional sewer authority, for the purpose of meeting the cost of advance planning and engineering work necessary or desirable for the development of a comprehensive plan for a regional sewage disposal system as defined in this Article. Such advances shall be subject to repayment by the recipient to the Department from the proceeds of bonds or other obligations for the regional sewage disposal system, or from other funds available to the recipient including grants, except when, in the judgment of the Department of Environment and Natural Resources, a proposed plan for development and construction of a countywide or other regional sewage disposal system is not feasible because of design and construction factors, or because of the effect that the sewage disposal system discharge will have upon water quality standards, or because construction of a proposed system is not economically feasible, (but not if the applicant decides not to proceed with construction that has been planned and which the Department of Environment and Natural Resources has declared to be feasible).

(b)   The Department of Administration shall not make any advance pursuant to this section without first referring the application and proposal to the Department of Environment and Natural Resources for determination as to whether the following conditions have been met:

(1)   The proposed area is suitable for development of a regional sewage disposal system from the standpoint of present and projected populations, industrial growth potential, and present and future sources of sewage.

(2)   The applicant proposes to undertake long-range comprehensive planning to meet present and projected needs for high quality sewage disposal through the construction of a regional sewage disposal system as defined in this Article. The determination by the Department of Environment and Natural Resources, that the proposed system would be a "regional system," as defined by this Article, shall be conclusive.

(3)   The applicant proposes to coordinate planning of the regional sewage disposal system with land-use planning in the area, in order that both planning efforts will be compatible.

(4)   The applicant proposes to employ an engineer licensed to practice in the State of North Carolina to prepare a comprehensive regional sewage

disposal plan, which plan will provide detailed information on the source or sources of sewage; the proposed system, including all facilities and appurtenances thereto for the collection, transmission, treatment, purification and disposal of sewage; any proposed interconnection with existing systems, and provisions for interconnections with other county, municipal and regional systems; the phased development of systems to achieve ultimate objectives if economic feasiblility is in question; projected sewage disposal service areas; proposed equipment; estimates of cost and projected revenues; and methods of financing.

(c) In addition to the above conditions, the Department of Administration shall not make any advance to any applicant until the following conditions have also been met:

(1) The Department has determined that there is a reasonable prospect of federal (or State) aid in the financing of the projected work if the undertaking is one that will be dependent upon federal (or State) aid.

(2) The Department has received firm assurances from the applicant that the work or project, if feasible, will be undertaken.

(3) The applicant has furnished evidence that it does not have funds available to finance the plan.

(d) All advances made pursuant to this section shall be repaid in full, upon receipt of any sewage disposal facilities planning grant funds from federal or State sources, or within one year of the start of construction on the projected system, or within six months after the issuance of bonds for the financing of construction of the system, or within six years from the date of the making of the advance, whichever comes first. The Department may, in its discretion, require the repayment of any advance in installments.

(e) The Department of Administration may adopt such rules and regulations with respect to the making of applications or the receipt of advances as are consistent with the terms and purpose of this section.

(f) The provisions of Chapter 159 of the General Statutes of North Carolina (Local Government Acts) shall not apply to advances made from the Regional Sewage Disposal Planning Revolving Fund as authorized in this Article. (1971, c. 870, s. 1; 1975, c. 251, ss. 3, 4; 1989, c. 727, ss. 216, 217; 1997-443, s. 11A.123.)

§ 162A-30. Construction of Article.

This Article shall be construed as providing supplemental authority in addition to the powers of the North Carolina Utilities Commission under Chapter 62 of the North Carolina General Statutes, the North Carolina Environmental Management Commission under Articles 21 and 38 of Chapter 143 of the North Carolina General Statutes, and the North Carolina Department of Environment and Natural Resources under General Statutes Chapter 130A, and any other provisions of law concerning local and regional sewage disposal. (1971, c. 870, s. 1; 1973, c. 476, s. 128; c. 1262, s. 23; 1997-443, s. 11A.116.)

Article 4.

Metropolitan Water Districts.

§ 162A-31. Short title.

This Article shall be known and may be cited as the Metropolitan Water Districts Act. (1971, c. 815, s. 1.)

§ 162A-32. Definitions; description of boundaries.

(a)   As used in this Article the following words and terms shall have the following meanings, unless the context shall indicate another or different meaning or intent:

(1)   "Board of commissioners" or "commissioners" shall mean the duly elected board of commissioners of the county in which a metropolitan water district shall be created under the provisions of this Article.

(2)   "City council" or "council" shall mean the duly elected city council of any municipality located within the State.

(3)   "Cost" as applied to a water system or sewerage system shall mean the cost of acquiring, constructing, reconstructing, improving, extending, enlarging, repairing and equipping any such system, and shall include the cost of all labor and materials, machinery and equipment, lands, property, rights, easements and franchises, plans and specifications, surveys and estimates of cost and of

revenues, and planning, engineering, financial advice, and legal services, financing charges, interest prior to and during construction and, if deemed advisable by a district board, for one year after the estimated date of completion of construction, and all other expenses necessary or incident to determining the feasibility or practicability of any such undertaking, administrative expense and such other expenses, including reasonable provision for working capital and a reserve for debt service, as may be necessary or incident to the financing herein authorized, and may also include any obligation or expense incurred by a district or by any political subdivision prior to the issuance of bonds under the provisions of this Article in connection with any such undertaking or any of the foregoing items of cost.

(4) "District" shall mean a metropolitan water district created under the provisions of this Article.

(5) "District board" shall mean the district board of the metropolitan water district created under the provisions of this Article.

(6) "General obligation bonds" shall mean bonds of a metropolitan water district for the payment of which and the interest thereon all the taxable property within said district is subject to the levy of an ad valorem tax without limitation of rate or amount.

(7) "Governing body" shall mean the board, board of trustees, commission, board of commissioners, council or other body, by whatever name it may be known, of a political subdivision including, but without limitation, other water or sewer districts or the trustees thereof within the State of North Carolina in which the general legislative powers thereof are vested.

(8) "Person" shall mean any and all persons including individuals, firms, partnerships, associations, public or private institutions, municipalities or political subdivisions, governmental agencies or private or public corporations organized and existing under the laws of the State or any other state or county.

(9) "Political subdivision" shall mean any county, city, town, incorporated village, sanitary district, water district, sewer district, special purpose district or other political subdivision or public corporation of this State now or hereafter created or established.

(10) "Revenue bonds" shall mean bonds the principal of and the interest on which are payable solely from revenues of a water system or systems or a

sewerage system or systems or both owned or operated by a metropolitan water district created under the provisions of this Article.

(11) "Revenues" shall mean all moneys received by a metropolitan water district from, in connection with, or as a result of its ownership or control or operation of a water system or systems or a sewerage system or systems, or both, including, without limitation and as deemed advisable by the district board, moneys received from the United States of America or any agency thereof, pursuant to an agreement with the district board pertaining to the water system or the sewerage system or both.

(12) "Sewerage system" shall embrace sewage collection and disposal systems of all types, including septic tank systems or other on-site collection or disposal facilities or systems and any part or parts thereof, either within or without the limits of a district, all property, rights, easements and franchises relating thereto, and any and all buildings and other structures deemed necessary or useful by a district board in connection with the operation or maintenance thereof.

(13) "Sewers" shall mean any mains, pipes and laterals, including pumping stations for the reception of sewage and carrying such sewage to an outfall or some part of a sewage disposal system, and all property, rights, easements, and franchises related thereto and deemed necessary or convenient by a district board for the operation and maintenance thereof.

(14) "Water distribution system" shall include aqueducts, mains, laterals, pumping stations, distributing reservoirs, standpipes, tanks, hydrants, services, meters, valves, and all necessary appurtenances, and all property, rights, easements, and franchises related thereto and deemed necessary or convenient by a district board for the operation and maintenance thereof.

(15) "Water system" shall mean and include all plants, systems, facilities or properties used or useful or having the present capacity for future use in connection with the supply or distribution of water, and any integral part thereof, including but not limited to water supply systems, water distribution systems, sources of water supply including lakes, reservoirs and wells, intakes, mains, laterals, aqueducts, pumping stations, standpipes, filtration plants, purification plants, hydrants, meters, valves, and all necessary appurtenances and equipment and all properties, rights, easements and franchises relating thereto and deemed necessary or convenient by a district board for the operation or maintenance thereof.

(16) "Water treatment or purification plant" shall mean any plant, system, facility, or property, used or useful or having the present capacity for future use in connection with the treatment or purification of water, or any integral part thereof; and all necessary appurtenances or equipment, and all property, rights, easements and franchises relating thereto and deemed necessary or convenient by a district board for the operation thereof.

(b) Whenever this Article requires that the boundaries of an area be described, it shall be sufficient if the boundaries are described in a manner which conveys an understanding of the location of the land and may be

(1) By reference to a map,

(2) By metes and bounds,

(3) By general description referring to natural boundaries, boundaries of political subdivisions, existing water or sewer districts, or portions thereof, or boundaries of particular tracts or parcels of land, or

(4) Any combination of the foregoing. (1971, c. 815, s. 2; 1979, c. 619, s. 9.)

§ 162A-33. Procedure for creation; resolutions and petitions for creation; notice to and action by Commission for Public Health; notice and public hearing; resolutions creating districts; actions to set aside proceedings.

Any two or more political subdivisions in a county, or any political subdivision or subdivisions, including any existing water or sewer district, and any unincorporated area or areas located within the same county, which political subdivisions or areas need not be contiguous, may petition the board of commissioners for the creation of a metropolitan water district under the provisions of this Article by filing with the board of commissioners:

(1) A resolution of the governing body of each such political subdivision stating the necessity for the creation of a metropolitan water district under the provisions of this Article in order to preserve and promote the public health and welfare within the area of the proposed district, and requesting the creation of a metropolitan water district having the boundaries set forth in said resolution, and

(2) If any unincorporated area is to be included in such district, a petition, signed by not less than fifteen per centum (15%) of the voters resident within such area, defining the boundaries of such area, stating the necessity for the creation of a metropolitan water district under the provisions of this Article in order to preserve and promote the public health and welfare within the proposed district, and requesting the creation of a metropolitan water district having the boundaries set forth in such petition for such district.

If any water district, sewer district or special purpose district shall encompass wholly or in part within its boundaries a city or town, no such water district, sewer district or special purpose district may petition for inclusion within a metropolitan water district unless the governing body of such city or town shall approve such petition or shall also petition for its inclusion within such metropolitan water district.

Upon the receipt of such resolutions and petitions requesting the creation of a metropolitan water district, the board of commissioners, through its chairman shall notify the Department of Environment and Natural Resources of the receipt of such resolutions and petitions, and shall request that a representative of the Department of Environment and Natural Resources hold a joint public hearing with the board of commissioners concerning the creation of the proposed metropolitan water district. The Secretary of Environment and Natural Resources and the chairman of the board of commissioners shall name a time and place within the proposed district at which the public hearing shall be held. The chairman of the board of commissioners shall give prior notice of such hearing by posting a notice at the courthouse door of the county and also by publication in a newspaper circulating in the proposed district at least once a week for four successive weeks, the first publication to be at least 30 days prior to such hearing. In the event all matters pertaining to the creation of such metropolitan water district cannot be concluded at such hearing, such hearing may be continued to a time and place within the proposed district determined by the board of commissioners with the concurrence of the representative of the Department of Environment and Natural Resources.

If, after such hearing, the Commission for Public Health and the board of commissioners shall deem it advisable to comply with the request of such resolutions and petitions, and determine that the preservation and promotion of the public health and welfare in the area or areas described in such resolutions and petitions require that a metropolitan water district should be created and established, the Commission for Public Health shall adopt a resolution to that effect, defining the boundaries of such district and declaring the territory within such boundaries to be a metropolitan water district under the name and style of "____ Metropolitan Water District of ____ County"; provided that the Commission for Public Health may make minor deviations in the boundaries from those prescribed in the resolutions and petitions upon the Commission for Public Health determining that such deviations are advisable in the interest of the public health, provided no such district shall include any political subdivision which has not petitioned for inclusion as provided for in this Article.

The Commission for Public Health shall cause copies of the resolution creating the metropolitan water district to be sent to the board of commissioners and to the governing body of each political subdivision included in the district. The board of commissioners shall cause a copy of such resolution of the Commission for Public Health to be published in a newspaper circulating within the district once in each of two successive weeks, and a notice substantially in the following form shall be published with such resolution:

"The foregoing resolution was passed by the Commission for Public Health on the ____ day of ____, ____, and was first published on the ____ day of ____, ____.

Any action or proceeding questioning the validity of said resolution or the creation of the metropolitan water district therein described must be commenced within 30 days after the first publication of said resolution.

Clerk, Board of Commissioners

for_____County."

Any action or proceeding in any court to set aside a resolution creating a metropolitan water district or to obtain any other relief upon the ground that such resolution or any proceeding or action taken with respect to the creation of such district is invalid, must be commenced within 30 days after the first publication of the resolution and said notice. After the expiration of such period of limitation, no right of action or defense founded upon the invalidity of the resolution or the creation of the metropolitan water district therein described shall be asserted, nor shall the validity of the resolution or of the creation of such metropolitan water district be open to question in any court upon any ground whatever, except in an action or proceeding commenced within such period.

Notwithstanding the provisions of G.S. 160-2(6), after the creation of a water district pursuant to the provisions of this Article a municipality or other political subdivision which owns or operates an existing water system or sewer system may lease, contract, assign or convey such system or systems to the district under and subject to such terms and conditions and for such considerations as it may deem advisable for the general welfare and benefit of its citizens. (1971, c. 815, s. 3; 1973, c. 476, s. 128; 1985, c. 462, s. 16; 1989, c. 727, s. 219(40); 1989 (Reg. Sess., 1990), c. 1004, s. 19(b); 1997-443, s. 11A.123; 1999-456, s. 59; 2007-182, s. 2.)

§ 162A-34. District board; composition, appointment, term, oaths and removal of members; organization; meetings; quorum; compensation and expenses of members.

(a) Immediately after the creation of the district, the board of commissioners shall appoint three members of the district board and the governing body of each political subdivision included in the district shall appoint one member, except that if any city or town has a population, according to the latest decennial census, in excess of the total population of the remaining cities and towns within the district, or where there are no other cities or towns involved, if the census population is in excess of the total population of the remainder of the district, the governing body shall appoint three members. No appointment of a member of the district board shall be made by or in behalf of any political subdivision of which the board of commissioners shall be the governing body, the three appointees designated by the board of commissioners shall be selected from within the district and shall be deemed to represent all such political subdivisions. The members of the district board first appointed shall have terms expiring one year, two years and three years, respectively, from the date of adoption of the resolution of the Commission for Public Health creating the district, as the board of commissioners shall determine, provided that of the three members appointed by any governing body, not more than one such member shall be appointed for a three-year term. Successive members shall each be appointed to serve only for the unexpired term and any member of the district board may be reappointed. Appointments of successor members shall, in each instance, be made by the governing body making the initial appointment or appointments. All members shall serve until their successors have been duly appointed and qualified, and any member of the district board may be removed for cause by the governing body appointing him.

Each member of the district board before entering upon his duties shall take and subscribe an oath or affirmation to support the Constitution and laws of the United States and of this State and to discharge faithfully the duties of his office, and a record of each such oath shall be filed with the clerk of the board of commissioners.

The district board shall elect one of its members as chairman and another as vice-chairman and shall appoint a secretary and a treasurer who may but need not be members of the district board. The offices of secretary and treasurer may be combined. The terms of office of the chairman, vice-chairman, secretary and treasurer shall be as provided in the bylaws of the district board.

The district board shall meet regularly at such places and dates as determined by the board. Special meetings may be called by the chairman on his own initiative and shall be called by him upon request of two or more members of the board. All members shall be notified in writing at least 24 hours in advance of such meeting. A majority of the members of the district board shall constitute a quorum and the affirmative vote of a majority of the members of the district board present at any meeting thereof shall be necessary for any action taken by the district board. No vacancy in the membership of the district board shall impair the right of a quorum to exercise all the rights and perform all the duties of the district board. Each member including the chairman shall be entitled to vote on any question. The members of the district board may receive compensation in an amount to be determined by the board, but not to exceed ten dollars ($10.00) for each meeting attended, and may be reimbursed the amount of actual expenses incurred by them in the performance of their duties.

(b)   Any metropolitan water district wholly within the corporate limits of two or more municipalities shall be governed by a district board consisting of members appointed by the governing body of each political subdivision (municipal corporation) included wholly or partially in the district and an additional at-large member appointed by the other members of the district board as provided in this subsection. The governing body of each constituent municipality shall initially appoint two members from its qualified electors, one for a term expiring the first day of July after the first succeeding regular election in which municipal officers shall be elected by the municipality from which he is appointed, and the other for a term expiring the first day of July after the second succeeding regular election of municipal officers in the municipality. Thereafter, subsequent to each ensuing regular election of municipal officers the governing body of each municipal corporation composing any part of the metropolitan water district shall appoint one member to the district board for a term of four years beginning on the first day of July. The one additional at-large member of the district board shall be a qualified elector of a constituent municipality of the district and appointed initially and quadrennially thereafter by majority vote of the other district board membership for a term of four years which shall expire on the first day of August in every fourth calendar year thereafter.

Any vacancy in district board membership shall be filled by appointment of the original appointing authority for the remainder of the unexpired term.

The provisions of subsection (a) in particular and of this Article generally not inconsistent with this subsection shall also apply.

(c)   In those cases where a district is created which includes a municipality which owns an existing water and sewer system and where the county commissioners are acting as or have been appointed as trustees of a separate water or sewer system, or both which will be included within the district along with an existing municipal system, the district board shall be comprised of seven members designated as follows: three county commissioners and three members of the city council of the municipality, said members to be selected by majority vote of the governing body on which they serve. These six members of the district board shall appoint a seventh member who shall also serve as chairman of the district board and whose term shall automatically expire upon the seating of either a new board of commissioners, or of a new council of the municipality.

The chairman of the district board will be eligible, however, for reappointment, upon the expiration of his or her current term, by the next district board selected upon and after the seating of either a new board of commissioners or new council of the municipality. The chairman of the district board shall take and subscribe an oath or affirmation to support the Constitution and laws of the United States and of this State, and to discharge faithfully the duties of his office, and a record of each such oath shall be filed with the clerk of the board of commissioners and the clerk of the municipality. The other six members will serve upon said board corollary to the responsibilities and duties of their respective elective offices and such service upon the district board will not constitute the holding of a public office. No compensation shall be paid to any member of the district board except for the chairman, and his compensation shall be fixed by the remaining six members. Except as provided above, no additional oath or affirmation shall be required of the members of the district board. No county commissioner or member of the council of the municipality shall continue to serve upon the district board subsequent to the termination of his or her current elective term, except upon reelection to said office.

The district board shall appoint a secretary and a treasurer who will not be members of the district board. The terms of office of the secretary and treasurer shall be as provided in the bylaws of the district board and the compensation of said officers shall be fixed by the district board. The treasurer shall furnish bond in some security company authorized to do business in North Carolina, the amount to be fixed by the district board in a sum not less than five thousand dollars ($5,000), which bond shall be approved by the district board and shall be continued upon the faithful performance of his duties. Every official, employee or agent of the district who handles or has custody of more than one hundred dollars ($100.00) of such district funds at any time, shall before assuming his duties as such be required to furnish bond in some security company authorized to do business in North Carolina, the amount to be fixed by the district board, which bond shall be approved by the district board and shall be continued upon the faithful performance of his duties in an amount sufficient to protect the district. All bonds required by this section shall be filed with the clerk of the municipality.

The district board shall meet regularly and no less than monthly, at such places and dates as determined by the board. Special meetings may be called by the chairman on his own initiative and shall be called by him upon request of two or more members of the board. All members shall be notified in writing at least 24 hours in advance of any meeting. A majority of the members of the district board shall constitute a quorum and the affirmative vote of a majority of the district board present at any meeting thereof shall be necessary for any action taken by the district board. No vacancy in the membership of the district board shall impair the right of a quorum to exercise all the rights and perform all the duties of the district board. Each member, including the chairman, shall be entitled to vote upon any question.

Any vacancy in district board membership, except that of the chairman, shall be filled by appointment of the original appointing authority for the remainder of the unexpired term. Each governing body may, by majority vote, replace at any time its representatives on said district board. (1971, c. 815, s. 4; 1973, c. 476, s. 128; 2007-182, s. 2.)

§ 162A-35. Procedure for inclusion of additional political subdivision or unincorporated area; notice and hearing; elections; actions questioning validity of elections.

If, at any time subsequent to the creation of a district, there shall be filed with the district board a resolution of the governing body of a political subdivision, or a petition, signed by not less than fifteen per centum (15%) of the voters resident within an unincorporated area, requesting inclusion in the district of such political subdivision or unincorporated area, and if the district board shall favor the inclusion in the district of such political subdivision or unincorporated area, the district board shall notify the board of commissioners and the board of commissioners, through its chairman, shall thereupon request that a representative of the Department of Environment and Natural Resources hold a joint public hearing with the board of commissioners concerning the inclusion of such political subdivision or unincorporated area in the district. The Secretary of Environment and Natural Resources and the chairman of the board of commissioners shall name a time and place within the district at which the public hearing shall be held. The chairman of the board of commissioners shall give prior notice of such hearing by posting a notice at the courthouse door of the county and also by publication in a newspaper circulating in the district and in any such political subdivision or unincorporated area at least once a week for four successive weeks, the first publication to be at least 30 days prior to such hearing. In the event all matters pertaining to the inclusion of such political subdivision or unincorporated area cannot be included at such hearing, such hearing may be continued to a time and place within the district determined by the board of commissioners with the concurrence of the representative of the Department of Environment and Natural Resources.

If, after such hearing, the Commission for Public Health and the board of commissioners shall determine that the preservation and promotion of the public health and welfare require that such political subdivision or unincorporated area be included in the district, the Commission for Public Health shall adopt a resolution to that effect, defining the boundaries of the district including such political subdivision or unincorporated area which has filed a resolution or petition as provided for in this section, and declaring such political subdivision or unincorporated area to be included in the district, subject to the approval, as to the inclusion of such political subdivision, of a majority of the qualified voters of such political subdivision, or as to the inclusion of such unincorporated area, of a majority of the qualified voters of such unincorporated area, voting at an election thereon to be called and held in such political subdivision or unincorporated area. When an election is required to be held within both a political subdivision and an unincorporated area, a separate election shall be called and held for the unincorporated area and a separate election shall be called and held for the political subdivision. Such separate elections, although independent one from the other, shall be called and held within each political subdivision and within the unincorporated area simultaneously on the same date.

If, at or prior to such public hearing, there shall be filed with the district board a petition signed by not less than fifteen percent (15%) of the registered voters of the district requesting an election to be held on the question of including the political subdivision or unincorporated area in the district, the district board shall certify the petition and if found adequate, shall request the county board of elections to hold the election in the district. The election in the district may be held at the same time as the election in the political subdivision or unincorporated area seeking to become a part of the district.

The county board of elections shall give notice of the elections as required in G.S. 163-33(8) and shall conduct the election.

The cost of the election in the district shall be paid by the district board and the cost of the municipal election by the municipality. The county shall pay the cost of an election in the unincorporated area. The governing body of the political subdivision shall file an accurate description of its boundaries, and those persons signing the petition for an unincorporated area shall file an accurate description of its boundaries with the board of elections at the time the petition is filed with the district board.

The elections shall be held and conducted in accordance with the applicable provisions of Articles 23 and 24 of Chapter 163 of the General Statutes.

The ballot shall contain the words:

"FOR inclusion in the ____ Metropolitan Water District of ____ County that area known as ____."

"AGAINST inclusion in the ____ Metropolitan Water District of ____ County that area known as ____."

If a majority of the votes cast in a political subdivision or unincorporated areas proposed to be included are in favor of inclusion, and a majority of the votes cast in the district favor inclusion, then from and after the date of the certification of the results such area or areas shall be a part of the district and subject to the debts of the district.

The results of the elections shall be certified to the district board.

If no election is required to be held in the district, then a favorable vote for inclusion in the political subdivision or unincorporated area shall be deemed to include such area or political subdivision as a part of the district and they shall be subject to the debts of the district.

No right of action or defense founded upon the invalidity of any such election shall be asserted, or open to question in any court upon any grounds unless the action or proceeding is commenced within 30 days after the results have been certified by the board of elections. (1971, c. 815, s. 5; 1973, c. 476, s. 128; 1981, c. 185; 1985, c. 462, s. 17; 1989, c. 727, s. 219(41); 1997-443, s. 11A.123; 2007-182, s. 2; 2011-31, s. 14.)

§ 162A-36. Powers generally; fiscal year.

(a)   Each district shall be deemed to be a public body and body politic and corporate, exercising public and essential governmental functions, to provide for the preservation and promotion of the public health and welfare, and said district is hereby authorized and empowered:

(1)   To adopt bylaws for the regulation of its affairs and the conduct of its business not in conflict with this or other law;

(2)   To adopt an official seal and alter the same at pleasure;

(3)   To maintain an office or offices at such place or places in the district as it may designate;

(4)   To sue and be sued in its own name, plead and be impleaded;

(5)   To acquire, lease as lessor or lessee, construct, reconstruct, improve, extend, enlarge, equip, repair, maintain and operate any water system or part thereof, and any sewerage system or part thereof, except interceptors, treatment plants and facilities constituting a system operated by a metropolitan sewage district within or without the district; provided, however, that no such water or sewerage system or part thereof, shall be located in any city, town or

incorporated village except with the consent of the governing body thereof, and each such governing body is hereby authorized to grant such consent;

(6) To issue general obligation bonds and revenue bonds of the district as hereinafter provided, to pay the costs of a water or sewerage system or systems;

(7) To issue general obligation refunding bonds and revenue refunding bonds of the district as hereinafter provided;

(8) To fix and revise from time to time and to collect rents, rates, fees and other charges for the use of the services and facilities furnished by any water or sewerage system;

(9) To cause taxes to be levied and collected upon all taxable property within the district sufficient to meet the obligations of the district, to pay the costs of maintaining, repairing and operating any water or sewerage system or systems, and to pay all obligations incurred by the district in the performance of its legal undertakings and functions;

(10) To acquire in the name of the district, either within or without the corporate limits of the district, by gift, purchase, lease or the exercise of the right of eminent domain, which right shall be exercised in accordance with the provisions of Chapter 40A of the General Statutes, any improved or unimproved lands or rights in lands, and to acquire by lease or purchase such personal property as it may deem necessary in connection with the acquisition, construction, reconstruction, improvement, extension, enlargement, repair, equipment, maintenance or operation of any water or sewerage system or systems, and to hold and dispose of real and personal property under its control;

(11) To make and enter into all contracts, leases and agreements necessary or incidental to the performance of its duties and the execution of its powers under this Article, including a trust agreement or trust agreements securing any revenue bonds issued hereunder;

(12) To employ such consulting and other engineers, superintendents, managers, construction and financial experts, accountants, attorneys, employees and agents as may, in the judgment of the district board, be deemed necessary, and to fix their compensation; provided, however, that the provisions

of G.S. 159-20 shall be complied with to the extent that the same shall be applicable;

(13) To receive and accept from the United States of America or the State of North Carolina, or any agency or instrumentality thereof loans, grants, advances or contributions for or in aid of the planning, acquisition, construction, reconstruction, improvement, extension, enlargement, repair, equipment, maintenance or operation of any water or sewerage system or systems, to agree to such reasonable conditions or requirements as may be imposed, and to receive and accept contributions from any source of either money, property, labor or other things of value, to be held, used and applied only for the purposes of which such loans, grants, advances or contributions may be made;

(14) To negotiate and pay close-out costs involved in the acquisition or lease of existing water supply or sewerage systems;

(15) To determine the extent to which local water distribution system and local sewerage system improvements will be financed out of district revenues and to contract with other political subdivisions for construction of facilities to be jointly financed and whose title would be vested in the district;

(16) To lease from any city or town or any other municipal corporation, or from any water or sewage district, any water or sewerage system or portions thereof upon such terms and conditions and for such considerations as may to the district board be deemed fair and reasonable;

(17) The metropolitan water district is authorized and empowered, through its district board, officers, agents and employees, to cause any user of water who shall fail to pay promptly his water rent or use bill for any month to be cut off, and his right to further use of water from said district to be discontinued until payment of any water rent or use arrearages;

(18) To do all acts and things necessary or convenient to carry out the powers granted by this Article.

(b) (1) Each metropolitan water district shall publish an annual financial report and its books shall be open for public inspection.

(2) Each district shall keep its accounts on the basis of a fiscal year commencing on the first day of July and ending on the thirtieth day of June of the following year.

(3) District revenues shall be used solely for the operation, improvement or benefit of the district's water and sewerage systems and the leasing of any portion thereof and to pay the principal and interest on bonds issued by the district. Said revenues shall not be used for the payment of interest or amortization of any utility bonds previously issued by any city, town or water or sewerage district.

(4) A district may provide water to a city or county or portion thereof within the district for governmental purposes without charge or at reduced rates. (1971, c. 815, s. 6; 1981, c. 919, s. 31.)

§ 162A-37. Bonds and notes authorized.

A metropolitan water district may from time to time issue bonds and notes under the Local Government Finance Act. (1971, c. 780, s. 37.5; c. 815, s. 7; 1973, c. 494, s. 46.)

§§ 162A-38 through 162A-44. Repealed by Session Laws 1971, c. 780, s. 37.5; 1973, c. 494, s. 46.

§ 162A-45. Determination of tax rate by district board; levy and collection of tax; remittance and deposit of funds.

After each assessment for taxes following the creation of the district, the board of commissioners shall file with the district board the valuation of assessable property within the district. The district board shall then determine the amount of funds to be raised by taxation for the ensuing year in excess of available funds to provide for the payment of the interest on and the principal of all outstanding general obligation bonds as the same shall become due and payable, to pay the cost of maintaining, repairing and operating any water system or sewerage system or both, and to pay all obligations incurred by the district in the performance of its lawful undertakings and functions.

The district board shall determine the number of cents per one hundred dollars ($100.00) necessary to raise said amount and certify such rate to the board of commissioners. The board of commissioners in its next annual levy shall include the number of cents per one hundred dollars ($100.00) certified by the district board in the levy against all taxable property within the district, which tax shall be collected as other county taxes are collected, and every month the amount of tax so collected shall be remitted to the district board and deposited by the district board in a separate account in a bank in the State of North Carolina. Such levy may include an amount for reimbursing the county for the additional cost to the county of levying and collecting such taxes, pursuant to such formula as may be agreed upon by the district board and the board of commissioners, to be deducted from the collections and stated with each remittance to the district board. The officer or officers having charge or custody of the funds of the district shall require such bank to furnish security for protection of such deposits as provided in G.S. 159-31. (1971, c. 815, s. 15; 1973, c. 1446, s. 13.)

§§ 162A-46 through 162A-48. Repealed by Session Laws 1971, c. 780, s. 37.5; 1973, c. 494, s. 46.

§ 162A-49. Rates and charges for services.

The district board may fix, and may revise from time to time, rents, rates, fees and other charges for the use of land for the services furnished or to be furnished by any water system or sewerage system or both. Such rents, rates, fees and charges shall not be subject to supervision or regulation by any bureau, board, commission, or other agency of the State or of any political subdivision. Any such rents, rates, fees and charges pledged to the payment of revenue bonds of the district shall be fixed and revised so that the revenues of the water system or sewerage system or both, together with any other available funds, shall be sufficient at all times to pay the cost of maintaining, repairing and operating the water system or the sewerage system or both, the revenues of which are pledged to the payment of such revenue bonds, including reserves for such purposes, and to pay the interest on and the principal of such revenue bonds as the same shall become due and payable and to provide reserves therefor. If any such rents, rates, fees and charges are pledged to the payment of any general obligation bonds issued under this Article, such rents, rates, fees and charges shall be fixed and revised so as to comply with the requirements of such pledge. The district board may provide methods for collection of such rents, rates, fees and charges and measures for enforcement of collection thereof, including penalties and the denial or discontinuance of service. (1971, c. 815, s. 19.)

§§ 162A-50 through 162A-52. Repealed by Session Laws 1971, c. 780, s. 37.5; 1973, c. 494, s. 46.

§ 162A-53. Authority of governing bodies of political subdivisions.

The governing body of any political subdivision is hereby authorized and empowered:

(1) Subject to the approval of the Local Government Commission, to transfer jurisdiction over, and to lease, lend, sell, grant or convey to a district, upon such terms and conditions as the governing body of such political subdivision may agree upon with the district board, the whole or any part of any water system or sewerage system or both, and such real or personal property as may be necessary or useful in connection with the acquisition, construction, reconstruction, improvement, extension, enlargement, equipment, repair, maintenance or operation of any new water system or sewerage system or both by the district, including public roads and other property already devoted to public use;

(2) To make and enter into contracts or agreements with a district, upon such terms and conditions and for such periods as such governing body and the district board may determine:

a. For the collection, treatment or disposal of sewage;

b. For the collecting by such political subdivision or by the district of rents, rates, fees or charges for the services and facilities provided to or for such political subdivision or its inhabitants by any water system or sewerage system or both and for the enforcement of collection of such rents, rates, fees and charges; and

c. For the imposition of penalties, including the shutting off of the supply of water furnished by any water system owned or operated by such political subdivision, in the event that the owner, tenant or occupant of any premises utilizing such water shall fail to pay any such rents, rates, fees or charges;

d. For the supply of raw or treated water on a regular retail or wholesale basis;

e. For the supply of raw or treated water on a standby wholesale basis;

f.   For the construction of jointly financed facilities whose title shall be vested in the district.

(3)   To fix, and revise from time to time, rents, rates, fees and other charges for the services furnished or to be furnished by a water system or sewerage system or both under any contract between the district and such political subdivision, and to pledge all or any part of the proceeds of such rents, rates, fees and charges to the payment of any obligation of such political subdivision to the district under such contract;

(4)   To pay any obligation of such political subdivision to the district under such contract from any available funds of the political subdivision and to levy and collect a tax ad valorem for the making of any such payment; and

(5)   In its discretion or if required by law, to submit to its qualified electors under the election laws applicable to such political subdivision any contract or agreement which such governing body is authorized to make and enter into with the district under the provisions of this Article.

Any such election upon a contract or agreement, may, at the discretion of the governing body, be called and held under the election laws applicable to the issuance of bonds by such political subdivision. (1971, c. 815, s. 23.)

§ 162A-54. Rights-of-way and easements in streets and highways.

A right-of-way or easement in, along, or across any State highway system road, or street, and along or across any city or town street within a district is hereby granted to a district in case such right-of-way is found by the district board to be necessary or convenient for carrying out any of the work of the district. Any work done in, along, or across any State highway system, road, street, or property shall be done in accordance with the rules and regulations and any reasonable requirements of the Department of Transportation, and any work done in, along, or across any municipal street or property shall be done in accordance with any reasonable requirements of the municipal governing body. (1971, c. 815, s. 24; 1973, c. 507, s. 5; 1977, c. 464, s. 34.)

§ 162A-55. Submission of preliminary plans to planning groups; cooperation with planning agencies.

Prior to the time final plans are made for the location and construction of any water system or sewerage system or both, the district board shall present preliminary plans for such improvement to the county, municipal or regional planning board for their consideration, if such facility is to be located within the planning jurisdiction of any such county, municipal or regional planning group. The district board shall make every effort to cooperate with the planning agency, if any, in the location and construction of a proposed facility authorized under this Article. The district board created under the authority of this Article is hereby directed, wherever possible, to coordinate its plans for the construction of a water system or sewerage system or both, with the overall plans for the development of the planning area, if such district is located wholly or in part within a county, municipal or regional planning area; provided, however, that the approval of any such county, municipal or regional planning board as to any such plan of the district shall not be required. (1971, c. 815, s. 25.)

§ 162A-56. Advances by political subdivisions for preliminary expenses of districts.

Any political subdivision is hereby authorized to make advances, from any moneys that may be available for such purpose, in connection with the creation of such district and to provide for the preliminary expenses of such district. Any such advances may be repaid to such political subdivision from the proceeds of bonds issued by said district or from other available funds of said district. (1971, c. 815, s. 26.)

§ 162A-57. Article regarded as supplemental.

This Article shall not be regarded as in derogation of or as repealing any powers now existing under any other law, either general, special or local; provided, however, that the issuance of bonds under the provisions of this Article need not comply with the requirements of any other law applicable to the issuance of bonds except as herein provided. (1971, c. 815, s. 27.)

§ 162A-58. Inconsistent laws declared inapplicable.

All general, special or local laws, or parts thereof inconsistent herewith are hereby declared to be inapplicable, unless otherwise specified, to the provisions of this Article. It is specifically provided that Chapter 399 of the 1933 Public-Local and Private Laws of North Carolina shall not be applicable to any metropolitan water district created pursuant to the provisions of this Article. (1971, c. 815, s. 28.)

§§ 162A-59 through 162A-63. Reserved for future codification purposes.

Article 5.

Metropolitan Sewerage Districts.

§ 162A-64. Short title.

This Article shall be known and may be cited as the "North Carolina Metropolitan Sewerage Districts Act." (1961, c. 795, s. 1; 1973, c. 822, s. 4.)

§ 162A-65. Definitions; description of boundaries.

(a) Definitions. - As used in this Article the following words and terms shall have the following meanings, unless the context shall indicate another or different meaning or intent:

(1) The term "board of commissioners" shall mean the board of commissioners of the county in which a metropolitan sewerage district shall be created under the provisions of this Article.

(2) The word "cost" as applied to a sewerage system shall mean the cost of acquiring, constructing, reconstructing, improving, extending, enlarging, repairing and equipping any such system, and shall include the cost of all labor and materials, machinery and equipment, lands, property, rights, easements and franchises, plans and specifications, surveys and estimates of cost and of revenues, and engineering and legal services, financing charges, interest prior to and during construction and, if deemed advisable by the district board, for one year after the estimated date of completion of construction, and all other expenses necessary or incident to determining the feasibility or practicability of any such undertaking, administrative expense and such other expenses,

including

reasonable provision for working capital and a reserve for interest, as may be necessary or incident to the financing herein authorized, and may also include any obligation or expense incurred by the district or by any political subdivision prior to the issuance of bonds under the provisions of this Article in connection with any such undertaking or any of the foregoing items of cost.

(3)   The word "district" shall mean a metropolitan sewerage district created under the provisions of this Article.

(4)   The term "district board" shall mean a sewerage district board established under the provisions of this Article as the governing body of a district or, if such sewerage district board shall be abolished, any board, body, or commission succeeding to the principal functions thereof or upon which the powers given by this Article to the sewerage district board shall be given by law.

(5)   The term "general obligation bonds" shall mean bonds of a district for the payment of which and the interest thereon all the taxable property within such district is subject to the levy of an ad valorem tax without limitation of rate or amount.

(6)   The term "governing body" shall mean the board, commission, council or other body, by whatever name it may be known, of a political subdivision in which the general legislative powers thereof are vested, including, but without limitation, as to any political subdivision other than the county, the board of commissioners for the county when the general legislative powers of such political subdivision are exercised by such board.

(7)   The word "person" shall mean any and all persons including individuals, firms, partnerships, associations, public or private institutions, municipalities, or political subdivisions, governmental agencies, or private or public corporations organized and existing under the laws of this State or any other state or county.

(8)   The term "political subdivision" shall mean any county, city, town, incorporated village, sanitary district, water district, sewer district, special purpose district or other political subdivision or public corporation of this State now or hereafter created or established.

(9) The term "revenue bonds" shall mean bonds the principal of and the interest on which are payable solely from revenues of a sewerage system or systems.

(9a) The word "revenues" shall mean all moneys received by a district from, in connection with or as a result of its ownership or operation of a sewerage system, including, without limitation and if deemed advisable by the district board, moneys received from the United States of America, or any agency thereof, pursuant to an agreement with the district board pertaining to the sewerage system.

(10) The word "sewage" shall mean the water-carried wastes created in and carried or to be carried away from residences, hotels, schools, hospitals, industrial establishments, commercial establishments or any other private or public buildings, together with such surface or groundwater or household and industrial wastes as may be present.

(11) The term "sewage disposal system" shall mean any plant, system, facility or property, either within or without the limits of the district, used or useful or having the present capacity for future use in connection with the collection, treatment, purification or disposal of sewage, or any integral part thereof, including but not limited to septic tank systems or other on-site collection or disposal facilities or systems, treatment plants, facilities for the generation and transmission of electric power and energy, pumping stations, intercepting sewers, trunk sewers, pressure lines, mains and all necessary appurtenances and equipment, and all property, rights, easements and franchises relating thereto and deemed necessary or convenient by the district board for the operation thereof.

(12) The term "sewerage system" shall embrace both sewers and sewage disposal systems and any part or parts thereof, either within or without the limits of the district, all property, rights, easements and franchises relating thereto, and any and all buildings and other structures necessary or useful in connection with the ownership, operation or maintenance thereof.

(13) The word "sewers" shall mean any mains, pipes and laterals, including pumping stations, either within or without the limits of the district, for the reception of sewage and carrying such sewage to an outfall or some part of a sewage disposal system.

(b) Description of Boundaries. - Whenever this Article requires that the boundaries of an area be described, it shall be sufficient if the boundaries are described in a manner which conveys an understanding of the location of the land and may be

(1) By reference to a map,

(2) By metes and bounds,

(3) By general description referring to natural boundaries, boundaries of political subdivisions, or boundaries of particular tracts or parcels of land, or

(4) Any combination of the foregoing. (1961, c. 795, s. 2; 1969, c. 993, s. 1; 1973, c. 822, s. 4; 1979, c. 619, s. 10; 1983, c. 333, s. 1.)

§ 162A-66. Procedure for creation; resolutions and petitions for creation; notice to and action by the Environmental Management Commission; notice and public hearing; resolutions creating districts; actions to set aside proceedings.

Any two or more political subdivisions in one or more counties, or any political subdivision or subdivisions and any unincorporated area or areas located within one or more counties, which political subdivisions or areas need not be contiguous, may petition for the creation of a metropolitan sewerage district under the provisions of this Article by filing with the board or boards of commissioners of the county or counties within which the proposed district will lie:

(1) A resolution of the governing body of each such political subdivision stating the necessity for the creation of a metropolitan sewerage district under the provisions of this Article in order to preserve and promote the public health and welfare within the area of the proposed district, and requesting the creation of a metropolitan sewerage district having the boundaries set forth in said resolution, and

(2) If any unincorporated area is to be included in such district, a petition, signed by not less than fifty-one per centum (51%) of the qualified voters resident within such area, defining the boundaries of such area, stating the necessity for the creation of a metropolitan sewerage district under the provisions of this Article in order to preserve and promote the public health and

welfare within the proposed district, and requesting the creation of a metropolitan sewerage district having the boundaries set forth in such petition for such district.

Upon the receipt of such resolutions and petitions requesting the creation of a metropolitan sewerage district, the board or boards of commissioners, through the chairman thereof, shall notify the North Carolina Environmental Management Commission of the receipt of such resolutions and petitions, and shall request that a representative of the Environmental Management Commission hold a joint public hearing with the board or boards of commissioners concerning the creation of the proposed metropolitan sewerage district. The chairman of the Environmental Management Commission and the chairman or chairmen of the board or boards of commissioners shall name a time and place within the proposed district at which the public hearing shall be held; provided, however, that where a proposed district lies within more than one county, the public hearing shall be held in the county within which the greater portion of the proposed district lies. The chairman or chairmen of the board or boards of commissioners shall give prior notice of such hearing by posting a notice at least 30 days prior to the hearing at the courthouse of the county or counties within which the district will lie and also by publication at least once a week for four successive weeks in a newspaper having general circulation in the proposed district, the first publication to be at least 30 days prior to such hearing. In the event all matters pertaining to the creation of such metropolitan sewerage district cannot be concluded at such hearing, such hearing may be continued to a time and place within the proposed district determined by the board or boards of commissioners with the concurrence of the representative of the Environmental Management Commission.

If, after such hearing, the Environmental Management Commission and the board or boards of commissioners shall deem it advisable to comply with the request of such resolutions and petitions, and determine that the creation of a metropolitan sewerage district would preserve and promote the public health and welfare in the area or areas described in such resolutions and petitions, the Environmental Management Commission shall adopt a resolution to that effect, defining the boundaries of such district and declaring the territory within such boundaries to be a metropolitan sewerage district under the name and style of "_____ Metropolitan Sewerage District of _____ [County] [Counties]"; provided, that the Environmental Management Commission may make minor deviations in the boundaries from those prescribed in the resolutions and petitions upon determination by the Environmental Management Commission that such deviations are advisable in the interest of the public health, and provided no such district shall include any political subdivision which has not petitioned for inclusion as provided in this Article.

The Environmental Management Commission shall cause copies of the resolution creating the metropolitan sewerage district to be sent to the board or boards of commissioners and to the governing body of each political subdivision included in the district. The board or boards of commissioners shall cause a copy of such resolution of the Environmental Management Commission to be published in a newspaper circulating within the district once in each of two successive weeks, and a notice substantially in the following form shall be published with such resolution:

The foregoing resolution was passed by the North Carolina Environmental Management Commission on the _____ day of _____, _____, and was first published on the _____ day of _____, ____.

Any action or proceeding questioning the validity of said resolution or the creation of the metropolitan sewerage district therein described must be commenced within 30 days after the first publication of said resolution.

_____

Clerk, Board of Commissioners for

_____ County.

Any action or proceeding in any court to set aside a resolution creating a metropolitan sewerage district, or to obtain any other relief upon the ground that such resolution or any proceeding or action taken with respect to the creation of such district is invalid, must be commenced within 30 days after the first publication of the resolution and said notice. After the expiration of such period of limitation, no right of action or defense founded upon the invalidity of the resolution or the creation of the metropolitan sewerage district therein described shall be asserted, nor shall the validity of the resolution or of the creation of such metropolitan sewerage district be open to question in any court upon any ground whatever, except in an action or proceeding commenced within such period. (1961, c. 795, s. 3; 1973, c. 512, s. 1; c. 822, s. 4; c. 1262, s. 23; 1977, c. 764, s. 1; 1999-456, s. 59.)

§ 162A-66.5. Approval of all political subdivisions required.

Prior to the adoption of a resolution under G.S. 162A-66 on or after April 1, 2013, the Environmental Management Commission shall receive a resolution supporting the establishment of a district board from (i) the board of commissioners of the county or counties lying wholly or partly within the boundaries of the proposed district and (ii) from the governing board of each political subdivision in the county or counties lying wholly or partly within the boundaries of the proposed district. If the Environmental Management Commission does not receive a resolution from each of those political subdivisions, the Environmental Management Commission may not adopt the resolution to create the district board. (2013-50, s. 5.5.)

§ 162A-67. District board; composition, appointment, terms, oaths and removal of members; organization; meetings; quorum; compensation and expenses of members.

(a) Appointment of Board for District Lying Wholly or Partly outside City or Town Limits. - The district board of a metropolitan sewerage district lying in whole or in part outside the corporate limits of a city or town shall be appointed immediately after the creation of the district in the following manner:

(1) If the district lies entirely within one county with a population of 25,000 or more, the board of commissioners of that county shall appoint to the district board three members who are qualified voters residing within the district. The initial members so appointed shall have terms expiring one year, two years and three years, respectively, from the date of adoption of the resolution of the Environmental Management Commission creating the district, and the board of commissioners shall designate the length of the term of each initial member. Successor members shall be appointed for a term of three years.

(1a) If the district lies entirely within one county with a population of less than 25,000, the board of commissioners of that county shall appoint to the district board five members who are qualified voters residing within the district. Of the initial members so appointed, one shall have a term expiring at the end of one year, two shall have terms expiring at the end of two years, and two shall have terms expiring at the end of three years from the date of adoption of the resolution of the Environmental Management Commission creating the district. In making initial appointments, the board of commissioners shall specify whether a member is to serve a term of one, two, or three years. Successor members shall be appointed for a term of three years.

(2) If the district lies in two counties, the board of commissioners of the county in which the largest portion of the district lies shall appoint to the district board two qualified voters residing in the county and district to serve for terms of one year and three years, respectively. The board of commissioners of the county in which the lesser portion of the district lies shall appoint to the district board one qualified voter residing in the county and district to serve for a term of two years. All successor members shall be appointed for a term of three years.

(3) If the district lies in three or more counties, the board of commissioners of each such county shall appoint one member of the district board. Each member so appointed shall be a qualified voter residing in the district and of the county from which he is appointed and shall serve for a term of three years. Successor members shall be appointed for a term of three years.

(4) The governing body of each political subdivision, other than counties, lying in whole or in part within the district, shall appoint one member of the district board. Except as provided in G.S. 162A-68, no appointment of a member of the district board shall be made by or in behalf of any political subdivision of which the board or boards of commissioners shall be the governing body. If any city or town within the district shall have a population, as determined from the latest decennial census, more than one-half the combined population of all other political subdivisions (other than counties) and unincorporated areas within the district, the governing body of any such city or town shall appoint three members.

(b) Appointment of Board for District Lying Wholly within City or Town Limits. - Any district lying entirely within the corporate limits of two or more cities or towns shall be governed by a district board consisting solely of members appointed by the governing bodies of such cities or towns and, in addition, one member elected by the appointed members of the district board. The governing body of each constituent city or town of the district shall appoint to the district board two qualified voters residing in the district and the city or town. The members so appointed shall elect, by majority vote, one additional member who shall be a qualified voter residing in the district and one of the constituent cities or towns.

One of the two members initially appointed by the governing body of each constituent city or town shall serve for a term which shall expire 30 days following the next regular election held for election of the governing body by which the member was appointed; and the other member shall serve for a term which shall expire two years thereafter. Successor members shall serve for a term of four years.

The member elected by the district board and his successors in office shall serve for a term of four years.

(c)   Reappointment; Vacancies; Removal; Term. - Members of a district board may be reappointed. If a vacancy shall occur on a district board, the governing body which appointed the member who previously filled the vacancy shall appoint a new member who shall serve for the remainder of the unexpired term. Any member of a district board may be removed for cause by the governing board that appointed him. All members shall serve until their successors have been duly appointed and qualified.

(d)   District Board Procedures. - Each member of the district board, before entering upon his duties, shall take and subscribe an oath or affirmation to support the Constitution and laws of the United States and of this State and to discharge faithfully the duties of his office; and a record of each such oath shall be filed with the clerk or clerks of the board or boards of commissioners.

The district board shall elect one of its members as chairman and another as vice-chairman and shall appoint a secretary and a treasurer who may, but need not, be members of the district board. The officers [offices] of secretary and treasurer may be combined. The district board may also appoint an assistant secretary and an assistant treasurer or, if the office is combined, an assistant secretary-treasurer who may, but need not, be members of the district board. The terms of office of the chairman, vice-chairman, secretary, treasurer, assistant secretary, and assistant treasurer shall be as provided in the bylaws of the district board.

The district board shall meet regularly at such places and dates as are determined by the board. Special meetings may be called by the chairman on his own initiative and shall be called by him upon request of two or more members of the board. All members shall be notified in writing at least 24 hours in advance of such meeting. A majority of the members of the district board shall constitute a quorum, and the affirmative vote of a majority of the members of the district board present at any meeting thereof shall be necessary for any action taken by the district board. No vacancy in the membership of the district board shall impair the right of a quorum to exercise all the rights and perform all the duties of the district board. Each member, including the chairman, shall be entitled to vote on any question. The members of the district board may receive compensation in an amount to be determined by the board, but not to exceed that compensation paid to members of Occupational Licensing Boards as provided in G.S. 93B-5(a) for each meeting of the board attended and for attendance at each regularly scheduled committee meeting of the board. The members of the district board may also be reimbursed the amount of actual expenses incurred by them in the performance of their duties. (1961, c. 795, s. 4; 1963, c. 471; 1973, c. 512, s. 2; c. 822, s. 4; c. 1262, s. 23; 1979, c. 471; 1983, c. 333, s. 2; 1991, c. 351, s. 1; 1995, c. 511, s. 2.1; 2012-203, s. 1.)

§ 162A-67.1: Reserved for future codification purposes.

§ 162A-67.2: Reserved for future codification purposes.

§ 162A-67.3: Reserved for future codification purposes.

§ 162A-67.4: Reserved for future codification purposes.

§ 162A-67.5. Determination of population and representation.

(a) For purposes of determining district board representation of political subdivisions for any appointment under this Article, population shall be determined by reference to the most recent decennial census.

(b) For purposes of determining population for district board representation, only that portion of the population residing within the district boundary itself shall be included for each political subdivision and each unincorporated area having district board representation at the time such determination is made.

(c) In determining district board representation, no appointment shall be made by or in behalf of a political subdivision which does not own or operate a public system for the collection of wastewater at the time of such appointment. (2012-203, s. 2.)

§ 162A-68. Procedure for inclusion of additional political subdivision or unincorporated area; notice and hearing; elections; actions to set aside proceedings.

(a) If, at any time subsequent to the creation of a district, there shall be filed with the district board a resolution of the governing body of a political subdivision, or a petition, signed by not less than fifty-one per centum (51%) of the qualified voters resident within an unincorporated area, requesting inclusion in the district of such political subdivision or unincorporated area, and if the district board shall favor the inclusion in the district of such political subdivision or unincorporated area, the district board shall notify the board or boards of commissioners of the county or counties within which the district lies and shall file with the board or boards of commissioners and with the Environmental Management Commission a report setting forth the plans of the district for extending sewerage service to the political subdivision or unincorporated area. The report shall include:

(1) A map or maps of the district and adjacent territory showing the present and proposed boundaries of the district; the existing major sewer interceptors and outfalls; and the proposed extension of such interceptors and outfalls.

(2) A statement setting forth the plans of the district for extending sewerage services to the territory proposed to be included, which plans shall:

a. Provide for extending sewerage service to the territory included on substantially the same basis and in the same manner as such services are provided within the rest of the district prior to inclusion of the new territory.

b. Set forth a proposed time schedule for extending sewerage service to the territory proposed to be included.

c. Set forth the estimated cost of extending sewerage service to the territory proposed to be included; the method by which the district proposes to finance the extension; the outstanding existing indebtedness of the district, if any; and the valuation of assessable property within the district and within the territory proposed to be included.

d. Contain a declaration of intent of the district board to conform with the plans set forth in the report in extending sewerage services to the territory proposed to be included; and a certification by the chairman of the district board to the effect that the matters and things set forth in the report are true to his knowledge or belief.

(b) The board or boards of commissioners, through the chairmen thereof, shall thereupon request that a representative of the Environmental Management

Commission hold a joint public meeting with the board or boards of commissioners concerning the inclusion of a political subdivision or an unincorporated area in the district. The chairman of the Environmental Management Commission and the chairman or chairmen of the board or boards of commissioners shall name a time and place within the district at which the public hearing shall be held. The chairman or chairmen of the board or boards of commissioners shall give prior notice of such hearing by posting a notice at the courthouse door of the county or counties at least 30 days prior to the hearing and also by publication at least once a week for four successive weeks in a newspaper having general circulation in the district and in any such political subdivision or unincorporated area, the first publication to be at least 30 days prior to such hearing. In the event all matters pertaining to the inclusion of such political subdivision or unincorporated area cannot be included at such hearing, such hearing may be continued to a time and place within the district determined by the board or boards of commissioners with the concurrence of the representative of the Environmental Management Commission.

(c)   If, after such hearing, the Environmental Management Commission and the board or boards of commissioners shall determine that the inclusion of the political subdivision or unincorporated area in the district will preserve and promote the public health and welfare, the Environmental Management Commission shall adopt a resolution to that effect, defining the boundaries of the district, including the political subdivision or unincorporated area which has filed a resolution or petition as provided for in this section, and declaring such political subdivision or unincorporated area to be included in the district.

(d)   If, at or prior to such public hearing, there shall be filed with the district board a petition, signed by not less than ten per centum (10%) of the qualified voters residing in the district, requesting an election to be held therein on the question of including the political subdivision or unincorporated area, the district board shall certify a copy of such petition to the board or boards of commissioners, and the board or boards of commissioners shall request the county board or boards of elections to submit such question to the qualified voters within the district in accordance with G.S. 163-287 and the other applicable provisions of Chapter 163 of the General Statutes; provided, that the election shall not be held unless the Environmental Management Commission has adopted a resolution approving the inclusion of the political subdivision or unincorporated area in the district.

Notice of such election, which shall contain a statement of the boundaries of the territory proposed to be included in the district and the boundaries of the district after inclusion, shall be given by publication once a week for three successive weeks in a newspaper or newspapers having general circulation within the district, the first publication to be at least 30 days prior to the election.

(e) Notice of the resolution of the Environmental Management Commission, or in the event that an election pursuant to this section is held, notice of the results of the election, approving the inclusion of the political subdivision or unincorporated area within the district shall be published as provided in G.S. 162A-66.

(f) Any action or proceeding in any court to set aside a resolution of the Environmental Management Commission or an election approving the inclusion of a political subdivision or unincorporated area within a district or to obtain any other relief upon the ground that such resolution or election or any proceeding or action taken with respect to the inclusion of the political subdivision or unincorporated area within the district is invalid, must be commenced within 30 days after the first publication of the notice. After the expiration of such period of limitation, no right of action or defense founded upon the invalidity of the resolution or the election or the inclusion of the political subdivision or unincorporated area in the district shall be asserted, nor shall the validity of the resolution or the election or the inclusion of the political subdivision or unincorporated area be open to question in any court upon any ground whatever, except in an action or proceeding commenced within such period.

(g) Any political subdivision or unincorporated area included within an existing district by resolution of the Environmental Management Commission or by such resolution and election shall be subject to all debts of the district.

(h) The annexation by a city or town within a metropolitan sewerage district of an area lying outside such district shall not be construed as the inclusion within the district of an additional political subdivision or unincorporated area within the meaning of the provisions of this section; but any such areas so annexed shall become a part of the district and shall be subject to all debts thereof.

(i) Immediately following the inclusion of any additional political subdivision within an existing district, members representing such additional political subdivision shall be appointed to the district board in the manner provided in this section:

(1) Any additional unincorporated area that is included within an existing district shall be represented by the members representing the county in which the unincorporated area lies as follows:

a. If inclusion of the additional unincorporated area extends the district into more than one county, members representing the unincorporated area in the new county shall be appointed immediately following the inclusion of the additional area. Upon the inclusion of the additional area, the board members appointed in accordance with G.S. 162A-67(a)(1) or G.S. 162A-67(a)(1a) shall continue to serve on the district board. The board of commissioners of the county in which the largest portion of the district lies shall appoint qualified voters residing in the county and district as their successors such that the county in which the largest portion of the district lies shall always have three members on the district board. The board of commissioners of the county in which the lesser portion of the district lies shall appoint to the district board two qualified voters residing in the county and district to serve a term of three years and shall appoint qualified voters residing in the county and district as their successors such that the county in which the lesser portion of the district lies shall always have two members on the district board. For purposes of this subdivision, the county in which the largest portion and lesser portion of the district lies shall be determined with reference to the land area of the district lying within the county as a percentage of land area of the entire district at the time such appointment or reappointment is made.

b. If the inclusion of the additional unincorporated area has the effect of changing the county in which the largest portion of the district lies, new members representing the county comprising the larger portion of the district shall be appointed in accordance with G.S. 162A-67(a)(2) immediately following the inclusion, and no reappointment shall be made by the county in which the lesser portion of the district lies upon expiration of the first term of a member representing that county following the inclusion.

(2) Following the inclusion of any additional political subdivision within an existing district, the political subdivisions added shall appoint members to the district board in accordance with G.S. 162A-67(a)(4) only if the governing body of the political subdivision owns or operates a public system for the collection of wastewater at the time of such appointment.

The terms of office of the members first appointed to represent such additional subdivision or area may be varied for a period not to exceed six months from the terms provided for in G.S. 162A-67, so that the appointment of successors to such members may more nearly coincide with the appointment of successors to members of the existing board; and all successor members shall be appointed for the terms provided for in G.S. 162A-67. (1961, c. 795, s. 5; 1973, c. 512, s. 3; c. 822, s. 4; c. 1262, s. 23; 1977, c. 764, s. 2; 1991 (Reg. Sess., 1992), c. 954, s. 1; 2012-203, s. 3; 2013-381, s. 10.30.)

§ 162A-69. Powers generally; fiscal year.

Each district shall be deemed to be a public body and body politic and corporate exercising public and essential governmental functions to provide for the preservation and promotion of the public health and welfare, and each district is hereby authorized and empowered:

(1) To adopt bylaws for the regulation of its affairs and the conduct of its business not in conflict with this or other law;

(2) To adopt an official seal and alter the same at pleasure;

(3) To maintain an office at such place or places in the district as it may designate;

(4) To sue and be sued in its own name, plead and be impleaded;

(5) To acquire, lease as lessor or lessee, construct, reconstruct, improve, extend, enlarge, equip, repair, maintain and operate any sewerage system or part thereof within or without the district; provided, however, that no such sewerage system or part thereof shall be located in any city, town or incorporated village outside the district except with the consent of the governing body thereof, and each such governing body is hereby authorized to grant such consent;

(6) To issue general obligation bonds and revenue bonds of the district as hereinafter provided to pay the cost of a sewerage system or systems;

(7) To issue general obligation refunding bonds and revenue refunding bonds of the district as hereinafter provided;

(8) To fix and revise from time to time and to collect rents, rates, fees and other charges for the use of or for the services and facilities furnished by any sewerage system;

(9) To cause taxes to be levied and collected upon all taxable property within the district sufficient to meet the obligations of the district, to pay the cost of maintaining, repairing and operating any sewerage system or systems, and to pay all obligations incurred by the district in the performance of its lawful undertakings and functions;

(10) To acquire in the name of the district, either within or without the corporate limits of the district, by gift, purchase or the exercise of the right of eminent domain, which right shall be exercised in accordance with the provisions of Chapter 40A of the General Statutes of North Carolina, any improved or unimproved lands or rights in land, and to acquire such personal property, as it may deem necessary in connection with the acquisition, construction, reconstruction, improvement, extension, enlargement, repair, equipment, maintenance or operation of any sewerage system, and to hold and dispose of all real and personal property under its control;

(11) To make and enter into all contracts and agreements necessary or incidental to the performance of its duties and the execution of its powers under this Article, including a trust agreement or trust agreements securing any revenue bonds issued hereunder;

(12) To employ such consulting and other engineers, superintendents, managers, construction and financial experts, accountants, attorneys, employees and agents as may, in the judgment of the district board be deemed necessary, and to fix their compensation; provided, however, that the provisions of G.S. 159-20 shall be complied with to the extent that the same shall be applicable;

(13) To receive and accept from the United States of America or the State of North Carolina or any agency or instrumentality thereof loans, grants, advances or contributions for or in aid of the planning, acquisition, construction, reconstruction, improvement, extension, enlargement, repair, equipment, maintenance or operation of any sewerage system or systems, to agree to such reasonable conditions or requirements as may be imposed, and to receive and accept contributions from any source of either money, property, labor or other things of value, to be held, used and applied only for the purposes for which such loans, grants, advances or contributions may be made;

(13a) To adopt ordinances to regulate and control the discharge of sewage into any sewerage system owned or operated by the district. Prior to the adoption of any ordinance or any amendment to any ordinance the district shall first pass a declaration of intent to adopt such ordinance or amendment. The declaration of intent shall describe the ordinance or amendment which it is proposed that the district adopt. The declaration of intent shall be submitted to each governing body for review and comment. The district shall take into consideration any comment and suggestions with respect to the proposed ordinance or amendment offered by any governing body and may modify such proposed ordinance or amendment to reflect comment and suggestions offered by any governing body. Thereafter, the district shall be authorized to adopt such ordinance or any amendment to it at any time after 60 days following the submission of the declaration of intent to each governing body;

(13b) To require the owners of improved property located within the district so as to be served by a sewer collection line owned or leased and operated by the district to connect their premises with the sewer line, and fix charges for these connections; and

(13c) To exercise any power of a Metropolitan Water District under Article 4 of this Chapter not set forth in this section.

(14) To do all acts and things necessary or convenient to carry out the powers granted by this Article.

Each district shall keep its accounts on the basis of a fiscal year commencing on the first day of July and ending on the thirtieth day of June of the following year. (1961, c. 795, s. 6; 1973, c. 822, s. 4; 1981, c. 919, s. 32; 1983, c. 333, s. 3; 1987, c. 396, ss. 1-3; 2012-203, s. 4.)

§ 162A-70. Bonds and notes authorized.

A metropolitan sewerage district shall have power from time to time to issue bonds and notes under the Local Government Finance Act. (1961, c. 795, s. 7; 1971, c. 780, s. 30; 1973, c. 822, s. 4.)

§ 162A-71. Determination of tax rate by district board; levy and collection of tax; remittance and deposit of funds.

After each assessment for taxes following the creation of the district, the board or boards of commissioners shall file with the district board the valuation of assessable property within the district. The district board shall then determine the amount of funds to be raised by taxation for the ensuing year in excess of available funds to provide for the payment of interest on and the principal of all outstanding general obligation bonds as the same shall become due and payable, to pay the cost of maintaining, repairing and operating any sewerage system or systems, and to pay all obligations incurred by the district in the performance of its lawful undertakings and functions.

The district board shall determine the number of cents per one hundred dollars ($100.00) necessary to raise said amount and certify such rate to the board or boards of commissioners. The board or boards of commissioners shall include the number of cents per one hundred dollars ($100.00) certified by the district board in its next annual levy against all taxable property within the district, which tax shall be collected as other county taxes are collected, and every month the amount of tax so collected shall be remitted to the district board and deposited by the district board in a separate account in a bank in the State of North Carolina. Such levy may include an amount for reimbursing the county for the additional cost to the county of levying and collecting such taxes, pursuant to such formula as may be agreed upon by the district board and the board or boards of commissioners, to be deducted from the collections and stated with each remittance to the district board. The officer or officers having charge or custody of the funds of the district shall require said bank to furnish security for protection of such deposits as provided in G.S. 159-28 and, after June 30, 1973, G.S. 159-31. (1961, c. 795, s. 15; 1973, c. 512, s. 4; c. 822, s. 4.)

§ 162A-72. Rates and charges for services.

The district board may fix, and may revise from time to time, rents, rates, fees and other charges for the use of and for the services furnished or to be furnished by any sewerage system. Such rents, rates, fees and charges shall not be subject to supervision or regulation by any bureau, board, commission, or other agency of the State or of any political subdivision. Any such rents, rates, fees and charges pledged to the payment of revenue bonds of the district shall be fixed and revised so that the revenues of the sewerage system, together with any other available funds, shall be sufficient at all times to pay the cost of maintaining, repairing and operating the sewerage system the revenues of which are pledged to the payment of such revenue bonds, including reserves for such purposes, and to pay the interest on and the principal of such revenue bonds as the same shall become due and payable and to provide reserves therefor. If any such rents, rates, fees and charges are pledged to the payment of any general obligation bonds issued under this Article, such rents, rates, fees and charges shall be fixed and revised so as to comply with the requirements of such pledge. The district board may provide methods for collection of such rents, rates, fees and charges and measures for enforcement of collection thereof, including penalties and the denial or discontinuance of service. (1961, c. 795, s. 19; 1973, c. 822, s. 4.)

§ 162A-73. Authority of governing bodies of political subdivisions.

The governing body of any political subdivision is hereby authorized and empowered:

(1)   Subject to the approval of the Local Government Commission, to transfer jurisdiction over, and to lease, lend, sell, grant or convey to a district, upon such terms and conditions as the governing body of such political subdivision may agree upon with the district board, the whole or any part of any existing sewerage system or systems or such real or personal property as may be necessary or useful in connection with the acquisition, construction, reconstruction, improvement, extension, enlargement, equipment, repair, maintenance or operation of any sewerage system by the district, including public roads and other property already devoted to public use;

(2)   To make and enter into contracts or agreements with a district, upon such terms and conditions and for such periods as such governing body and the district board may determine:

a.   For the collection, treatment or disposal of sewage;

b.   For the collecting by such political subdivision or by the district of rents, rates, fees or charges for the services and facilities provided to or for such political subdivision or its inhabitants by any sewerage system, and for the enforcement of collection of such rents, rates, fees and charges; and

c.   For the imposition of penalties, including the shutting off of the supply of water furnished by any water system owned or operated by such political subdivision, in the event that the owner, tenant or occupant of any premises utilizing such water shall fail to pay any such rents, rates, fees or charges;

(3)   To fix, and revise from time to time, rents, rates, fees and other charges for the services furnished or to be furnished by a sewerage system under any contract between the district and such political subdivision, and to pledge all or

any part of the proceeds of such rents, rates, fees and charges to the payment of any obligation of such political subdivision to the district under such contract;

(4)   To pay any obligation of such political subdivision to the district under such contract from any available funds of the political subdivision and to levy and collect a tax ad valorem for the making of any such payment; and

(5)   In its discretion or if required by law, to submit to its qualified electors under the election laws applicable to such political subdivision any contract or agreement which such governing body is authorized to make and enter into with the district under the provisions of this Article.

Any such election upon a contract or agreement may, at the discretion of the governing body, be called and held under the election laws applicable to the issuance of bonds by such political subdivision. (1961, c. 795, s. 23; 1973, c. 822, s. 4.)

§ 162A-74. Rights-of-way and easements in streets and highways.

A right-of-way or easement in, along, or across any State highway system, road, or street, and along or across any city or town street within a district is hereby granted to a district in case such right-of-way is found by the district board to be necessary or convenient for carrying out any of the work of the district. Any work done in, along, or across any State highway system, road, street, or property shall be done in accordance with the rules and regulations and any reasonable requirements of the Department of Transportation, and any work done in, along, or across any municipal street or property shall be done in accordance with any reasonable requirements of the municipal governing body. (1961, c. 795, s. 24; 1973, c. 507, s. 5; c. 822, s. 4; 1977, c. 464, s. 34.)

§ 162A-75. Submission of preliminary plans to planning groups; cooperation with planning agencies.

Prior to the time final plans are made for the location and construction of any sewerage system, the district board shall present preliminary plans for such improvement to the county, municipal or regional planning board for their consideration, if such facility is to be located within the planning jurisdiction of any such county, municipal or regional planning group. The district board shall make every effort to cooperate with the planning agency, if any, in the location and construction of a proposed facility authorized under this Article. Any district board created under the authority of this Article is hereby directed, wherever possible, to coordinate its plans for the construction of sewerage system improvements with the overall plans for the development of the planning area, if such district is located wholly or in part within a county, municipal or regional planning area; provided, however, that the approval of any such county, municipal or regional planning board as to any such plan of the district shall not be required. (1961, c. 795, s. 25; 1973, c. 822, s. 4.)

§ 162A-76. Water system acting as billing and collecting agent for district; furnishing meter readings.

The owner or operator, including any political subdivision, of a water system supplying water to the owners, lessees or tenants of real property which is or will be served by any sewerage system owned or operated by a district is authorized to act as the billing and collecting agent of the district for any rents, rates, fees or charges imposed by the district for the services and facilities provided by such sewerage system, and such district is authorized to arrange with such owner or operator to act as the billing and collecting agent of the district for such purpose. Any such owner or operator shall, if requested by a district, furnish to the district copies of such regular periodic meter reading and water consumption records and other pertinent data as the district may require to do its own billing and collecting. The district shall pay to such owner or operator the reasonable additional expenses incurred by such owner or operator in rendering such services to the district. (1961, c. 795, s. 26; 1973, c. 822, s. 4.)

§ 162A-77. District may assume sewerage system indebtedness of political subdivision; approval of voters; actions founded upon invalidity of election; tax to pay assumed indebtedness.

A district may assume all outstanding indebtedness of any political subdivision in the district lawfully incurred for paying all or any part of the cost of a sewerage system, subject to approval thereof by a majority of the qualified voters of the district voting at an election thereon. Any such election shall be called and held in accordance with the provisions of the Local Government Finance Act, insofar as the same may be made applicable, and the returns of such election shall be canvassed and a statement of the result thereof prepared, recorded and published as provided in the Local Government Finance Act. No right of action or defense founded upon the invalidity of the election shall be asserted nor shall the validity of the election be open to question in any court upon any ground whatever, except in an action or proceeding commenced within 30 days after the publication of such statement of result. In the event that any such indebtedness of a political subdivision is assumed by the district, there shall be annually levied and collected a tax ad valorem upon all the taxable property in the district sufficient to pay such assumed indebtedness and the interest thereon as the same become due and payable; provided, however, that such tax may be reduced by the amount of other moneys actually available for such purpose. Such tax shall be determined, levied and collected in the manner provided by G.S. 162A-71 and subject to the provisions of said section.

Nothing herein shall prevent any political subdivision from levying taxes to provide for the payment of its debt service requirements as to indebtedness incurred for paying all or any part of the cost of a sewerage system if such debt service requirements shall not have been otherwise provided for. (1961, c. 795, s. 27; 1973, c. 512, s. 5; c. 822, s. 4.)

§ 162A-77.1. Special election upon the question of the merger of metropolitan sewerage districts into cities or towns.

Any district lying entirely within the corporate limits of a city or town may be merged into such city or town in accordance with the provisions of this section.

The governing body of a city or town, with the approval of the district board, shall call and conduct a special election within such city or town on the question of the merger of the district into the city or town. A vote in favor of such merger shall constitute a vote for such city or town to assume the obligations of the district. Such special election may be called and conducted by the governing body of a city or town upon its own motion after passage of a resolution of the district board requesting or approving the special election. Any special election shall be conducted in accordance with G.S. 163-287.

A new registration of voters shall not be required for the special election. The special election shall be conducted in accordance with the provisions of law applicable to regular elections in the city or town.

If a majority of the votes are in favor of the merger, then:

(1) All property, real and personal and mixed, including accounts receivable, belonging to such district shall vest in, belong to, and be the property

of, such city or town. All district boards are hereby authorized to take such actions and to execute such documents as will carry into effect the provisions and the intent of this section.

(2) All judgments, liens, rights of liens, and causes of action of any nature in favor of such district shall vest in and remain and inure to the benefit of such city or town.

(3) All taxes, assessments, sewer charges, and any other debts, charges or fees, owing to such district shall be owed to and collected by such city or town.

(4) All actions, suits and proceedings pending against, or having been instituted by, such district shall not be abated by this section or by the merger herein provided for, but all such actions, suits, and proceedings shall be continued and completed in the same manner as if merger had not occurred, and such city or town shall be a party to all such actions, suits, and proceedings in the place and stead of the district and shall pay or cause to be paid any judgments rendered against the district in any such actions, suits, or proceedings. No new process need be served in any such action, suit, or proceeding.

(5) All obligations of the district, including outstanding indebtedness, shall be assumed by such city or town, and all such obligations and outstanding indebtedness shall constitute obligations and indebtedness of such city or town, and the full faith and credit of such city or town shall be deemed to be pledged for the punctual payment of the principal of and the interest on any general obligation bonds or bond anticipation notes of such district, and all the taxable property within such city or town, as well as that formerly located within the district, shall be and remain subject to taxation for such payment.

(6) All ordinances, rules, regulations, and policies of such district shall continue in full force and effect until repealed or amended by the governing body of such city or town.

(7) Such district shall be abolished, and shall no longer be constituted a public body or a body politic and corporate, except for the purposes of carrying into effect the provisions and the intent of this section.

If a majority of the votes are against the merger, then such merger shall not be effective unless approved by a majority of the qualified voters who vote thereon in a subsequent special election conducted under authority of this section.

Any action or proceeding in any court to set aside a special election held under authority of this section or the result thereof, or to obtain any other relief upon the ground that such election or any proceeding or action taken with respect to the holding of such election is invalid, must be commenced within 30 days after the day of such special election. After the expiration of such period of limitation, no right of action or defense founded upon the invalidity of the election or the result thereof shall be asserted, nor shall the validity of the election or of the result thereof be open to question in any court upon any ground whatever, except in an action or proceeding commenced within such period. (1975, c. 448; 2013-381, s. 10.31.)

§ 162A-78. Advances by political subdivisions for preliminary expenses of districts.

Any political subdivision is hereby authorized to make advances, from any moneys that may be available for such purpose, in connection with the creation of such district and to provide for the preliminary expenses of such district. Any such advances may be repaid to such political subdivision from the proceeds of bonds issued by such district or from other available funds of the district. (1961, c. 795, s. 28; 1973, c. 822, s. 4.)

§ 162A-79. Article regarded as supplemental.

This Article shall be deemed to provide an additional and alternative method for the doing of the things authorized hereby and shall be regarded as supplemental and additional to powers conferred by other laws, and shall not be regarded as in derogation of or as repealing any powers now existing under any other law, either general, special or local; provided, however, that the issuance of bonds under the provisions of this Article need not comply with the requirements of any other law applicable to the issuance of bonds except as herein provided. (1961, c. 795, s. 29; 1973, c. 822, s. 4.)

§ 162A-80. Inconsistent laws declared inapplicable.

All general, special or local laws, or parts thereof, inconsistent herewith are hereby declared to be inapplicable, unless otherwise specified, to the provisions of this Article. (1961, c. 795, s. 30; 1973, c. 822, s. 4.)

§ 162A-81. Adoption and enforcement of ordinances.

(a) A district shall have the same power as a city under G.S. 160A-175 to assess civil fines and penalties for violation of its ordinances, and may secure injunctions to further insure compliance with its ordinances as provided by this section.

(b) An ordinance may provide that its violation shall subject the offender to a civil penalty of not more than one thousand dollars ($1,000) to be recovered by the district in a civil action in the nature of debt if the offender does not pay the penalty within a prescribed period of time after he has been cited for violation of the ordinance. Any person assessed a civil penalty by the district shall be notified of the assessment by registered or certified mail, and the notice shall specify the reasons for the assessment. If the person assessed fails to pay the amount of the assessment to the district within 30 days after receipt of notice, or such longer period, not to exceed 180 days, as the district may specify, the district may institute a civil action in the General Court of Justice of the county in which the violation occurred or, in the discretion of the district, in the General Court of Justice of the county in which the person assessed has his or its principal place of business, to recover the amount of the assessment. The validity of the district's action may be appealed directly to General Court of Justice in the county in which the violation occurred, or may be raised at any time in the action to recover the assessment. Neither failure to contest the district's action directly nor failure to raise the issue of validity in the action to recover an assessment precludes the other.

(c) An ordinance may provide that it may be enforced by an appropriate equitable remedy issuing from court of competent jurisdiction. In such case, the General Court of Justice shall have jurisdiction to issue such orders as may be appropriate and it shall not be a defense to the application of the district for equitable relief that there is an adequate remedy at law.

(d) Subject to the express terms of an ordinance, a district ordinance may be enforced by any one, all, or a combination of the remedies authorized and prescribed by this section.

(e) An ordinance may provide, when appropriate, that each day's continuing violation shall be a separate and distinct offense. (1983, c. 333, s. 4.)

§§ 162A-82 through 162A-85. Reserved for future codification purposes.

Article 5A.

Metropolitan Water and Sewerage Districts.

§ 162A-85.1. Definitions.

(a) Definitions. - As used in this Article, the following definitions shall apply:

(1) Board of commissioners. - The duly elected board of commissioners of the county or counties in which a metropolitan water and sewerage district shall be created under the provisions of this Article.

(2) City council or Council. - The duly elected city council of any municipality.

(3) Cost. - As defined in G.S. 162A-65.

(4) District. - A metropolitan water and sewerage district created under the provisions of this Article.

(5) District board. - A water and sewerage district board established under the provisions of this Article.

(6) General obligation bonds. - As defined in G.S. 162A-65.

(7) Governing body. - As defined in G.S. 162A-32.

(8) Person. - As defined in G.S. 162A-65.

(9) Political subdivision. - As defined in G.S. 162A-65.

(10) Revenue bonds. - Any bonds the principal of and the interest on which are payable solely from revenues of a water and sewerage system or systems.

(11) Revenues. - All moneys received by a district from, in connection with, or as a result of its ownership or operation of a water and sewerage system, including moneys received from the United States of America, or any agency

thereof, pursuant to an agreement with the district board pertaining to the water and sewerage system, if deemed advisable by the district board.

(12) Sewage. - As defined in G.S. 162A-65.

(13) Sewage disposal system. - As defined in G.S. 162A-65.

(14) Sewerage system. - As defined in G.S. 162A-65.

(15) Sewers. - As defined in G.S. 162A-65.

(16) Water distribution system. - As defined in G.S. 162A-32.

(17) Water system. - As defined in G.S. 162A-32.

(18) Water treatment or purification plant. - As defined in G.S. 162A-32.

(b) Description of Boundaries. - Whenever this Article requires the boundaries of an area be described, it shall be sufficient if the boundaries are described in a manner which conveys an understanding of the location of the land and may be by any of the following:

(1) By reference to a clearly identified map recorded in the appropriate register of deeds office.

(2) By metes and bounds.

(3) By general description referring to natural boundaries, boundaries of political subdivisions, or boundaries of particular tracts or parcels of land.

(4) Any combination of the foregoing. (2013-50, s. 2.)

§ 162A-85.2. Creation.

(a) Except as provided by operation of law, the governing bodies of two or more political subdivisions may establish a metropolitan water and sewerage district if all of the political subdivisions adopt a resolution setting forth all of the following:

(1) The names of the appointees to the district board.

(2) The date on which the district board shall be established.

(3) The boundaries of the district board.

(b) Prior to the adoption of a resolution under subsection (a) of this section, the governing body shall hold at least two public hearings on the matter, held at least 30 days apart, after publication of the notices of public hearing in a newspaper of general circulation, published at least 10 days before each public hearing. (2013-50, s. 2.)

§ 162A-85.3. District board.

(a) Appointment. - The district board shall consist of members appointed as follows:

(1) Two individuals by the governing body of each county served, wholly or in part, by the district.

(2) One individual by the governing body of each municipality served by the district located in any county served by the district with a population greater than 200,000.

(3) Two individuals by the governing body of any municipality served by the district with a population greater than 75,000, in addition to any appointments under subdivision (2) of this subsection.

(4) One individual by the governing body of any county served by the district with a population greater than 200,000, in addition to any appointments under subdivision (1) of this subsection.

(5) One individual by the governing body of a county in which a watershed serving the district board is located in a municipality not served by the district, upon recommendation of that municipality. The municipality shall provide to the governing body of the county a list of three names within 30 days of written request by the county, from which the county must select an appointee if the names are provided within 30 days of written request.

(6) One individual by the governing body of any elected water and sewer district wholly contained within the boundaries of the district.

(b) Terms; Reappointment. - Terms shall be for three years. A member shall serve until a successor has been duly appointed and qualified.

(c) Vacancies; Removal. - If a vacancy shall occur on a district board, the governing body which appointed the vacating member shall appoint a new member who shall serve for the remainder of the unexpired term. Any member of a district board may be removed by the governing board that appointed that member.

(d) Oath of Office. - Each member of the district board, before entering upon the duties, shall take and subscribe an oath or affirmation to support the Constitution and laws of the United States and of this State and to discharge faithfully the duties of the office. A record of each such oath shall be filed with the clerk or clerks of the governing boards appointing the members.

(e) Chair; Officers. - The district board shall elect one of its members as chairman and another as vice-chairman. The district board shall appoint a secretary and a treasurer who may, but need not, be members of the district board. The offices of secretary and treasurer may be combined. The district board may also appoint an assistant secretary and an assistant treasurer or, if the office is combined, an assistant secretary-treasurer who may, but need not, be members of the district board. The terms of office of the chairman, vice-chairman, secretary, treasurer, assistant secretary, and assistant treasurer shall be as provided in the bylaws of the district board.

(f) Meetings; Quorum. - The district board shall meet regularly at such places and dates as are determined by the district board. All meetings shall comply with Article 33C of Chapter 143 of the General Statutes. A majority of the members of the district board shall constitute a quorum, and the affirmative vote of a majority of the members of the district board present at any meeting thereof shall be necessary for any action taken by the district board. No vacancy in the membership of the district board shall impair the right of a quorum to exercise all the rights and perform all the duties of the district board. Each member, including the chairman, shall be entitled to vote on any question.

(g) Compensation. - The members of the district board may receive compensation in an amount to be determined by the district board but not to exceed that compensation paid to members of Occupational Licensing Boards as provided in G.S. 93B-5(a) for each meeting of the district board attended and for attendance at each regularly scheduled committee meeting of the district board. The members of the district board may also be reimbursed the amount of actual expenses incurred by that member in the performance of that member's duties. (2013-50, s. 2.)

§ 162A-85.4. Expansion of district board after creation.

(a)   After creation pursuant to G.S. 162A-85.2, the district board may expand to include other political subdivisions if the district board and the political subdivision adopt identical resolutions indicating the political subdivision will become a participant in the district board.

(b)   Prior to adopting the resolution under subsection (a) of this section, the district board and the political subdivision shall hold at least two public hearings on the matter, held at least 30 days apart, after publication of the notices of public hearing in a newspaper of general circulation, published at least 10 days before each public hearing.

(c)   Upon adoption of the identical resolutions, the political subdivision shall appoint a district member in accordance with G.S. 162A-85.3(a), if that political subdivision is entitled to an appointment under that section. (2013-50, s. 2.)

§ 162A-85.5. Powers generally.

(a)   Each district shall be deemed to be a public body and body politic and corporate exercising public and essential governmental functions to provide for the preservation and promotion of the public health and welfare, and each district is hereby authorized and empowered to do all of the following:

(1)   To exercise any power of a Metropolitan Water District under G.S. 162A-36, except subdivision (9) of that section.

(2)   To exercise any power of a Metropolitan Sewer District under G.S. 162A-69, except subdivision (9) of that section.

(3)   To do all acts and things necessary or convenient to carry out the powers granted by this Article.

(b)   Each district shall keep its accounts on the basis of a fiscal year commencing on the first day of July and ending on the 30th day of June of the following year. (2013-50, s. 2.)

§ 162A-85.6: Reserved for future codification purposes.

§ 162A-85.7. Bonds and notes authorized.

A metropolitan water and sewerage district shall have power from time to time to issue bonds and notes under the Local Government Finance Act. (2013-50, s. 2.)

§ 162A-85.8: Reserved for future codification purposes.

§ 162A-85.9: Reserved for future codification purposes.

§ 162A-85-10: Reserved for future codification purposes.

§ 162A-85-11: Reserved for future codification purposes.

§ 162A-85-12: Reserved for future codification purposes.

§ 162A-85.13. Rates and charges for services.

(a) The district board may fix, and may revise from time to time, rents, rates, fees, and other charges for the use of and for the services furnished or to be furnished by any water system or sewerage system. Such rents, rates, fees, and charges may not apply differing treatment within and outside the corporate limits of any city or county within the jurisdiction of the district board. Such rents, rates, fees, and charges shall not be subject to supervision or regulation by any bureau, board, commission, or other agency of the State or of any political subdivision.

(b) Any such rents, rates, fees, and charges pledged to the payment of revenue bonds of the district shall be fixed and revised so that the revenues of the water system or sewerage system, together with any other available funds, shall be sufficient at all times to pay the cost of maintaining, repairing, and operating the water system or sewerage system, the revenues of which are pledged to the payment of such revenue bonds, including reserves for such purposes, and to pay the interest on and the principal of such revenue bonds as the same shall become due and payable and to provide reserves therefor. If any such rents, rates, fees, and charges are pledged to the payment of any general obligation bonds issued under this Article, such rents, rates, fees, and charges shall be fixed and revised so as to comply with the requirements of such pledge.

(c)   The district board may provide methods for collection of such rents, rates, fees, and charges and measures for enforcement of collection thereof, including penalties and the denial or discontinuance of service. (2013-50, s. 2.)

§ 162A-85.14: Reserved for future codification purposes.

§ 162A-85.17. Rights-of-way and easements.

A right-of-way or easement in, along, or across any State highway system, road, or street, and along or across any city or town street within a district is hereby granted to a district in case such right-of-way is found by the district board to be necessary or convenient for carrying out any of the work of the district. Any work done in, along, or across any State highway system, road, street, or property shall be done in accordance with the rules and regulations and any reasonable requirements of the Department of Transportation, and any work done in, along, or across any municipal street or property shall be done in accordance with any reasonable requirements of the municipal governing body. (2013-50, s. 2.)

§ 162A-85.18: Reserved for future codification purposes.

§ 162A-85.19. Authority of governing bodies of political subdivisions.

(a)   The governing body of any political subdivision is hereby authorized and empowered to do any of the following:

(1)   Subject to the approval of the Local Government Commission regarding the disposition of any outstanding debt related to the water system or sewer system, or both, to transfer jurisdiction over and to lease, lend, sell, grant, or convey to a district, upon such terms and conditions as the governing body of such political subdivision may agree upon with the district board, the whole or any part of any existing water system or systems or sewerage system or systems or such real or personal property as may be necessary or useful in connection with the acquisition, construction, reconstruction, improvement, extension, enlargement, equipment, repair, maintenance, or operation of any

water system or sewerage system by the district, including public roads and other property already devoted to public use.

(2) To make and enter into contracts or agreements with a district, upon such terms and conditions and for such periods as such governing body and the district board may determine for any of the following:

a. For the collection, treatment, or disposal of sewage.

b. For the supply of raw or treated water on a regular retail or wholesale basis.

c. For the supply of raw or treated water on a standby wholesale basis.

d. For the construction of jointly financed facilities whose title shall be vested in the district.

e. For the collecting by such political subdivision or by the district of rents, rates, fees, or charges for the services and facilities provided to or for such political subdivision or its inhabitants by any water system or sewerage system and for the enforcement of collection of such rents, rates, fees, and charges.

f. For the imposition of penalties, including the shutting off of the supply of water furnished by any water system owned or operated by such political subdivision, in the event that the owner, tenant, or occupant of any premises utilizing such water shall fail to pay any such rents, rates, fees, or charges.

(3) To fix and revise from time to time, rents, rates, fees, and other charges for the services furnished or to be furnished by a water system or sewerage system under any contract between the district and such political subdivision and to pledge all or any part of the proceeds of such rents, rates, fees, and charges to the payment of any obligation of such political subdivision to the district under such contract.

(4) To pay any obligation of such political subdivision to the district under such contract from any available funds of the political subdivision and to levy and collect a tax ad valorem for the making of any such payment.

(5) In its discretion or if required by law, to submit to its qualified electors under the election laws applicable to such political subdivision any contract or

agreement which such governing body is authorized to make and enter into with the district under the provisions of this Article.

(b)   Any such election upon a contract or agreement called under subsection (a) of this section may, at the discretion of the governing body, be called and held under the election laws applicable to the issuance of bonds by such political subdivision. (2013-50, s. 2.)

§ 162A-85.20: Reserved for future codification purposes.

§ 162A-85.21. Submission of preliminary plans to planning groups; cooperation with planning agencies.

(a)   Prior to the time final plans are made for the extension of any water system or sewerage system, the district board shall present preliminary plans for such improvement to the county or municipal governing board for their consideration if such facility is to be located within the jurisdiction of any such county or municipality. The district board shall make every effort to cooperate with the county or municipality in the location and construction of any new proposed facility authorized under this Article.

(b)   Any district board created under the authority of this Article is hereby directed, wherever possible, to coordinate its plans for the construction of any new water system or sewerage system improvements with the overall plans for the development of the planning area if such district is located wholly or in part within a county or municipal planning area.

(c)   This section shall not apply to renovations, repairs, or regular maintenance of water systems or sewer systems. (2013-50, s. 2.)

§ 162A-85.22: Reserved for future codification purposes.

§ 162A-85.23: Reserved for future codification purposes.

§ 162A-85.24: Reserved for future codification purposes.

§ 162A-85.25. Adoption and enforcement of ordinances.

(a) A district shall have the same power as a city under G.S. 160A-175 to assess civil fines and penalties for violation of its ordinances and may secure injunctions to further ensure compliance with its ordinances as provided by this section.

(b) An ordinance may provide that its violation shall subject the offender to a civil penalty of not more than one thousand dollars ($1,000) to be recovered by the district in a civil action in the nature of debt if the offender does not pay the penalty within a prescribed period of time after he has been cited for violation of the ordinance. Any person assessed a civil penalty by the district shall be notified of the assessment by registered or certified mail, and the notice shall specify the reasons for the assessment. If the person assessed fails to pay the amount of the assessment to the district within 30 days after receipt of notice, or such longer period, not to exceed 180 days, as the district may specify, the district may institute a civil action in the General Court of Justice of the county in which the violation occurred or, in the discretion of the district, in the General Court of Justice of the county in which the person assessed has his or its principal place of business, to recover the amount of the assessment. The validity of the district's action may be appealed directly to General Court of Justice in the county in which the violation occurred or may be raised at any time in the action to recover the assessment. Neither failure to contest the district's action directly nor failure to raise the issue of validity in the action to recover an assessment precludes the other.

(c) An ordinance may provide that it may be enforced by an appropriate equitable remedy issuing from court of competent jurisdiction. In such case, the General Court of Justice shall have jurisdiction to issue such orders as may be appropriate, and it shall not be a defense to the application of the district for equitable relief that there is an adequate remedy at law.

(d) Subject to the express terms of an ordinance, a district ordinance may be enforced by any one, all, or a combination of the remedies authorized and prescribed by this section.

(e) An ordinance may provide, when appropriate, that each day's continuing violation shall be a separate and distinct offense. (2013-50, s. 2.)

§ 162A-85.26: Reserved for future codification purposes.

§ 162A-85.27: Reserved for future codification purposes.

§ 162A-85.28: Reserved for future codification purposes.

§ 162A-85.29. No privatization.

The district board may not in any way privatize the provision of water or sewer to the customers of the district unless related to administrative matters only. (2013-50, s. 2.)

Article 6.

County Water and Sewer Districts.

§ 162A-86. Formation of district; hearing.

(a) The board of commissioners of any county may create a county water and sewer district.

(a1) The governing board of a consolidated city-county, as defined by G.S. 160B-2(1), may create a water and sewer district pursuant to this Article. For the purposes of this Article, the term "board of county commissioners" shall also mean the governing board of a consolidated city-county and the term "county water and sewer district" also means a water and sewer district created by the governing board of a consolidated city-county.

(b) Before creating such a district, the board of commissioners shall hold a public hearing. Notice of the hearing shall state the date, hour, and place of the hearing and its subject and shall set forth a description of the territory to be included within the proposed district. The notice shall be published once a week for three weeks in a newspaper that circulates in the proposed district and in addition shall be posted in at least three public places in the district. The notice shall be posted and published the first time not less than 20 days before the hearing.

(b1) Before creating such a district, the board of commissioners shall hold a public hearing. Notice of the hearing shall state the date, hour, and place of the hearing and its subject and shall set forth a description of the territory to be included within the proposed district. The notice shall be published once in a newspaper that circulates in the proposed district and in addition shall be posted in at least three public places in the district. The notice shall be posted and published not more than 30 nor less than 14 days before the hearing. The newspaper notice and the public hearing may cover more than one district covered by this subsection.

This subsection applies only when the local Health Director or the State Health Director has certified that there is a present or imminent serious public health hazard caused by the failure of a low-pressure pipe sewer system within the area of the proposed district, and in such case the board of commissioners may proceed either under subsection (a) of this section or under this subsection.

(c) At the public hearing, the commissioners shall hear all interested persons and may adjourn the hearing from time to time. (1977, c. 466, s. 1; 1979, c. 624, ss. 2, 3; 1993 (Reg. Sess., 1994), c. 696, s. 1; c. 714, s. 1; 1995, c. 461, s. 7.)

§ 162A-87. Creation of district; standards; limitation of actions.

(a) Following the public hearing, the board of commissioners may, by resolution, create a county water and sewer district if the board finds that:

(1) There is a demonstrable need for providing in the district water services, or sewer services, or both;

(2) The residents of all the territory to be included in the district will benefit from the district's creation; and

(3) It is economically feasible to provide the proposed service or services in the district without unreasonable or burdensome annual tax levies.

Territory lying within the corporate limits of a city or town may not be included in the district unless the governing body of the city or town agrees by resolution to such inclusion. Otherwise, the board of commissioners may define as the district all or any portion of the territory described in the notice of the public hearing.

(b) Upon adoption of a resolution creating a county water and sewer district, the board of commissioners shall cause the resolution to be published once in each of two successive weeks in the newspaper in which the notices of the hearing were published. In addition, the commissioners shall cause to be published with the resolution a notice in substantially the following form:

"The foregoing resolution was adopted by the _____ County Board of Commissioners on _____ and was first published on _____.

Any action or proceeding questioning the validity of this resolution or the creation of the _____ Water and Sewer District of _____ County or the inclusion in the district of any of the territory described in the resolution must be commenced within 30 days after the first publication of the resolution.

_____

Clerk, _____County Board of

Commissioners"

Any action or proceeding in any court to set aside a resolution creating a county water and sewer district, or questioning the validity of such a resolution, the creation of such a district, or the inclusion in such a district of any of the territory described in the resolution creating the district must be commenced within 30 days after the first publication of the resolution and notice. After the expiration of this period of limitation, no right of action or defense founded upon the invalidity of the resolution, the creation of the district, or the inclusion of any territory in the district may be asserted, nor may the validity of the resolution, the creation of the district, or the inclusion of the territory be open to question in any court upon any ground whatever, except in an action or proceeding commenced within that period.

Notwithstanding any other provision of this section, in the case of any county water and sewer districts created under G.S. 162A-86(b1):

(1)   A resolution may cover the creation of more than one district;

(2)   The board of commissioners shall cause the resolution to be published once in the newspaper in which the notice of the hearing was published; and

(3)   References in this subsection to "30 days" are instead "21 days". (1977, c. 466, s. 1; 1979, c. 624, s. 4; 1993 (Reg. Sess., 1994), c. 696, s. 2; c. 714, s. 2.)

§ 162A-87.1. Extension of water and sewer districts.

(a) Standards. - The board of commissioners may, by resolution, annex territory to any water and sewer district upon a finding that:

(1) The area to be annexed is contiguous to the district, with at least one eighth of the area's aggregate external boundary coincident with the existing boundary of the district;

(2) The residents of the territory to be annexed will benefit from the annexation; and

(3) It is economically feasible to provide the proposed service or services in the annexed district without unreasonable or burdensome annual tax levies.

(b) Annexation by Petition. - The board of commissioners may, by resolution, extend by annexation the boundaries of any water or sewer district when one hundred percent (100%) of the real property owners of the area to be annexed have petitioned the board for annexation to the water and sewer district.

(c) Annexation of Property within a City or Sanitary District. - Territory lying within the corporate limits of a city or sanitary district may not be annexed to a water and sewer district unless the governing body of the city or sanitary district agrees, by resolution, to the annexation.

(d) Report. - Before the public hearing required by subsection (e) of this section, the board of commissioners shall have prepared a report containing:

(1) A map of the water and sewer district and the adjacent territory, showing the present and proposed boundaries of the district; and

(2) A statement showing that the area to be annexed meets the standards and requirements established in subsections (a), (b), or (c) of this section.

The report shall be available for public inspection in the office of the clerk of the board of commissioners for at least two weeks before the date of the public hearing required by subsection (e) of this section.

(e) Hearing and Notice. - The board of commissioners shall hold a public hearing before adopting any resolution extending the boundaries of a water and sewer district. Notice of the hearing shall state the date, hour, and place of the hearing and its subject, and shall include a statement that the report required by subsection (d) of this section is available for inspection in the office of the clerk of the board of commissioners. The notice shall be published at least once not less than one week before the date of the hearing. In addition, unless the hearing is because of a petition for annexation submitted under subsection (b) of this section, the notice shall be mailed, at least four weeks before the date of the hearing, to the owners, as shown by the county tax records as of the preceding January 1, of all property located within the area to be annexed. The notice may be mailed by any class of U.S. mail which is fully prepaid. The person designated by the board of commissioners to mail the notice shall certify to the board of commissioners that the mailing has been completed, and his certificate shall be conclusive in the absence of fraud.

(f) Effective Date. - The resolution extending the boundaries of the district shall take effect at the beginning of a fiscal year commencing after its passage, as determined by the board of commissioners. (1985, c. 627, s. 1; 1989, c. 543.)

§ 162A-87.1A. Initial boundaries of district.

(a) The initial boundaries of a district may exclude areas contained solely within the external boundaries of the district.

(b) The initial boundaries of a district may include noncontiguous portions, as long as the closest distance from a noncontiguous piece to the part of the district containing the greatest area does not exceed one mile.

(c) This section does not invalidate any district created prior to the effective date of this section. (1993 (Reg. Sess., 1994), c. 696, s. 3; c. 714, s. 3.)

§ 162A-87.1B. Transfer of State-owned property from one district to another.

If any property owned by the State is located in a county water and sewer district, the board of commissioners of that county by resolution may transfer the property to another county water and sewer district in that county. This section only applies if the State acquired the property from the county. Any such resolution shall become effective on the date specified in the resolution, and a copy of the resolution shall be sent to the Department of Administration. (2005-127, s. 1; 2006-226, s. 29.)

§ 162A-87.2. Abolition of water and sewer districts.

(a) Upon finding that there is no longer a need for a water and sewer district and that there are no outstanding bonds or notes issued to finance projects in the district, the board of commissioners may, by resolution, abolish that district. The board of commissioners shall hold a public hearing before adopting a resolution abolishing a district. Notice of the hearing shall state the date, hour, and place of the hearing and its subject, and shall be published at least once not less than one week before the date of the hearing. The abolition of any water and sewer district shall take effect at the end of a fiscal year following passage of the resolution, as determined by the board of commissioners.

(b) If the:

(1) Terms of any contract between a county water and sewer district and a city provide that upon certain conditions, all the property of the district is conveyed to that city; and

(2) District has at the time of abolition no existing bonds or notes issued as authorized by G.S. 162A-90 to finance projects in the district,

then such contract may also provide that no earlier than such conveyance the district may be abolished by action of the governing board of the city. If the district has any other indebtedness, a contract providing for conveyance of all of the assets of a district to a city must provide for assumption of such other indebtedness by the city. If the district is owed any assessments, then the right to collect such assessments becomes that of the city. The governing board of the city shall hold a public hearing before adopting a resolution abolishing a district. Notice of the hearing shall state the date, hour, and place of the hearing and its subject, and shall be published at least once not less than one week before the date of the hearing. The abolition of any water and sewer district shall take effect at the end of a fiscal year of the district following passage of the resolution, as determined by the governing board. This subsection applies only to a county water and sewer district created under G.S. 162A-86(b1).

(c) If the:

(1) Terms of any contract between a county water and sewer district and a private person provide that upon certain conditions, all the property of the district is conveyed to that private person; and

(2) District has at the time of abolition no existing bonds or notes issued as authorized by G.S. 162A-90 to finance projects in the district,

such contract may also provide that no earlier than such conveyance the district may be abolished by action of the Utilities Commission. If the district has any other indebtedness, a contract providing for conveyance of all of the assets of a district to a private person must provide for assumption of such other indebtedness by the private person. If the district is owed any assessments, then the private person may collect the assessment under the same procedures as if it was the district. The Utilities Commission shall hold a public hearing before adopting a resolution abolishing a district. Notice of the hearing shall state the date, hour, and place of the hearing and its subject, and shall be published at least once not less than one week before the date of the hearing. The abolition of any water and sewer district shall take effect at the end of a fiscal year of the district following passage of the resolution, as determined by the Utilities Commission. This subsection applies only to a county water and sewer district created under G.S. 162A-86(b1).

(d) Any resolution of abolition adopted under this section on or after the effective date of this section shall be filed with the Secretary of State. (1985, c. 627, s. 2; 1993 (Reg. Sess., 1994), c. 696, s. 4; c. 714, s. 4.)

§ 162A-87.3. Services outside the district.

(a) A county water and sewer district may provide water or sewer services, or both, to customers outside the district, but in no case shall the county water and sewer district be held liable for damages to those outside the district for failure to furnish such services.

(b) A county water and sewer district may provide a different schedule of rents, rates, fees, and charges for services provided outside the district.

(c) A county water and sewer district may not extend service to customers lying within the corporate limits of a city or sanitary district unless the governing body of a city or sanitary district agrees, by resolution, to the extension.

(d) A county water and sewer district may not extend service to customers lying within another county unless the board of commissioners of that county agrees, by resolution, to the extension. (1989, c. 726, s. 1.)

§ 162A-88. District is a municipal corporation.

The inhabitants of a county water and sewer district created pursuant to this Article are a body corporate and politic by the name specified by the board of commissioners. Under that name they are vested with all the property and rights of property belonging to the corporation; have perpetual succession; may sue and be sued; may contract and be contracted with; may acquire and hold any property, real and personal, devised, sold, or in any manner conveyed, dedicated to, or otherwise acquired by them, and from time to time may hold, invest, sell, or dispose of the same; may have a common seal and alter and renew it at will; may establish, revise and collect rates, fees or other charges and penalties for the use of or the services furnished or to be furnished by any sanitary sewer system, water system or sanitary sewer and water system of the district; and may exercise those powers conferred on them by this Article. (1977, c. 466, s. 1; 1979, c. 624, s. 5; 2011-284, s. 124.)

§ 162A-88.1. Contracts with private entities.

A county water and sewer district may contract with and appropriate money to any person, association, or corporation, in order to carry out any public purpose that the county water and sewer district is authorized by law to engage in. (1993 (Reg. Sess., 1994), c. 696, s. 5; c. 714, s. 5.)

§ 162A-89. Governing body of district; powers.

(a)   The board of commissioners of the county in which a county water and sewer district is created is the governing body of the district.

(b)   The governing board of a consolidated city-county in which a water and sewer district is created is the governing body of the district. (1977, c. 466, s. 1; 1995, c. 461, s. 8.)

§ 162A-89.1. Eminent domain power authorized.

A county water and sewer district shall have the power of eminent domain, to be exercised in accordance with the provisions of Chapter 40A of the General Statutes, over the acquisition of any improved or unimproved lands or rights in land, within or without the district. (1977, c. 466, s. 1; 1983, c. 735, s. 1.; 1987, c. 2, s. 2)

§ 162A-90. Bonds and notes authorized.

A county water and sewer district may from time to time issue general obligation and revenue bonds and bond anticipation notes pursuant to the Local Government Finance Act, for the purposes of providing sanitary sewer systems or water systems or both.

A county water and sewer district may from time to time issue tax and revenue anticipation notes pursuant to Chapter 159, Article 9, Part 2. (1977, c. 466, s. 1.)

§ 162A-91. Taxes authorized.

The governing body of a county water and sewer district may levy property taxes within the district in order to finance the operation and maintenance of the district's water system or sewer system or both and in order to finance debt service on any general obligation bonds or notes issued by the district. No voter approval is necessary in order for such taxes to be levied. (1977, c. 466, s. 1.)

§ 162A-92. Special assessments authorized.

A county water and sewer district may make special assessments against benefited property within the district for all or part of the costs of:

(1) Constructing, reconstructing, extending, or otherwise building or improving water systems;

(2) Constructing, reconstructing, extending, or otherwise building or improving sewage disposal systems.

A district shall exercise the authority granted by this section according to the provisions of Chapter 153A, Article 9. For the purposes of this section references in that Article to the "county" and the "board of commissioners" are deemed to refer, respectively, to the "district" and the "governing body of the district." (1977, c. 466, s. 1.)

§ 162A-93. Certain city actions prohibited.

(a) No city may duplicate water or sewer services provided by a district under this Article by installing parallel lines and requiring owners of improved property in territory annexed by the city to connect, except with consent of the district governing body.

(b) The provisions of subsection (a) shall not apply if the city council adopts an annexation ordinance including an area served by a district and finds, after a public hearing, that adequate fire protection cannot be provided in the area because of the level of available water service. Notice of the public hearing shall be provided by first class mail to each affected customer and by publication in a newspaper having general circulation in the area, each not less than 10 days before the hearing. The clerk's certification of the mailing shall be deemed conclusive in the absence of fraud. Any resident of the annexed area aggrieved by such a finding of the council may file a petition for review in the superior court in the nature of certiorari, within 30 days after the finding. The petition for review in the nature of certiorari shall comply with G.S. 160A-393.

(c) Provision of public water and sewer services by a district under this Article to an area annexed by a city shall satisfy the city's obligation to provide for water and sewer services under G.S. 160A-35 and G.S. 160A-47. The city may negotiate for purchase of the lines or systems owned and operated by the district.

(d) Upon annexation by a city of an area served by a district under this Article, the city may provide for installation of and use fire hydrants on the district water lines, by arrangement with the district and at the city's cost. (1989, c. 741, s. 1; 2009-421, s. 4.)

§ 162A-94. Certain actions validated.

Any contract entered into by a county water and sewer district on or before February 1, 1995, is not invalid because of failure to comply with Article 8 of Chapter 143 of the General Statutes. (1995, c. 266, s. 1.)

§§ 162A-95 through 162A-100. Reserved for future codification purposes.

Article 7.

Assumption of Indebtedness of Certain Districts.

§ 162A-101. Assumption of indebtedness of certain districts.

Subject to approval by a majority of the qualified voters of the county voting at an election thereon, a county may assume all indebtedness, incurred for paying all or any part of the cost of a water supply and distribution system, a sewerage system, or both, of any:

(1)   Water and sewer authority organized under Article 1 of this Chapter;

(2)   Metropolitan water district organized under Article 4 of this Chapter;

(3)   Metropolitan sewerage district organized under Article 5 of this Chapter; or

(4)   County water and sewer district organized under Article 6 of this Chapter.

An election under this Article shall be called and held in accordance with the provisions of the Local Government Finance Act, insofar as the same may be made applicable, and the returns of the election shall be canvassed and a statement of the result thereof prepared, recorded and published as provided in the Local Government Finance Act. No right of action or defense founded upon the invalidity of the election shall be asserted nor shall the validity of the election be open to question in any court upon any ground whatever, except in an action or proceeding commenced within 30 days after the publication of the statement of result. In the event that any indebtedness of a water and sewer authority, metropolitan water district, metropolitan sewerage district, or county water and sewer district is assumed by the county, there shall be annually levied and collected an ad valorem tax upon all the taxable property in the county sufficient to pay the assumed indebtedness and the interest thereon as it becomes due and payable; provided, however, the tax may be reduced by the amount of other moneys actually available for this purpose. The tax shall be determined, levied and collected in the manner provided by law. (1989, c. 573.)

Chapter 162B.

Continuity of Local Government in Emergency.

Article 1.

In General.

§ 162B-1. Designated emergency location of government.

The governing body of each political subdivision of this State is hereby authorized to designate by ordinance, resolution or other manner, alternate sites or places, within or without the territorial limits of such political subdivision and within or without this State, as the emergency location of government. (1959, c. 349.)

§ 162B-2. Emergency meetings.

Whenever the Governor and Council of State acting together declare an emergency to exist by reason of actual or impending hostile attack upon the State of North Carolina and, due to the emergency so declared, it becomes imprudent or impossible to conduct the affairs of local government at the regular or usual place or places thereof, the governing body of each political subdivision of this State is hereby authorized to meet from time to time upon call of the presiding officer or a majority of the members thereof at the designated emergency location of government during the period of the emergency and until the emergency is declared terminated by the Governor and Council of State. (1959, c. 349.)

§ 162B-3. Emergency public business; nature and conduct.

Whenever the public business of any political subdivision is being conducted at a designated emergency location outside the territorial limits thereof, the members of the governing body may exercise such executive and legislative powers and functions as are pertinent to continued operation of the local government upon return to within the respective political subdivision. Any action taken by any local governing body at a designated emergency location shall apply and be effective only within the territorial limits of the political subdivision which such governing body represents. During the period of time in which the public business is being conducted at a designated emergency location, the governing body may, when emergency conditions make impossible compliance with legally prescribed procedural requirements relating to the conduct of meetings and transaction of business, waive such compliance by adoption of an ordinance or resolution reciting the facts and conditions showing the impossibility of compliance. (1959, c. 349.)

§ 162B-4. Provisions of Article control over local law.

The provisions of this Article shall be effective in the event it shall be employed notwithstanding any statutory, charter or ordinance provision to the contrary or in conflict herewith. (1959, c. 349.)

Article 2.

Emergency Interim Succession to Local Offices.

§ 162B-5. Short title.

This Article shall be known and may be cited as the North Carolina "Emergency Interim Local Government Executive Succession Act of 1959." (1959, c. 314, s. 1.)

§ 162B-6. Policy and purpose.

Because of the existing possibility of attack upon the State of North Carolina of unprecedented size and destructiveness, and in order, in the event of such an attack, to assure continuity of local government through legally constituted leadership, authority and responsibility in offices of political subdivisions of the State of North Carolina; to provide for the effective operation of local governments during an emergency; and to facilitate the early resumption of functions temporarily suspended, it is found and declared to be necessary to provide for emergency interim succession to governmental offices of political subdivisions in the event the incumbents thereof and their deputies, assistants or other subordinate officers authorized, pursuant to law, to exercise all of the powers and discharge the duties of such offices (hereinafter referred to as deputies) are unavailable to perform the duties and functions of such offices. (1959, c. 314, s. 2.)

§ 162B-7. Definitions.

Unless otherwise clearly required by the context, as used in this Article:

(1) "Attack" means any attack or series of attacks by an enemy of the United States upon the State of North Carolina causing, or which may cause, substantial damage or injury to civilian property or persons in the State in any manner by sabotage or by the use of bombs, missiles, shellfire, or atomic, radiological, chemical, bacteriological or biological means or other weapons or processes.

(2) "Emergency interim successor" means a person designated pursuant to this Article, in the event the officer is unavailable, to exercise the powers and discharge the duties of an office until a successor is appointed or elected and qualified as may be provided by the statutes, charters and ordinances or until the lawful incumbent is able to resume the exercise of the powers and discharge the duties of the office.

(3) "Office" includes all local offices, the powers and duties of which are defined by statutes, charters and ordinances.

(4) "Political subdivision" includes counties, cities, towns, townships, districts, authorities and other municipal corporations and entities whether organized and existing under charter or general law.

(5) "Unavailable" means either that a vacancy in office exists and there is no deputy authorized to exercise all of the powers and discharge the duties of the office, or that the lawful incumbent of the office (including any deputy exercising the powers and discharging the duties of an office because of a vacancy) and his duly authorized deputy are absent or unable to exercise the powers and discharge the duties of the office. (1959, c. 314, s. 3.)

§ 162B-8. Enabling authority for emergency interim successors for local offices.

With respect to local offices for which the governing bodies of cities, towns, townships, and counties may enact resolutions or ordinances relative to the manner in which vacancies will be filled or temporary appointments to office made, such governing bodies are hereby authorized to enact resolutions or ordinances providing for emergency interim successors to offices of the aforementioned governmental units. Such resolutions and ordinances shall not be inconsistent with the provisions of this Article. (1959, c. 314, s. 4.)

§ 162B-9. Emergency interim successors for local officers.

The provisions of this section shall be applicable to officers of political subdivisions (including, but not limited to counties, cities, towns and townships as well as school, fire, drainage and other municipal corporate districts) not included in G.S. 162B-8. Such governing bodies, pursuant to such regulations as they may adopt, shall upon approval of this Article, designate by title (if feasible) or by named person, emergency interim successors and specify their order of succession. The local governing body shall review and revise, as necessary, designations made pursuant to this Article to insure their current status. The governing body will designate a sufficient number of persons so that there will be not less than three, nor more than seven, deputies or emergency interim successors or combination thereof at any time. In the event that any officer of any political subdivision (or his deputy provided for pursuant to law) is unavailable, the powers of the office shall be exercised and duties shall be discharged by his designated emergency interim successors in the order specified. The emergency interim successor shall exercise the powers and discharge the duties of the office to which designated until such time as a vacancy which may exist shall be filled in accordance with the Constitution or statutes; or until the officer (or his deputy or a preceding emergency interim successor) again becomes available to exercise the powers and discharge the duties of his office. (1959, c. 314, s. 5.)

§ 162B-10. Formalities of taking office.

At the time of their assumption of office, emergency interim successors shall take such oath as may be required for them to exercise the powers and discharge the duties of the office to which they may succeed. Notwithstanding any other provision of law, no person, as a prerequisite to the exercise of the powers or discharge of the duties of an office to which he succeeds, shall be required to comply with any other provision of law relative to taking office. (1959, c. 314, s. 6.)

§ 162B-11. Period in which authority may be exercised.

Emergency interim successors, authorized to act pursuant to this Article, are empowered to exercise the powers and discharge the duties of an office as herein authorized only after an attack upon the State of North Carolina, as defined herein, has occurred. The local governing body, by a duly adopted resolution, may at any time terminate the authority of said emergency interim successors to exercise the powers and discharge the duties of office as herein provided. (1959, c. 314, s. 7.)

§ 162B-12. Removal of designees.

Until such time as the persons designated as emergency interim successors are authorized to exercise the powers and discharge the duties of an office in accordance with this Article, including G.S. 162B-11 hereof, said persons shall serve in their designated capacities at the pleasure of the designating authority and may be removed or replaced by said designating authority at any time, with or without cause. (1959, c. 314, s. 8.)

§ 162B-13. Disputes.

Any dispute concerning a question of fact arising under this Article with respect to an office in any political subdivision shall be adjudicated by the local governing body and their decision shall be final. (1959, c. 314, s. 9.)

Chapter 163.

Elections and Election Laws.

SUBCHAPTER I. TIME OF PRIMARIES AND ELECTIONS.

Article 1.

Time of Primaries and Elections.

§ 163-1. Time of regular elections and primaries.

(a) Unless otherwise provided by law, elections for the officers listed in the tabulation contained in this section shall be conducted in all election precincts of the territorial units specified in the column headed "Jurisdiction" on the dates indicated in the column headed "Date of Election." Unless otherwise provided by law, officers shall serve for the terms specified in the column headed "Term of Office."

(b) On Tuesday next after the first Monday in May preceding each general election to be held in November for the officers referred to in subsection (a) of this section, there shall be held in all election precincts within the territory for which the officers are to be elected a primary election for the purpose of nominating candidates for each political party in the State for those offices, and nonpartisan candidates as to offices elected under the provisions of Article 25 of this Chapter.

(c) On Tuesday next after the first Monday in November in the year 1968, and every four years thereafter, or on such days as the Congress of the United States shall direct, an election shall be held in all of the election precincts of the State for the election of electors of President and Vice-President of the United States. The number of electors to be chosen shall be equal to the number of Senators and Representatives in Congress to which this State may be entitled. Presidential electors shall not be nominated by primary election; instead, they shall be nominated in a State convention of each political party as defined in G.S. 163-96 unless otherwise provided by the plan of organization of the political party; provided, that in the case of a candidate for President of the United States who has qualified to have his name printed on the general election ballot as an unaffiliated candidate under G.S. 163-122, that candidate shall nominate presidential electors. One presidential elector shall be nominated from each congressional district and two from the state-at-large, and in addition, the State convention of each party and the unaffiliated candidate shall each nominate first and second alternate electors who shall serve if their slate is elected as provided by G.S. 163-209 and if there is a vacancy as provided by G.S. 163-210.

(d) If primaries for the State Senate or State House of Representatives are temporarily moved from the date provided in subsection (b) of this section for any election year, all primaries shall be held on the same day.

OFFICE	JURISDICTION	DATE OF ELECTION	TERM OF OFFICE
Governor	State	Tuesday next after the first Monday	Four years, from first day of

		in November 1968 and every four years thereafter	January after
Lieutenant Governor	State	Tuesday next after the first Monday in November 1968 and every four years thereafter	Four years, from first day of January after
Secretary of State	State	Tuesday next after the first Monday in November 1968 and every four years thereafter	Four years, from first day of January after
Auditor	State	Tuesday next after the first Monday in November 1968	Four years, from first day of January after

(Row labels include "next election" continuations beneath Governor, Lieutenant Governor, Secretary of State, and Auditor entries.)

173

election		and every four years thereafter	after
Treasurer	State	Tuesday next after the first Monday in November 1968 and every four years thereafter	Four years, from first day of January next after election
Superintendent of Public Instruction	State	Tuesday next after the first Monday in November 1968 and every four years thereafter	Four years, from first day of January next after election
Attorney General	State	Tuesday next after the first Monday in November 1968	Four years, from first day of January next

174

election		and every four years thereafter	after
Commissioner of Agriculture	State	Tuesday next after the first Monday in November 1968	Four years, from first day of January next
election		and every four years thereafter	after
Commissioner of Labor	State	Tuesday next after the first Monday in November 1968	Four years, from first day of January next
election		and every four years thereafter	after
Commissioner of Insurance	State	Tuesday next after the first Monday in November 1968	Four years, from first day of January next
election		and every four	after

		years thereafter	
All other years, from State officers next whose terms election last for four years	State	Tuesday next after the first Monday in November 1968 and every four years thereafter	Four first day of January after
All other years, from State officers next whose terms election are not specified by law	State	Tuesday next after the first Monday in November 1968 and every two years thereafter	Two first day of January after
State Senator years	Senatorial district	Tuesday next after the first Monday in November 1968	Two

176

Office	District	Time of Election	Term
Member of State House of Representatives	Representative district	Tuesday next after the first Monday in November 1968 and every two years thereafter	Two years
Justices and Judges of the Appellate Division	State	At the regular election for members of the General Assembly immediately preceding the termination of each regular term	Eight years, from first day of January next after election
Judges of the superior courts	Superior Court District	At the regular election for members of the	Eight years, from first day of January next after

election		General Assembly immediately preceding the termination of each regular term	after
Judges of the district courts	District court district	At the regular election for members of the General Assembly immediately preceding the termination of each regular term	Four years, from the first day in January next after election
District Attorney	District Attorney district	At the regular election for members of the General Assembly immediately preceding	Four years, from first day of January next after election

		the termination of each regular term	
Members of years House of Representatives of the Congress of the United States	Congressional district, except as modified by G.S. 163-104	Tuesday next after the first Monday in November 1968 and every two years thereafter	Two
United States Senators	State	At the regular election immediately preceding the termination of each regular term	Six years
County commissioners	County	At the regular election for	Two years, from the first

Office		Term	When elected	
	in December next		members of the General Assembly immediately preceding election	Monday after the termination of each regular term
Clerk of superior court	County	Four years, from the first Monday in December next	At the regular election for members of the General Assembly immediately preceding election	Four the first Monday after the termination of each regular term
Register of deeds	County	Four years, from the first Monday in December next	At the regular election for members of the General Assembly	Four the first Monday

		immediately	after
election			
		preceding the	
		termination of	
		each regular term	
Sheriff years, from	County	At the regular	Four
		election for	the first
		members of the	Monday
in			
		General Assembly	
December next			
		immediately	after
election			
		preceding the	
		termination of	
		each regular term	
Coroner years, from	County	At the regular	Four
		election for	the first
		members of the	Monday
in			
		General Assembly	
December next			

election		immediately preceding the termination of a regular term	after
County treasurer (in counties in which elected)	County years, from in December next which election	Tuesday next after the first Monday in November 1968 and every two years thereafter	Two the first Monday after
All other county officers to be elected by the people	County years, from in December next	Tuesday next after the first Monday in November 1968 and every two years thereafter	Two the first Monday after

(Const., art. 4, s. 24; 1901, c. 89, ss. 1-4, 73, 74, 77; Rev., ss. 4293, 4294, 4296-4299; 1915, c. 101, s. 1; 1917, c. 218; C.S., ss. 5914, 5915, 5917-5920, 6018; 1935, c. 362; 1939, c. 196; 1943, c. 134, s. 4; 1947, c. 505, s. 1; 1951, c. 1009, s. 2; 1953, c. 1191, s. 1; 1967, c. 775, s. 1; cc. 1264, 1271; 1969, c. 44, s. 80; 1971, c. 170; 1973, c. 793, s. 93; 1977, c. 265, s. 1; c. 661, s. 1; 1991 (Reg. Sess., 1992), c. 782, s. 1; 1993 (Reg. Sess., 1994), c. 738, s. 2; 1996, 2nd Ex. Sess., c. 9, s. 2; 2003-434, 1st Ex. Sess., s. 6; 2004-127, s. 12; 2005-425, s. 3.2.)

§ 163-2: Repealed by Session Laws 2001-460, s. 2.

§ 163-3. Special elections.

Special elections shall be called as permitted by law and conducted in accordance with G.S. 163-287. (2013-381, s. 10.2.)

§ 163-4: Reserved for future codification purposes.

§ 163-5: Reserved for future codification purposes.

§ 163-6: Reserved for future codification purposes.

§ 163-7: Reserved for future codification purposes.

Article 2.

Time of Elections to Fill Vacancies.

§ 163-8. Filling vacancies in State executive offices.

If the office of Governor or Lieutenant Governor shall become vacant, the provisions of G.S. 147-11.1 shall apply. If the office of any of the following officers shall be vacated by death, resignation, or otherwise than by expiration of term, it shall be the duty of the Governor to appoint another to serve until his successor is elected and qualified: Secretary of State, Auditor, Treasurer, Superintendent of Public Instruction, Attorney General, Commissioner of Agriculture, Commissioner of Labor, and Commissioner of Insurance. Each such vacancy shall be filled by election at the first election for members of the General Assembly that occurs more than 60 days after the vacancy has taken place, and the person chosen shall hold the office for the remainder of the unexpired four-year term: Provided, that when a vacancy occurs in any of the offices named in this section and the term expires on the first day of January succeeding the next election for members of the General Assembly, the Governor shall appoint to fill the vacancy for the unexpired term of the office.

Upon the occurrence of a vacancy in the office of any one of these officers for any of the causes stated in the preceding paragraph, the Governor may appoint an acting officer to perform the duties of that office until a person is appointed or elected pursuant to this section and Article III, Section 7 of the State Constitution, to fill the vacancy and is qualified. (1901, c. 89, ss. 4, 73; Rev., s. 4299; C.S., s. 5920; 1967, c. 775, s. 1; 1981, c. 504, s. 14; 1983, c. 324, s. 1; 1985 (Reg. Sess., 1986), c. 920, s. 5.)

§ 163-9. Filling vacancies in State and district judicial offices.

(a) Vacancies occurring in the offices of Justice of the Supreme Court, judge of the Court of Appeals, and judge of the superior court for causes other than expiration of term shall be filled by appointment of the Governor. An appointee to the office of Justice of the Supreme Court or judge of the Court of Appeals shall hold office until January 1 next following the election for members of the General Assembly that is held more than 60 days after the vacancy occurs, at which time an election shall be held for an eight-year term and until a successor is elected and qualified.

(b) Except for judges specified in the next paragraph of this subsection, an appointee to the office of judge of superior court shall hold his place until the next election for members of the General Assembly that is held more than 60 days after the vacancy occurs, at which time an election shall be held to fill the unexpired term of the office.

Appointees for judges of the superior court from any district:

(1) With only one resident judge; or

(2) In which no county is subject to section 5 of the Voting Rights Act of 1965,

shall hold the office until the next election of members of the General Assembly that is held more than 60 days after the vacancy occurs, at which time an election shall be held to fill an eight-year term.

(c) When the unexpired term of the office in which the vacancy has occurred expires on the first day of January succeeding the next election for members of the General Assembly, the Governor shall appoint to fill that vacancy for the unexpired term of the office.

(d) Vacancies in the office of district judge which occur before the expiration of a term shall not be filled by election. Vacancies in the office of district judge shall be filled in accordance with G.S. 7A-142. (1901, c. 89, ss. 4, 73; Rev. s. 4299; C.S., s. 5920; 1967, c. 775, s. 1; 1969, c. 44, s. 81; 1979, c. 494; 1981, c. 763, s. 3; 1985 (Reg. Sess., 1986), c. 920, s. 6; 1995, c. 98, s. 1; 1996, 2nd Ex. Sess., c. 9, s. 21.)

§ 163-10. Filling vacancy in office of district attorney.

Any vacancy occurring in the office of district attorney for causes other than expiration of term shall be filled by appointment of the Governor. An appointee shall hold his place until the next election for members of the General Assembly that is held more than 60 days after the vacancy occurs, at which time an election shall be held to fill the unexpired term of the office: Provided, that when the unexpired term of the office in which the vacancy has occurred expires on the first day of January succeeding the next election for members of the General Assembly, the Governor shall appoint to fill that vacancy for the unexpired term of the office. (1901, c. 89, ss. 4, 73; Rev., s. 4299; C.S., s. 5920; 1967, c. 775, s. 1; 1973, c. 47, s. 2; 1977, c. 265, s. 2; 1981, c. 504, s. 16; 1985 (Reg. Sess., 1986), c. 920, s. 7.)

§ 163-11. Filling vacancies in the General Assembly.

(a) If a vacancy shall occur in the General Assembly by death, resignation, or otherwise than by expiration of term, the Governor shall immediately appoint for the unexpired part of the term the person recommended by the political party executive committee provided by this section. The Governor shall make the appointment within seven days of receiving the recommendation of the appropriate committee. If the Governor fails to make the appointment within the required period, he shall be presumed to have made the appointment and the legislative body to which the appointee was recommended is directed to seat the appointee as a member in good standing for the duration of the unexpired term.

(b)   If the district consists solely of one county and includes all of that county, the Governor shall appoint the person recommended by the county executive committee of the political party with which the vacating member was affiliated when elected, it being the party executive committee of the county which the vacating member was resident.

(c)   If the district consists solely of one county but includes less than all of the county, the Governor shall appoint the person recommended by the county executive committee of the political party with which the vacating member was affiliated when elected, it being the county executive committee of the county which the vacating member was resident, provided that in voting only those county executive committee members who reside in the district shall be eligible to vote.

(d)   If the district consists of more than one county, the Governor shall appoint for the unexpired portion of the term the person recommended by the State House of Representatives district committee or the Senatorial district committee of the political party with which the vacating member was affiliated when elected. In the case where all of a county is included within a district, the county convention or county executive committee of that political party shall elect or appoint at least one member from that county to serve on the State House of Representatives district executive committee or State Senatorial district executive committee. In the case where only part of a county is included within a district, the county convention or county executive committee of that political party shall elect or appoint at least one member from that county to serve on the State House of Representatives district committee or the State Senatorial district committee, but only the delegates to the county convention or the members of the county executive committee who reside in the district may vote in electing the district committee member. When the State House of Representatives district committee or the State Senatorial district committee meets, a member shall be entitled to cast for his county (or the part of his county within the district) one vote for each 300 persons or major fraction thereof residing within that county, or in the case where less than the whole county is in the district one vote for each 300 persons or major fraction thereof residing in that part of the district within the county.

A county convention or county executive committee may elect more than one member to the district committee but in the event that more than one member is selected from that county, then each member shall cast an equal share of the votes allotted to the county.

(e) No person is eligible for appointment to fill a vacancy in the Senate or the House of Representatives under this section, unless that person would have been qualified to vote as an elector for that office if an election were to be held on the date of appointment. This section is intended to implement the provisions of Section 8 of Article VI of the Constitution. (1901, c. 89, s. 74; Rev., s. 4298; C.S., s. 5919; 1947, c. 505, s. 1; 1953, c. 1191, s. 1; 1967, c. 775, s. 1; 1973, c. 35; 1981 (Reg. Sess., 1982), c. 1265, s. 3; 2007-391, s. 27(b).)

§ 163-12. Filling vacancy in United States Senate.

Whenever there shall be a vacancy in the office of United States Senator from this State, whether caused by death, resignation, or otherwise than by expiration of term, the Governor shall appoint to fill the vacancy until an election shall be held to fill the office. If the Senator was elected as the nominee of a political party, the person appointed by the Governor shall be a person affiliated with that same political party. The Governor shall issue a writ for the election of a Senator to be held at the time of the first election for members of the General Assembly that is held more than 60 days after the vacancy occurs. The person elected shall hold the office for the remainder of the unexpired term. The election shall take effect from the date of the canvassing of the returns. (1913, c. 114, ss. 1, 2; C.S., ss. 6002, 6003; 1929, c. 12, s. 2; 1955, c. 871, s. 6; 1967, c. 775, s. 1; 1985, c. 759, s. 2; 2013-381, s. 8.1.)

§ 163-13. Filling vacancy in United States House of Representatives.

(a) Special Election. - If at any time after expiration of any Congress and before another election, or if at any time after an election, there shall be a vacancy in this State's representation in the House of Representatives of the United States Congress, the Governor shall issue a writ of election, and by proclamation fix the date on which an election to fill the vacancy shall be held in the appropriate congressional district.

(b) Nominating Procedures. - If a congressional vacancy occurs beginning on the tenth day before the filing period ends under G.S. 163-106(c) preceding the next succeeding general election, candidates for the special election to fill the vacancy shall not be nominated in primaries. Instead, nominations may be made by the political party congressional district executive committees in the district in which the vacancy occurs. The chairman and secretary of each political party congressional district executive committee nominating a candidate shall immediately certify his name and party affiliation to the State Board of Elections so that it may be printed on the special election ballots.

If the congressional vacancy occurs before the tenth day before the filing period ends under G.S. 163-106(c) prior to the next succeeding general election, the Governor shall call a special primary for the purpose of nominating candidates to be voted on in a special election called by the Governor in accordance with the provisions of subsection (a) of this section. Such a primary election shall be conducted in accordance with the general laws governing primaries, except that the opening and closing dates for filing notices of candidacy with the State Board of Elections shall be fixed by the Governor in his call for the special primary. The Governor may also fix the absentee voting period for the special election and for the special first primary, but such period shall not be less than 30 days. (1901, c. 89, s. 60; Rev., s. 4369; C.S., s. 6007; 1947, c. 505, s. 5; 1967, c. 775, s. 1; 1985, c. 759, ss. 3-5.)

§§ 163-14 through 163-18. Reserved for future codification purposes.

SUBCHAPTER II. ELECTION OFFICERS.

Article 3.

State Board of Elections.

§ 163-19. State Board of Elections; appointment; term of office; vacancies; oath of office.

All of the terms of office of the present members of the State Board of Elections shall expire on May 1, 1969, or when their successors in office are appointed and qualified.

The State Board of Elections shall consist of five registered voters whose terms of office shall begin on May 1, 1969, and shall continue for four years, and until their successors are appointed and qualified. The Governor shall appoint the members of this Board and likewise shall appoint their successors every four years at the expiration of each four-year term. Not more than three members of the Board shall be members of the same political party. The Governor shall appoint the members from a list of nominees submitted to him by the State party chairman of each of the two political parties having the highest number of registered affiliates as reflected by the latest registration statistics published by the State Board of Elections. Each party chairman shall submit a list of five nominees who are affiliated with that political party. No person may serve more than two consecutive four-year terms.

Any vacancy occurring in the Board shall be filled by the Governor, and the person so appointed shall fill the unexpired term. The Governor shall fill the vacancy from a list of three nominees submitted to him by the State party chairman of the political party that nominated the vacating member as provided by the preceding paragraph. The three nominees must be affiliated with that political party.

At the first meeting held after new appointments are made, the members of the State Board of Elections shall take the following oath:

"I, _____, do solemnly swear (or affirm) that I will support the Constitution of the United States; that I will be faithful and bear true allegiance to the State of North Carolina, and to the constitutional powers and authorities which are or may be established for the government thereof; that I will endeavor to support, maintain and defend the Constitution of said State, and that I will well and truly execute the duties of the office of member of the State Board of Elections according to the best of my knowledge and ability, according to law, so help me, God."

After taking the prescribed oath, the Board shall organize by electing one of its members chairman and another secretary.

No person shall be eligible to serve as a member of the State Board of Elections who holds any elective or appointive office under the government of the United States, or of the State of North Carolina or any political subdivision thereof. No person who holds any office in a political party, or organization, or who is a candidate for nomination or election to any office, or who is a campaign manager or treasurer of any candidate in a primary or election shall be eligible to serve as a member of the State Board of Elections. (1901, c. 89, ss. 5, 7; Rev., ss. 2760, 4300, 4301; C.S., ss. 5921, 5922; 1933, c. 165, s. 1; 1953, c. 428; 1967, c. 775, s. 1; 1975, c. 286; 1985, c. 62, ss. 1, 1.1; 2005-276, s. 23A.3; 2006-262, s. 4.2; 2013-381, s. 45.1(a).)

§ 163-20. Meetings of Board; quorum; minutes.

(a) Call of Meeting. - The State Board of Elections shall meet at the call of the chairman whenever necessary to discharge the duties and functions imposed upon it by this Chapter. The chairman shall call a meeting of the Board upon the written application or applications of any two members thereof. If there is no chairman, or if the chairman does not call a meeting within three days after receiving a written request or requests from two members, any three members of the Board shall have power to call a meeting of the Board, and any duties imposed or powers conferred on the Board by this Chapter may be performed or exercised at that meeting, although the time for performing or exercising the same prescribed by this Chapter may have expired.

(b) Place of Meeting. - Except as provided in subsection (c), below, the State Board of Elections shall meet in its offices in the City of Raleigh, or at another place in Raleigh to be designated by the chairman. However, subject to the limitation imposed by subsection (c), below, upon the prior written request of any four members, the State Board of Elections shall meet at any other place in the State designated by the four members.

(c) Meetings to Investigate Alleged Violations of This Chapter. - When called upon to investigate or hear sworn alleged violations of this Chapter, the State Board of Elections shall meet and hear the matter in the county in which the violations are alleged to have occurred.

(d) Quorum. - A majority of the members constitutes a quorum for the transaction of business by the State Board of Elections. If any member of the Board fails to attend a meeting, and by reason thereof there is no quorum, the members present shall adjourn from day to day for not more than three days, by the end of which time, if there is no quorum, the Governor may summarily remove any member failing to attend and appoint his successor.

(e) Minutes. - The State Board of Elections shall keep minutes recording all proceedings and findings at each of its meetings. The minutes shall be recorded in a book which shall be kept in the office of the Board in Raleigh. (1901, c. 89,

s. 7; Rev., ss. 2760, 4301, 4302; C.S., ss. 5922, 5923; 1933, c. 165, s. 1; 1945, c. 982; 1967, c. 775, s. 1; 1973, c. 793, s. 3; c. 1223, s. 1.)

§ 163-21. Compensation of Board members.

The members of the State Board of Elections shall be compensated for the time they are actually engaged in the discharge of their duties and for their traveling and other expenses necessary and incidental to the discharge of their duties in accordance with the provisions of Chapter 138 of the General Statutes. (1901, c. 89, s. 7; Rev., ss. 2760, 4301; C.S., s. 5922; 1933, c. 165, s. 1; 1967, c. 775, s. 1.)

§ 163-22. Powers and duties of State Board of Elections.

(a)   The State Board of Elections shall have general supervision over the primaries and elections in the State, and it shall have authority to make such reasonable rules and regulations with respect to the conduct of primaries and elections as it may deem advisable so long as they do not conflict with any provisions of this Chapter.

(b)   From time to time, the Board shall publish and furnish to the county boards of elections and other election officials a sufficient number of indexed copies of all election laws and Board rules and regulations then in force. It shall also publish, issue, and distribute to the electorate such materials explanatory of primary and election laws and procedures as the Board shall deem necessary.

(c)   The State Board of Elections shall appoint, in the manner provided by law, all members of the county boards of elections and advise them as to the proper methods of conducting primaries and elections. The Board shall require such reports from the county boards and election officers as are provided by law, or as are deemed necessary by the Board, and shall compel observance of the requirements of the election laws by county boards of elections and other election officers. In performing these duties, the Board shall have the right to hear and act on complaints arising by petition or otherwise, on the failure or neglect of a county board of elections to comply with any part of the election laws imposing duties upon such a board. The State Board of Elections shall have power to remove from office any member of a county board of elections for incompetency, neglect or failure to perform duties, fraud, or for any other satisfactory cause. Before exercising this power, the State Board shall notify the county board member affected and give that member an opportunity to be heard. When any county board member shall be removed by the State Board of Elections, the vacancy occurring shall be filled by the State Board of Elections.

(d) The State Board of Elections shall investigate when necessary or advisable, the administration of election laws, frauds and irregularities in elections in any county and municipality and special district, and shall report violations of the election laws to the Attorney General or district attorney or prosecutor of the district for further investigation and prosecution.

(e) The State Board of Elections shall determine, in the manner provided by law, the form and content of ballots, instruction sheets, pollbooks, tally sheets, abstract and return forms, certificates of election, and other forms to be used in primaries and elections. The Board shall furnish to the county boards of elections the registration application forms required pursuant to G.S. 163-82.3. The State Board of Elections shall direct the county boards of elections to purchase a sufficient quantity of all forms attendant to the registration and elections process. In addition, the State Board shall provide a source of supply from which the county boards of elections may purchase the quantity of pollbooks needed for the execution of its responsibilities. In the preparation of ballots, pollbooks, abstract and return forms, and all other forms, the State Board of Elections may call to its aid the Attorney General of the State, and it shall be the duty of the Attorney General to advise and aid in the preparation of these books, ballots and forms.

(f) The State Board of Elections shall prepare, print, distribute to the county boards of elections all ballots for use in any primary or election held in the State which the law provides shall be printed and furnished by the State to the counties. The Board shall instruct the county boards of elections as to the printing of county and local ballots.

(g) The State Board of Elections shall certify to the appropriate county boards of elections the names of candidates for district offices who have filed notice of candidacy with the Board and whose names are required to be printed on county ballots.

(h) It shall be the duty of the State Board of Elections to tabulate the primary and election returns, to declare the results, and to prepare abstracts of the votes cast in each county in the State for offices which, according to law, shall be tabulated by the Board.

(i)   The State Board of Elections shall make recommendations to the Governor and legislature relative to the conduct and administration of the primaries and elections in the State as it may deem advisable.

(j)   Notwithstanding the provisions of any other section of this Chapter, the State Board of Elections is empowered to have access to any ballot boxes and their contents, any voting machines and their contents, any registration records, pollbooks, voter authorization cards or voter lists, any lists of absentee voters, any lists of presidential registrants under the Voting Rights Act of 1965 as amended, and any other voting equipment or similar records, books or lists in any precinct, county, municipality or electoral district over whose elections it has jurisdiction or for whose elections it has responsibility.

(k)   Notwithstanding the provisions contained in Article 20 or Article 21A of Chapter 163 the State Board of Elections shall be authorized, by resolution adopted prior to the printing of the primary ballots, to reduce the time by which absentee ballots are required to be printed and distributed for the primary election from 50 days to 45 days. This authority shall not be authorized for absentee ballots to be voted in the general election, except if the law requires ballots to be available for mailing 60 days before the general election, and they are not ready by that date, the State Board of Elections shall allow the counties to mail them out as soon as they are available.

(l)   Notwithstanding any other provision of law, in order to obtain judicial review of any decision of the State Board of Elections rendered in the performance of its duties or in the exercise of its powers under this Chapter, the person seeking review must file his petition in the Superior Court of Wake County.

(m)   Repealed by Session Laws 2001-398, s. 4, effective January 1, 2002.

(n)   The State Board of Elections shall provide specific training to county boards of elections regarding rules for registering students.

(o)   The State Board of Elections shall promulgate minimum requirements for the number of pollbooks, voting machines and curbside ballots to be available at each precinct, such that more of such will be available at general elections and a sufficient number will be available to allow voting without excessive delay. The State Board of Elections shall provide for a training and screening program for chief judges and judges. The State Board of Elections shall provide additional testing of voting machines to ensure that they operate properly even with complicated ballots.

(p)   The State Board of Elections shall require counties with voting systems to have sufficient personnel available on election day with technical expertise to make repairs in such equipment, to investigate election day problems, and assist in curbside voting.

(q)   The State Board of Elections may assign responsibility for enumerated administrative matters to the Executive Director by resolution, if that resolution provides a process for the State Board to review any administrative decision made by the Executive Director. (1901, c. 89, ss. 7, 11; Rev., ss. 4302, 4305; 1913, c. 138; C.S., ss. 5923, 5926; 1921, c. 181, s. 1; 1923, c. 196; 1933, c. 165, ss. 1, 2; 1945, c. 982; 1953, c. 410, s. 2; 1967, c. 775, s. 1; 1973, c. 47, s. 2; c. 793, s. 2; 1975, c. 19, s. 65; 1977, c. 661, s. 6; 1979, c. 411, s. 1; 1981, c. 556; 1985 (Reg. Sess., 1986), c. 986, ss. 2, 3; 1987, c. 485, ss. 2, 5; c. 509, s. 9; c. 642, s. 3; 1989, c. 635, s. 5; 1991, c. 727, ss. 5.2, 7; 1993 (Reg. Sess., 1994), c. 762, s. 12; 1995, c. 509, s. 114; 1999-424, s. 7(a); 2001-398, s. 4; 2009-537, s. 10; 2009-541, s. 1; 2011-31, s. 15; 2011-182, s. 3.)

§ 163-22.1: Repealed by Session Laws 2001-398, s. 2.

§ 163-22.2. Power of State Board to promulgate temporary rules and regulations.

In the event any portion of Chapter 163 of the General Statutes or any State election law or form of election of any county board of commissioners, local board of education, or city officer is held unconstitutional or invalid by a State or federal court or is unenforceable because of objection interposed by the United States Justice Department under the Voting Rights Act of 1965 and such ruling adversely affects the conduct and holding of any pending primary or election, the State Board of Elections shall have authority to make reasonable interim rules and regulations with respect to the pending primary or election as it deems advisable so long as they do not conflict with any provisions of Chapter 163 of the General Statutes and such rules and regulations shall become null and void 60 days after the convening of the next regular session of the General Assembly. The State Board of Elections shall also be authorized, upon recommendation of the Attorney General, to enter into agreement with the courts in lieu of protracted litigation until such time as the General Assembly convenes. (1981, c. 741; 1982, 2nd Ex. Sess., c. 3, s. 19.1; 1985, c. 563, s. 15; 1986, Ex. Sess., c. 3, s. 1.)

§ 163-22.3. State Board of Elections littering notification.

At the time an individual files with the State Board of Elections a notice of candidacy pursuant to G.S. 163-106, 163-112, 163-291, 163-294.2, or 163-323, is certified to the State Board of Elections by a political party executive committee to fill a nomination vacancy pursuant to G.S. 163-114, is certified to the State Board of Elections by a new political party as that party's nominee pursuant to G.S. 163-98, qualifies with the State Board of Elections as an unaffiliated or write-in candidate pursuant to Article 11 of this Chapter, or formally initiates a candidacy with the State Board of Elections pursuant to any statute or local act, the State Board of Elections shall notify the candidate of the provisions concerning campaign signs in G.S. 136-32 and G.S. 14-156, and the rules adopted by the Department of Transportation pursuant to G.S. 136-18. (2001-512, s. 7.)

§ 163-23. Powers of chairman in execution of Board duties.

In the performance of the duties enumerated in this Chapter, the chairman of the State Board of Elections shall have power to administer oaths, issue subpoenas, summon witnesses, and compel the production of papers, books, records and other evidence. Upon the written request or requests of two or more members of the State Board of Elections, he shall issue subpoenas for designated witnesses or identified papers, books, records and other evidence. In the absence of the chairman or upon his refusal to act, any two members of the State Board of Elections may issue subpoenas, summon witnesses, and compel the production of papers, books, records and other evidence. In the absence of the chairman or upon his refusal to act, any member of the Board may administer oaths. (1901, c. 89, s. 7; Rev., s. 4302; C.S., s. 5923; 1933, c. 165, s. 1; 1945, c. 982; 1967, c. 775, s. 1; 1973, c. 793, s. 4.)

§ 163-24. Power of State Board of Elections to maintain order.

The State Board of Elections shall possess full power and authority to maintain order, and to enforce obedience to its lawful commands during its sessions, and shall be constituted an inferior court for that purpose. If any person shall refuse to obey the lawful commands of the State Board of Elections or its chairman, or by disorderly conduct in its hearing or presence shall interrupt or disturb its proceedings, it may, by an order in writing, signed by its chairman, and attested by its secretary, commit the person so offending to the common jail of the county for a period not exceeding 30 days. Such order shall be executed by any sheriff to whom the same shall be delivered, or if a sheriff shall not be present, or shall refuse to act, by any other person who shall be deputed by the State Board of Elections in writing, and the keeper of the jail shall receive the person so committed and safely keep him for such time as shall be mentioned in the commitment: Provided, that any person committed under the provisions of this section shall have the right to post a two hundred dollar ($200.00) bond with the clerk of the superior court and appeal to the superior court for a trial on the merits of his commitment. (1901, c. 89, s. 72; Rev., s. 4376; C.S., s. 5977; 1955, c. 871, s. 4; 1967, c. 775, s. 1; 1995, c. 379, s. 14(e).)

§ 163-25. Authority of State Board to assist in litigation.

The State Board of Elections shall possess authority to assist any county board of elections in any matter in which litigation is contemplated or has been initiated, provided, the county board of elections in such county petitions, by majority resolution, for such assistance from the State Board of Elections and, provided further, that the State Board of Elections determines, in its sole discretion by majority vote, to assist in any such matter. It is further stipulated that the State Board of Elections shall not be authorized under this provision to enter into any litigation in assistance to counties, except in those instances where the uniform administration of Chapter 163 of the General Statutes of North Carolina has been, or would be threatened.

The Attorney General shall provide the State Board of Elections with legal assistance in execution of its authority under this section or, in the Attorney General's discretion, recommend that private counsel be employed.

If the Attorney General recommends employment of private counsel, the State Board may employ counsel with the approval of the Governor. (1969, c. 408, s. 1; 1973, c. 793, s. 6; 1983, c. 324, s. 2; 2011-31, s. 16.)

§ 163-26. Executive Director of State Board of Elections.

There is hereby created the position of Executive Director of the State Board of Elections, who shall perform all duties imposed upon him by statute and such duties as might be assigned to him by the State Board of Election [Elections]. (1973, c. 1272, s. 4; 2001-319, s. 11.)

§ 163-27. Executive Director to be appointed by Board.

The appointment of the Executive Director of the State Board of Elections is extended to May 15, 1989, unless removed for proper cause, and thereafter the Board shall appoint an Executive Director for a term of four years with compensation to be determined by the Department of Personnel. He shall serve, unless removed for cause, until his successor is appointed. Such Executive Director shall be responsible for staffing, administration, execution of the Board's decisions and orders and shall perform such other responsibilities as may be assigned by the Board. In the event of a vacancy, the vacancy shall be filled for the remainder of the term. (1973, c. 1409, s. 3; 1985, c. 62, s. 2; 2001-319, s. 11.)

§ 163-27.1. Emergency powers.

The Executive Director, as chief State elections official, may exercise emergency powers to conduct an election in a district where the normal schedule for the election is disrupted by any of the following:

(1)   A natural disaster.

(2)   Extremely inclement weather.

(3)   An armed conflict involving Armed Forces of the United States, or mobilization of those forces, including North Carolina National Guard and reserve components of the Armed Forces of the United States.

In exercising those emergency powers, the Executive Director shall avoid unnecessary conflict with the provisions of this Chapter. The Executive Director shall adopt rules describing the emergency powers and the situations in which the emergency powers will be exercised. (1999-455, s. 23; 2001-319, s. 11; 2011-183, s. 110.)

§ 163-28. State Board of Elections independent agency.

The State Board of Elections shall be and remain an independent regulatory and quasi-judicial agency and shall not be placed within any principal administrative department. The State Board of Elections shall exercise its statutory powers, duties, functions, authority, and shall have all powers and duties conferred upon the heads of principal departments under G.S. 143B-10. (1973, c. 1409, s. 2.)

§ 163-29. Reserved for future codification purposes.

Article 4.

County Boards of Elections.

§ 163-30. County boards of elections; appointments; terms of office; qualifications; vacancies; oath of office; instructional meetings.

In every county of the State there shall be a county board of elections, to consist of three persons of good moral character who are registered voters in the county in which they are to act. Members of county boards of elections shall be appointed by the State Board of Elections on the last Tuesday in June 1985, and every two years thereafter, and their terms of office shall continue for two years from the specified date of appointment and until their successors are appointed and qualified. Not more than two members of the county board of elections shall belong to the same political party.

No person shall be eligible to serve as a member of a county board of elections who holds any elective office under the government of the United States, or of the State of North Carolina or any political subdivision thereof.

No person who holds any office in a state, congressional district, county or precinct political party or organization, or who is a campaign manager or treasurer of any candidate or political party in a primary or election, shall be eligible to serve as a member of a county board of elections, provided however that the position of delegate to a political party convention shall not be considered an office for the purpose of this section.

No person shall be eligible to serve as a member of a county board of elections who is a candidate for nomination or election.

No person shall be eligible to serve as a member of a county board of elections who is the wife, husband, son, son-in-law, daughter, daughter-in-law, mother, mother-in-law, father, father-in-law, sister, sister-in-law, brother, brother-in-law, aunt, uncle, niece, or nephew of any candidate for nomination or election. Upon any member of the board of elections becoming ineligible, that member's seat shall be declared vacant. This paragraph only applies if the county board of elections is conducting the election for which the relative is a candidate.

The State chairman of each political party shall have the right to recommend to the State Board of Elections three registered voters in each county for appointment to the board of elections for that county. If such recommendations are received by the Board 15 or more days before the last Tuesday in June 1985, and each two years thereafter, it shall be the duty of the State Board of Elections to appoint the county boards from the names thus recommended.

Whenever a vacancy occurs in the membership of a county board of elections for any cause the State chairman of the political party of the vacating member shall have the right to recommend two registered voters of the affected county for such office, and it shall be the duty of the State Board of Elections to fill the vacancy from the names thus recommended.

At the meeting of the county board of elections required by G.S. 163-31 to be held on Tuesday following the third Monday in July in the year of their appointment the members shall take the following oath of office:

"I, _____, do solemnly swear (or affirm) that I will support the Constitution of the United States; that I will be faithful and bear true allegiance to the State of North Carolina and to the constitutional powers and authorities which are or may be established for the government thereof; that I will endeavor to support, maintain and defend the Constitution of said State, not inconsistent with the Constitution of the United States; and that I will well and truly execute the duties of the office of member of the _____ County Board of Elections to the best of my knowledge and ability, according to law; so help me God."

Each member of the county board of elections shall attend each instructional meeting held pursuant to G.S. 163-46, unless excused for good cause by the chairman of the board, and shall be paid the sum of twenty-five dollars ($25.00) per day for attending each of those meetings. (1901, c. 89, ss. 6, 11; Rev., ss.

4303, 4304, 4305; 1913, c. 138; C.S., ss. 5924, 5925, 5926; 1921, c. 181, s. 1; 1923, c. 111, s. 1; c. 196; 1933, c. 165, s. 2; 1941, c. 305, s. 1; 1945, c. 758, ss. 1, 2; 1949, c. 672, s. 1; 1953, c. 410, ss. 1, 2; c. 1191, s. 2; 1955, c. 871, s. 1; 1957, c. 182, s. 1; 1959, c. 1203, s. 1; 1967, c. 775, s. 1; 1969, c. 208, s. 1; 1973, c. 793, s. 7; c. 1094; c. 1344, s. 4; 1975, c. 19, s. 66; c. 159, s. 1; 1981, c. 954, s. 1; 1983, c. 617, ss. 1, 2; 1985, c. 472, s. 4; 1997-211, s. 1.)

§ 163-31. Meetings of county boards of elections; quorum; minutes.

In each county of the State the members of the county board of elections shall meet at the courthouse or board office at noon on the Tuesday following the third Monday in July in the year of their appointment by the State Board of Elections and, after taking the oath of office provided in G.S. 163-30, they shall organize by electing one member chairman and another member secretary of the county board of elections. On the Tuesday following the third Monday in August of the year in which they are appointed the county board of elections shall meet and appoint precinct chief judges and judges of elections. The board may hold other meetings at such times as the chairman of the board, or any two members thereof, may direct, for the performance of duties prescribed by law. A majority of the members shall constitute a quorum for the transaction of board business. The chairman shall notify, or cause to be notified, all members regarding every meeting to be held by the board.

The county board of elections shall keep minutes recording all proceedings and findings at each of its meetings. The minutes shall be recorded in a book which shall be kept in the board office and it shall be the responsibility of the secretary, elected by the board, to keep the required minute book current and accurate. The secretary of the board may designate the director of elections to record and maintain the minutes under his supervision. (1901, c. 89, s. 11; Rev., ss. 4304, 4306; C.S., ss. 5925, 5927; 1921, c. 181, s. 2; 1923, c. 111, s. 1; 1927, c. 260, s. 1; 1933, c. 165, s. 2; 1941, c. 305, s. 1; 1945, c. 758, s. 2; 1953, c. 410, s. 1; c. 1191, s. 2; 1957, c. 182, s. 1; 1959, c. 1203, s. 1; 1966, Ex. Sess., c. 5, s. 2; 1967, c. 775, s. 1; 1969, c. 208, s. 2; 1975, c. 159, s. 2; 1977, c. 626; 1983, c. 617, s. 3; 1993 (Reg. Sess., 1994), c. 762, s. 13; 1995, c. 243, s. 1.)

§ 163-32. Compensation of members of county boards of elections.

In full compensation of their services, members of the county board of elections (including the chairman) shall be paid by the county twenty-five dollars ($25.00) per meeting for the time they are actually engaged in the discharge of their duties, together with reimbursement of expenditures necessary and incidental to the discharge of their duties; provided that members are not entitled to be compensated for more than one meeting held in any one 24-hour period. In its discretion, the board of county commissioners of any county may pay the chairman and members of the county board of elections compensation in addition to the per meeting and expense allowance provided in this paragraph.

In all counties the board of elections shall pay its clerk, assistant clerks, and other employees such compensation as it shall fix within budget appropriations. Counties which adopt full-time and permanent registration shall have authority to pay directors of elections whatever compensation they may fix within budget appropriations. (1901, c. 89, s. 11; Rev., s. 4303; C.S., s. 5925; 1923, c. 111, s. 1; 1933, c. 165, s. 2; 1941, c. 305, s. 1; 1945, c. 758, s. 2; 1953, c. 410, s. 1; c. 843; c. 1191, s. 2; 1955, c. 800; 1957, c. 182, s. 1; 1959, c. 1203, s. 1; 1963, c. 303, s. 1; 1967, c. 775, s. 1; 1971, c. 1166, s. 1; 1973, c. 793, s. 8; c. 1344, s. 5; 1977, c. 626, s. 1; 1991, c. 338, s. 1; 1993 (Reg. Sess., 1994), c. 762, s. 14; 1995, c. 243, s. 1.)

§ 163-33. Powers and duties of county boards of elections.

The county boards of elections within their respective jurisdictions shall exercise all powers granted to such boards in this Chapter, and they shall perform all the duties imposed upon them by law, which shall include the following:

(1)   To make and issue such rules, regulations, and instructions, not inconsistent with law, with directives promulgated under the provisions of G.S. 163-132.4, or with the rules, orders, and directives established by the State Board of Elections, as it may deem necessary for the guidance of election officers and voters.

(2)   To appoint all chief judges, judges, assistants, and other officers of elections, and designate the precinct in which each shall serve; and, after notice and hearing, to remove any chief judge, judge of elections, assistant, or other officer of election appointed by it for incompetency, failure to discharge the duties of office, failure to qualify within the time prescribed by law, fraud, or for any other satisfactory cause. In exercising the powers and duties of this subdivision, the board may act only when a majority of its members are present at any meeting at which such powers or duties are exercised.

(3) To investigate irregularities, nonperformance of duties, and violations of laws by election officers and other persons, and to report violations to the State Board of Elections. In exercising the powers and duties of this subdivision, the board may act only when a majority of its members are present at any meeting at which such powers or duties are exercised. Provided that in any hearing on an irregularity no board of elections shall consider as evidence the testimony of a voter who cast a ballot, which ballot that voter was not eligible to cast, as to how that voter voted on that ballot.

(4) As provided in G.S. 163-128, to establish, define, provide, rearrange, discontinue, and combine election precincts as it may deem expedient, and to fix and provide for places of registration and for holding primaries and elections.

(5) To review, examine, and certify the sufficiency and validity of petitions and nomination papers.

(6) To advertise and contract for the printing of ballots and other supplies used in registration and elections; and to provide for the delivery of ballots, pollbooks, and other required papers and materials to the voting places.

(7) To provide for the purchase, preservation, and maintenance of voting booths, ballot boxes, registration and pollbooks, maps, flags, cards of instruction, and other forms, papers, and equipment used in registration, nominations, and elections; and to cause the voting places to be suitably provided with voting booths and other supplies required by law.

(8) To provide for the issuance of all notices, advertisements, and publications concerning elections required by law. If the election is on a State bond issue, an amendment to the Constitution, or approval of an act submitted to the voters of the State, the State Board of Elections shall reimburse the county boards of elections for their reasonable additional costs in placing such notices, advertisements, and publications. In addition, the county board of elections shall give notice at least 20 days prior to the date on which the registration books or records are closed that there will be a primary, general or special election, the date on which it will be held, and the hours the voting places will be open for voting in that election. The notice also shall describe the nature and type of election, and the issues, if any, to be submitted to the voters at that election. Notice shall be given by advertisement at least once weekly during the 20-day period in a newspaper having general circulation in the county and by posting a copy of the notice at the courthouse door. Notice may additionally be made on a radio or television station or both, but such notice

shall be in addition to the newspaper and other required notice. This subdivision shall not apply in the case of bond elections called under the provisions of Chapter 159.

(9) To receive the returns of primaries and elections, canvass the returns, make abstracts thereof, transmit such abstracts to the proper authorities, and to issue certificates of election to county officers and members of the General Assembly except those elected in districts composed of more than one county.

(10) To appoint and remove the board's clerk, assistant clerks, and other employees; and to appoint and remove precinct transfer assistants as provided in G.S. 163-82.15(g).

(11) To prepare and submit to the proper appropriating officers a budget estimating the cost of elections for the ensuing fiscal year.

(12) To perform such other duties as may be prescribed by this Chapter, by directives promulgated pursuant to G.S. 163-132.4, or by the rules, orders, and directives of the State Board of Elections.

(13) Notwithstanding the provisions of any other section of this Chapter, to have access to any ballot boxes and their contents, any voting machines and their contents, any registration records, pollbooks, voter authorization cards or voter lists, any lists of absentee voters, any lists of presidential registrants under the Voting Rights Act of 1965 as amended, and any other voting equipment or similar records, books or lists in any precinct or municipality over whose elections it has jurisdiction or for whose elections it has responsibility.

(14) To make forms available for near relatives or personal representatives of a deceased voter's estate to provide signed statements of the status of a deceased voter to return to the board of elections of the county in which the deceased voter was registered. Forms may be provided, upon request, to any of the following: near relatives, personal representatives of a deceased voter's estate, funeral directors, or funeral service licensees. (1901, c. 89, s. 11; Rev., s. 4306; C.S., s. 5927; 1921, c. 181, s. 2; 1927, c. 260, s. 1; 1933, c. 165, s. 2; 1966, Ex. Sess., c. 5, s. 2; 1967, c. 775, s. 1; 1973, c. 793, ss. 9-11; 1983, c. 392, s. 1; 1989, c. 93, s. 1; 1993 (Reg. Sess., 1994), c. 762, s. 15; 1995 (Reg. Sess., 1996), c. 694, s. 1; 1997-510, s. 1; 1999-424, s. 7(b); 2009-541, s. 2; 2013-381, s. 39.1(a).)

§ 163-33.1. Power of chairman to administer oaths.

The chairman of the county board of elections is authorized to administer to election officials specified in Articles 4, 5, and 20 of this Chapter the required oath, and may also administer the required oath to witnesses appearing before the county board at a duly called public hearing. (1981, c. 154; 2007-391, s. 5; 2008-187, s. 33(a).)

§ 163-33.2. Chairman and county board to examine voting machines.

Prior to each primary and general election the chairman and members of the county board of elections, in counties where voting machines are used, shall test vote, in a reasonable number of combinations, no less than ten percent (10%) of all voting machines programmed for each primary or election, such machines to be selected at random by the board after programming has been completed, and further, the board shall record the serial numbers of the machines test voted in the official minutes of the board. In the alternative, the board may cause the test voting required herein to be performed by persons qualified to program and test voting equipment. (1981, c. 303.)

§ 163-33.3. County board of elections littering notification.

At the time an individual files with a county board of elections a notice of candidacy pursuant to G.S. 163-106, 163-112, 163-291, or 163-294.2, is certified to a county board of elections by a political party executive committee to fill a nomination vacancy pursuant to G.S. 163-114, qualifies with a county board of elections as an unaffiliated or write-in candidate pursuant to Article 11 of this Chapter, or formally initiates with a county board of elections a candidacy pursuant to any statute or local act, the county board of elections shall notify the candidate of the provisions concerning campaign signs in G.S. 136-32 and G.S. 14-156 and the rules adopted by the Department of Transportation pursuant to G.S. 136-18. (2001-512, s. 8.)

§ 163-34. Power of county board of elections to maintain order.

Each county board of elections shall possess full power to maintain order, and to enforce obedience to its lawful commands during its sessions, and shall be constituted an inferior court for that purpose. If any person shall refuse to obey the lawful commands of any county board of elections, or by disorderly conduct in its hearing or presence shall interrupt or disturb its proceedings, it may, by an order in writing, signed by its chairman, and attested by its secretary, commit the person so offending to the common jail of the county for a period not exceeding 30 days. Such order shall be executed by any sheriff to whom the same shall be delivered, or if a sheriff shall not be present, or shall refuse to act, by any other person who shall be deputed by the county board of elections in writing, and the keeper of the jail shall receive the person so committed and safely keep him for such time as shall be mentioned in the commitment: Provided, that any person committed under the provisions of this section shall have the right to post a two hundred dollar ($200.00) bond with the clerk of the superior court and appeal to the superior court for a trial on the merits of his commitment. (1901, c. 89, s. 72; Rev., s. 4376; C.S., s. 5977; 1955, c. 871, s. 4; 1967, c. 775, s. 1; 2004-203, s. 57.)

§ 163-35. Director of elections to county board of elections; appointment; compensation; duties; dismissal.

(a)   In the event a vacancy occurs in the office of county director of elections in any of the county boards of elections in this State, the county board of elections shall submit the name of the person it recommends to fill the vacancy, in accordance with provisions specified in this section, to the Executive Director of the State Board of Elections who shall issue a letter of appointment. A person shall not serve as a director of elections if he:

(1)   Holds any elective public office;

(2)   Is a candidate for any office in a primary or election;

(3)   Holds any office in a political party or committee thereof;

(4)   Is a campaign chairman or finance chairman for any candidate for public office or serves on any campaign committee for any candidate;

(5)   Has been convicted of a felony in any court unless his rights of citizenship have been restored pursuant to the provisions of Chapter 13 of the General Statutes of North Carolina;

(6)   Has been removed at any time by the State Board of Elections following a public hearing; or

(7) Is a member or a spouse, child, spouse of child, parent, sister, or brother of a member of the county board of elections by whom he would be employed.

(b) Appointment, Duties; Termination. - Upon receipt of a nomination from the county board of elections stating that the nominee for director of elections is submitted for appointment upon majority selection by the county board of elections the Executive Director shall issue a letter of appointment of such nominee to the chairman of the county board of elections within 10 days after receipt of the nomination. Thereafter, the county board of elections shall enter in its official minutes the specified duties, responsibilities and designated authority assigned to the director by the county board of elections. The specified duties and responsibilities shall include adherence to the duties delegated to the county board of elections pursuant to G.S. 163-33. A copy of the specified duties, responsibilities and designated authority assigned to the director shall be filed with the State Board of Elections.

The county board of elections may, by petition signed by a majority of the board, recommend to the Executive Director of the State Board of Elections the termination of the employment of the county board's director of elections. The petition shall clearly state the reasons for termination. Upon receipt of the petition, the Executive Director shall forward a copy of the petition by certified mail, return receipt requested, to the county director of elections involved. The county director of elections may reply to the petition within 15 days of receipt thereof. Within 20 days of receipt of the county director of elections' reply or the expiration of the time period allowed for the filing of the reply, the State Executive Director shall render a decision as to the termination or retention of the county director of elections. The decision of the Executive Director of the State Board of Elections shall be final unless the decision is, within 20 days from the official date on which it was made, deferred by the State Board of Elections. If the State Board defers the decision, then the State Board shall make a final decision on the termination after giving the county director of elections an opportunity to be heard and to present witnesses and information to the State Board, and then notify the Executive Director of its decision in writing. Any one or more members of the State Board designated by the remaining members of the State Board may conduct the hearing and make a final determination on the termination. For the purposes of this subsection, the member(s) designated by the remaining members of the State Board shall possess the same authority conferred upon the chairman pursuant to G.S. 163-23. If the decision, rendered after the hearing, results in concurrence with the decision entered by the Executive Director, the decision becomes final. If the decision rendered after the hearing is contrary to that entered by the Executive Director, then the Executive Director shall, within 15 days from the written notification, enter an amended decision consistent with the results of the decision by the State Board of Elections or its designated member(s).

Upon majority vote on the recommendation of the Executive Director, the State Board of Elections may initiate proceedings for the termination of a county director of elections for just cause. If the State Board votes to initiate proceedings for termination, the State Board shall state the reasons for the termination in writing and send a copy by certified mail, return receipt requested, to the county director of elections. The director has 15 days to reply in writing to the notice. The State Board of Elections shall also notify the chair of the county board of elections and the chair of the county board of commissioners that the State Board has initiated termination proceedings. The State Board shall make a final decision on the termination after giving the county director of elections an opportunity to be heard, present witnesses, and provide information to the State Board. Any one or more members of the State Board designated by the remaining members of the State Board may conduct the hearing and make a final decision. For the purposes of this subsection, the member(s) designated by the remaining members of the State Board shall possess the same authority conferred upon the chairman pursuant to G.S. 163-23.

A county director of elections may be suspended, with pay, without warning for causes relating to personal conduct detrimental to service to the county or to the State Board of Elections, pending the giving of written reasons, in order to avoid the undue disruption of work or to protect the safety of persons or property or for other serious reasons. Any suspension may be initiated by the Executive Director but may not be for more than five days. Upon placing a county director of elections on suspension, the Executive Director shall, as soon as possible, reduce to writing the reasons for the suspension and forward copies to the county director of elections, the members of the county board of elections, the chair of the county board of commissioners, and the State Board of Elections. If no action for termination has been taken within five days, the county director of elections shall be fully reinstated.

Termination of any county director of elections shall comply with this subsection.

(c) Compensation of Directors of Elections. - Compensation paid to directors of elections in all counties maintaining full-time registration (five days per week) shall be in the form of a salary in an amount recommended by the county board of elections and approved by the Board of County Commissioners and shall be commensurate with the salary paid to directors in counties similarly situated and similar in population and number of registered voters.

The Board of County Commissioners in each county, whether or not the county maintains full-time or modified full-time registration, shall compensate the director of elections at a minimum rate of twelve dollars ($12.00) per hour for hours worked in attendance to his or her duties as prescribed by law, including rules and regulations adopted by the State Board of Elections. In addition, the county shall pay to the director an hourly wage of at least twelve dollars ($12.00) per hour for all hours worked in excess of those prescribed in rules and regulations adopted by the State Board of Elections, when such additional hours have been approved by the county board of elections and such approval has been recorded in the official minutes of the county board of elections.

In addition to the compensation provided for herein, the director of elections to the county board of elections shall be granted the same vacation leave, sick leave, and petty leave as granted to all other county employees. It shall also be the responsibility of the Board of County Commissioners to appropriate sufficient funds to compensate a replacement for the director of elections when authorized leave is taken.

(d) Duties. - The director of elections may be empowered by the county board of elections to perform such administrative duties as might be assigned by the board and the chairman. In addition, the director of elections may be authorized by the chairman to execute the responsibilities devolving upon the chairman provided such authorization by any chairman shall in no way transfer the responsibility for compliance with the law. The chairman shall remain liable for proper execution of all matters specifically assigned to him by law.

The county board of elections shall have authority, by resolution adopted by majority vote, to delegate to its director of elections so much of the administrative detail of the election functions, duties, and work of the board, its officers and members, as is now, or may hereafter be vested in the board or its members as the county board of elections may see fit: Provided, that the board shall not delegate to a director of elections any of its quasi-judicial or policy-making duties and authority. Such a resolution shall require adherence to the duties delegated to the county board of elections pursuant to G.S. 163-33. Within the limitations imposed upon the director of elections by the resolution of the county board of elections the acts of a properly appointed director of elections shall be deemed to be the acts of the county board of elections, its officers and members.

(e) Training and Certification. - The State Board of Elections shall conduct a training program consisting of four weeks for each new county director of elections. The director shall complete that program. Each director appointed after May 1995 shall successfully complete a certification program as provided in G.S. 163-82.24(b) within three years after appointment or by January 1, 2003, whichever occurs later. (1953, c. 843; 1955, c. 800; 1963, c. 303, s. 1; 1967, c. 775, s. 1; 1971, c. 1166, s. 2; 1973, c. 859, s. 1; 1975, c. 211, ss. 1, 2; c. 713; 1977, c. 265, s. 21; c. 626, s. 1; c. 1129, s. 1; 1981, cc. 84, 221; 1983, c. 697; 1985, c. 763; 1991, c. 338, s. 2; 1993 (Reg. Sess., 1994), c. 762, s. 16; 1995, c. 243, s. 1; 1999-426, s. 7(a); 2001-319, ss. 1(a), 1(b), 11; 2004-203, s. 58; 2009-541, ss. 3, 4(a).)

§ 163-36. Modified full-time offices.

The State Board of Elections shall promulgate rules permitting counties that have fewer than 6,501 registered voters to operate a modified full-time elections office to the extent that the operation of a full-time office is not necessary. Nothing in this section shall preclude any county from keeping an elections office open at hours consistent with the hours observed by other county offices. (1993 (Reg. Sess., 1994), c. 762, s. 6; 1999-426, s. 8(a).)

§ 163-37. Duty of county board of commissioners.

The respective boards of county commissioners shall appropriate reasonable and adequate funds necessary for the legal functions of the county board of elections, including reasonable and just compensation of the director of elections. (1999-424, s. 3(a).)

Article 4A.

Political Activities by Board of Elections Members and Employees.

§ 163-38. Applicability of Article.

This Article applies to members and employees of the State Board of Elections and of each county board of elections. With regard to prohibitions in this Article concerning candidates, referenda, and committees, the prohibitions do not apply if the candidate or referendum will not be on the ballot in an area within the jurisdiction of the board, or if the political committee or referendum committee is not involved with an election or referendum that will be on the ballot in an area within the jurisdiction of the board. (2000-114, s. 1; 2007-391, s. 14(a); 2011-31, s. 17.)

§ 163-39. Limitation on political activities.

No individual subject to this Article shall:

(1)   Make written or oral statements intended for general distribution or dissemination to the public at large supporting or opposing the nomination or election of one or more clearly identified candidates for public office.

(2)   Make written or oral statements intended for general distribution or dissemination to the public at large supporting or opposing the passage of one or more clearly identified referendum proposals.

(3)   Solicit contributions for a candidate, political committee, or referendum committee.

Individual expressions of opinion, support, or opposition not intended for general public distribution shall not be deemed a violation of this Article. Nothing in this Article shall be deemed to prohibit participation in a political party convention as a delegate. Nothing in this Article shall be deemed to prohibit a board member or board employee from making a contribution to a candidate, political committee, or referendum committee. Nothing in this Article shall be deemed to prohibit a board member or board employee from advising other government entities as to technical matters related to election administration or revision of electoral district boundaries. (2000-114, s. 1; 2007-391, s. 14(a).)

§ 163-40. Violation may be ground for removal.

A violation of this Article may be a ground to remove a State Board of Elections member under G.S. 143B-16 or a county board of elections member under G.S. 163-22(c). A violation of this Article may be a ground for dismissal of an employee of the State Board of Elections or of a county board of elections. No criminal penalty shall be imposed for a violation of this Article. (2000-114, s. 1; 2007-391, s. 14(a); 2011-31, s. 18.)

§ 163-40.1. Definitions.

The provisions of Article 22A of this Chapter apply to the definition and proof of terms used in this Article. (2000-114, s. 1.)

Article 5.

Precinct Election Officials.

§ 163-41. Precinct chief judges and judges of election; appointment; terms of office; qualifications; vacancies; oaths of office.

(a) Appointment of Chief Judge and Judges. - At the meeting required by G.S. 163-31 to be held on the Tuesday following the third Monday in August of the year in which they are appointed, the county board of elections shall appoint one person to act as chief judge and two other persons to act as judges of election for each precinct in the county. Their terms of office shall continue for two years from the specified date of appointment and until their successors are appointed and qualified, except that if a nonresident of the precinct is appointed as chief judge or judge for a precinct, that person's term of office shall end if the board of elections appoints a qualified resident of the precinct of the same party to replace the nonresident chief judge or judge. It shall be their duty to conduct the primaries and elections within their respective precincts. Persons appointed to these offices must be registered voters and residents of the county in which the precinct is located, of good repute, and able to read and write. Not more than one judge in each precinct shall belong to the same political party as the chief judge.

The term "precinct official" shall mean chief judges and judges appointed pursuant to this section, and all assistants appointed pursuant to G.S. 163-42, unless the context of a statute clearly indicates a more restrictive meaning.

No person shall be eligible to serve as a precinct official, as that term is defined above, who holds any elective office under the government of the United States, or of the State of North Carolina or any political subdivision thereof.

No person shall be eligible to serve as a precinct official who is a candidate for nomination or election.

No person shall be eligible to serve as a precinct official who holds any office in a state, congressional district, county, or precinct political party or political organization, or who is a manager or treasurer for any candidate or political party, provided however that the position of delegate to a political party convention shall not be considered an office for the purpose of this subsection.

The chairman of each political party in the county where possible shall recommend two registered voters in each precinct who are otherwise qualified, are residents of the precinct, have good moral character, and are able to read and write, for appointment as chief judge in the precinct, and he shall also recommend where possible the same number of similarly qualified voters for appointment as judges of election in that precinct. If such recommendations are received by the county board of elections no later than the fifth day preceding the date on which appointments are to be made, it must make precinct appointments from the names of those recommended. Provided that if only one name is submitted by the fifth day preceding the date on which appointments are to be made, by a party for judge of election by the chairman of one of the two political parties in the county having the greatest numbers of registered voters in the State, the county board of elections must appoint that person.

If the recommendations of the party chairs for chief judge or judge in a precinct are insufficient, the county board of elections by unanimous vote of all of its members may name to serve as chief judge or judge in that precinct registered voters in that precinct who were not recommended by the party chairs. If, after diligently seeking to fill the positions with registered voters of the precinct, the county board still has an insufficient number of officials for the precinct, the county board by unanimous vote of all of its members may appoint to the positions registered voters in other precincts in the same county who meet the qualifications other than residence to be precinct officials in the precinct, provided that where possible the county board shall seek and adopt the recommendation of the county chairman of the political party affected. In making its appointments, the county board shall assure, wherever possible, that no precinct has a chief judge and judges all of whom are registered with the same party. In no instance shall the county board appoint nonresidents of the precinct to a majority of the three positions of chief judge and judge in a precinct.

If, at any time other than on the day of a primary or election, a chief judge or judge of election shall be removed from office, or shall die or resign, or if for any other cause there be a vacancy in a precinct election office, the chairman of the county board of elections shall appoint another in his place, promptly notifying him of his appointment. If at all possible, the chairman of the county board of elections shall consult with the county chairman of the political party of the vacating official, and if the chairman of the county political party nominates a qualified voter of that precinct to fill the vacancy, the chairman of the county board of elections shall appoint that person. In filling such a vacancy, the chairman shall appoint a person who belongs to the same political party as that to which the vacating member belonged when appointed. If the chairman of the county board of elections did not appoint a person upon recommendation of the chairman of the party to fill such a vacancy, then the term of office of the person appointed to fill the vacancy shall expire upon the conclusion of the next canvass held by the county board of elections under this Chapter, and any successor must be a person nominated by the chairman of the party of the vacating officer.

If any person appointed chief judge shall fail to be present at the voting place at the hour of opening the polls on primary or election day, or if a vacancy in that office shall occur on primary or election day for any reason whatever, the precinct judges of election shall appoint another to act as chief judge until such time as the chairman of the county board of elections shall appoint to fill the vacancy. If such appointment by the chairman of the county board of elections is not a person nominated by the county chairman of the political party of the vacating officer, then the term of office of the person appointed to fill the vacancy shall expire upon the conclusion of the next canvass held by the county board of elections under this Chapter. If a judge of election shall fail to be present at the voting place at the hour of opening the polls on primary or election day, or if a vacancy in that office shall occur on primary or election day for any reason whatever, the chief judge shall appoint another to act as judge until such time as the chairman of the county board of elections shall appoint to fill the vacancy. Persons appointed to fill vacancies shall, whenever possible, be chosen from the same political party as the person whose vacancy is being filled, and all such appointees shall be sworn before acting.

As soon as practicable, following their training as prescribed in G.S. 163-82.24, each chief judge and judge of election shall take and subscribe the following oath of office to be administered by an officer authorized to administer oaths and file it with the county board of elections:

"I, _____, do solemnly swear (or affirm) that I will support the Constitution of the United States; that I will be faithful and bear true allegiance to the State of North Carolina, and to the constitutional powers and authorities which are or may be established for the government thereof; that I will endeavor to support, maintain and defend the Constitution of said State not inconsistent with the Constitution of the United States; that I will administer the duties of my office as chief judge of (judge of election in) _____ precinct, _____ County, without fear or favor; that I will not in any manner request or seek to persuade or induce any voter to vote for or against any particular candidate or proposition; and that I will not keep or make any memorandum of anything occurring within a voting booth, unless I am called upon to testify in a judicial proceeding for a violation of the election laws of this State; so help me, God."

Notwithstanding the previous paragraph, a person appointed chief judge by the judges of election under this section, or appointed judge of election by the chief judge under this section may take the oath of office immediately upon appointment.

Before the opening of the polls on the morning of the primary or election, the chief judge shall administer the oath set out in the preceding paragraph to each assistant, and any judge of election not previously sworn, substituting for the words "chief judge of" the words "assistant in" or "judge of election in" whichever is appropriate.

(b)   Special Registration Commissioners Abolished; Optional Training. - The office of special registration commissioner is abolished. The State Board of Elections and county boards of elections may provide training to persons assisting in voter registration.

(b1)   Repealed by Session Laws 1985, c. 387, s. 1.1.

(c)   Publication of Names of Precinct Officials. - Immediately after appointing chief judges and judges as herein provided, the county board of elections shall publish the names of the persons appointed in some newspaper having general circulation in the county or, in lieu thereof, at the courthouse door, and shall notify each person appointed of his appointment, either by letter or by having a notice served upon him by the sheriff. Notice may additionally be made on a radio or television station or both, but such notice shall be in addition to the newspaper and other required notice. (1901, c. 89, ss. 8, 9, 16; Rev., ss. 4307, 4308, 4309; C.S., ss. 5928, 5929, 5930; 1923, c. 111, s. 2; 1929, c. 164, s. 18; 1933, c. 165, s. 3; 1947, c. 505, s. 2; 1953, c. 843; c. 1191, s. 3; 1955, c. 800; 1957, c. 784, s. 1; 1963, c. 303, s. 1; 1967, c. 775, s. 1; 1973, c. 435; c. 1223, s. 2; 1975, c. 159, ss. 3, 4; c. 711; c. 807, s. 1; 1979, c. 766, s. 1; c. 782; 1981, c. 628, ss. 1, 2; c. 954, ss. 2, 4; 1981 (Reg. Sess., 1982), c. 1265, s. 7; 1983, c. 617, s. 5; 1985, c. 387; c. 563, ss. 9, 10; c. 600, s. 7.1; c. 759, ss. 7, 7.1, 8;

1987, c. 80; c. 491, s. 4.1; 1987 (Reg. Sess., 1988), c. 1028, s. 12; 1989, c. 93, s. 2; 1993 (Reg. Sess., 1994), c. 762, s. 3; 1995 (Reg. Sess., 1996), c. 734, s. 1.)

§ 163-41.1. Certain relatives prohibited from serving together.

(a)   The following categories of relatives are prohibited from serving as precinct officials of the same precinct: spouse, child, spouse of a child, sister or brother.

(b)   No precinct official who is the wife, husband, mother, father, son, daughter, brother or sister of any candidate for nomination or election may serve as precinct official during any primary or election in which such candidate participates. The county board of elections shall temporarily disqualify any such official for the specific primary or election involved and shall have authority to appoint a substitute official, from the same political party, to serve only during the primary or election at which such conflict exists. (1975, c. 745; 1979, c. 411, s. 2.)

§ 163-41.2. Discharge of precinct official unlawful.

(a)   No employer may discharge or demote any employee because the employee has been appointed as a precinct official and is serving as a precinct official on election day or canvass day.

(b)   An employee discharged or demoted in violation of this section shall be entitled to be reinstated to that employee's former position. The burden of proof shall be upon the employee.

(c)   The statute of limitations for actions under this section shall be one year pursuant to G.S. 1-54.

(d)   This section does not apply unless the employee provides the employer with not less than 30 days written notice, before the date the leave is to begin, of the employee's intention to take leave to serve as a precinct official.

(e)   As used in this section, "precinct official" has the same meaning as in G.S. 163-41(a). (2001-169, s. 1.)

215

§ 163-42. Assistants at polls; appointment; term of office; qualifications; oath of office.

(a) Each county board of elections is authorized, in its discretion, to appoint two or more assistants for each precinct to aid the chief judge and judges. Not more than two assistants shall be appointed in precincts having 500 or less registered voters. Assistants shall be qualified voters of the county in which the precinct is located. When the board of elections determines that assistants are needed in a precinct an equal number shall be appointed from different political parties, unless the requirement as to party affiliation cannot be met because of an insufficient number of voters of different political parties within the county.

In the discretion of the county board of elections, a precinct assistant may serve less than the full day prescribed for chief judges and judges in G.S. 163-47(a).

(b) The chairman of each political party in the county shall have the right to recommend from three to 10 registered voters in each precinct for appointment as precinct assistants in that precinct. If the recommendations are received by it no later than the thirtieth day prior to the primary or election, the board shall make appointments of the precinct assistants for each precinct from the names thus recommended. If the recommendations of the party chairs for precinct assistant in a precinct are insufficient, the county board of elections by unanimous vote of all of its members may name to serve as precinct assistant in that precinct registered voters in that precinct who were not recommended by the party chairs. If, after diligently seeking to fill the positions with registered voters of the precinct, the county board still has an insufficient number of precinct assistants for the precinct, the county board by unanimous vote of all of its members may appoint to the positions registered voters in other precincts in the same county who meet the qualifications other than residence to be precinct officials in the precinct. In making its appointments, the county board shall assure, wherever possible, that no precinct has precinct officials all of whom are registered with the same party. In no instance shall the county board appoint nonresidents of the precinct to a majority of the positions as precinct assistant in a precinct.

(c) In addition, a county board of elections by unanimous vote of all of its members may appoint any registered voter in the county as emergency election-day assistant, as long as that voter is otherwise qualified to be a precinct official. The State Board of Elections shall determine for each election the number of emergency election-day assistants each county may have, based on population, expected turnout, and complexity of election duties. The county board by unanimous vote of all of its members may assign emergency election-day assistants on the day of the election to any precinct in the county where the number of precinct officials is insufficient because of an emergency occurring within 48 hours of the opening of the polls that prevents an appointed precinct official from serving. A person appointed to serve as emergency election-day assistant shall be trained and paid like other precinct assistants in accordance with G.S. 163-46. A county board of elections shall apportion the appointments as emergency election-day assistant among registrars of each political party so as to make possible the staffing of each precinct with officials of more than one party, and the county board shall make assignments so that no precinct has precinct officials all of whom are registered with the same party.

(d)   Before entering upon the duties of the office, each assistant shall take the oath prescribed in G.S. 163-41(a) to be administered by the chief judge of the precinct for which the assistant is appointed. Assistants serve for the particular primary or election for which they are appointed, unless the county board of elections appoints them for a term to expire on the date appointments are to be made pursuant to G.S. 163-41. (1929, c. 164, s. 35; 1933, c. 165, s. 24; 1953, c. 1191, s. 3; 1967, c. 775, s. 1; 1973, c. 793, s. 95; c. 1359, ss. 1-3; 1975, c. 19, s. 67; 1977, c. 95, ss. 1, 2; 1981, c. 954, s. 3; 1983, c. 617, s. 4; 1985, c. 563, ss. 8, 8.1; 1993 (Reg. Sess., 1994), c. 762, s. 17; 1995 (Reg. Sess., 1996), c. 554, s. 1; c. 734, s. 2; 2011-31, s. 19.)

§ 163-42.1. Student election assistants.

A student of at least 17 years of age at the time of any election or primary in which the student works shall be eligible to be appointed as a student election assistant. To be eligible a student must have all the following qualifications:

(1)   Be a United States citizen.

(2)   Be a resident of the county in which the student is appointed.

(3)   Be enrolled in a secondary educational institution, including a home school as defined in G.S. 115C-563(a), with an exemplary academic record as determined by that institution.

(4)   Be recommended by the principal or director of the secondary educational institution in which the student is enrolled.

(5) Have the consent of a parent, legal custodian, or guardian.

The county board of elections may appoint student election assistants, following guidelines which shall be issued by the State Board of Elections. No more than two student election assistants shall be assigned to any voting place. Every student election assistant shall work under the direct supervision of the election judges. The student election assistants shall attend the same training as a precinct assistant, shall be sworn in the same manner as a precinct assistant, and shall be compensated in the same manner as precinct assistants. The county board of elections shall prescribe the duties of a student election assistant, following guidelines which shall be issued by the State Board of Elections. Under no circumstances may students ineligible to register to vote be appointed and act as precinct judges or observers in any election. The date of birth of a student election assistant shall be kept confidential. (2003-278, s. 1; 2004-127, s. 17(e).)

§ 163-43. Ballot counters; appointment; qualifications; oath of office.

The county board of elections of any county may authorize the use of precinct ballot counters to aid the chief judges and judges of election in the counting of ballots in any precinct or precincts within the county. The county board of elections shall appoint the ballot counters it authorizes for each precinct or, in its discretion, the board may delegate authority to make such appointments to the precinct chief judge, specifying the number of ballot counters to be appointed for each precinct. A ballot counter must be a resident of the county in which the precinct is located.

No person shall be eligible to serve as a ballot counter, who holds any elective office under the government of the United States, or of the State of North Carolina or any political subdivision thereof.

No person shall be eligible to serve as a ballot counter, who serves as chairman of a state, congressional district, county, or precinct political party or political organization.

No person who is the wife, husband, mother, father, son, daughter, brother or sister of any candidate for nomination or election may serve as ballot counter during any primary or election in which such candidate qualifies.

No person shall be eligible to serve as a ballot counter who is a candidate for nomination or election.

Upon acceptance of appointment, each ballot counter shall appear before the precinct chief judge at the voting place immediately at the close of the polls on the day of the primary or election and take the following oath to be administered by the chief judge:

"I, _____, do solemnly swear (or affirm) that I will support the Constitution of the United States; that I will be faithful and bear true allegiance to the State of North Carolina, and to the constitutional powers and authorities which are or may be established for the government thereof; that I will endeavor to support, maintain and defend the Constitution of said State not inconsistent with the Constitution of the United States; that I will honestly discharge the duties of ballot counter in _____ precinct, _____County for primary (or election) held this day, and that I will fairly and honestly tabulate the votes cast in said primary (or election); so help me, God."

The names and addresses of all ballot counters serving in any precinct, whether appointed by the county board of elections or by the chief judge, shall be reported by the chief judge to the county board of elections at the county canvass following the primary or election. (1953, c. 843; 1955, c. 800; 1963, c. 303, s. 1; 1967, c. 775, s. 1; 1981, c. 954, s. 5; 1985, c. 563, s. 10.1; 1993 (Reg. Sess., 1994), c. 762, s. 18; 1995 (Reg. Sess., 1996), c. 734, s. 3.)

§ 163-44. Repealed by Session Laws 1973, c. 793, s. 13.

§ 163-45. Observers; appointment.

(a) The chair of each political party in the county shall have the right to designate two observers to attend each voting place at each primary and election and such observers may, at the option of the designating party chair, be relieved during the day of the primary or election after serving no less than four hours and provided the list required by this section to be filed by each chair contains the names of all persons authorized to represent such chair's political party. The chair of each political party in the county shall have the right to designate 10 additional at-large observers who are residents of that county who may attend any voting place in that county. The list submitted by the chair of the political party may be amended between the one-stop period under G.S. 163-

227.2 and general election day to substitute one or all at-large observers for election day. Not more than two observers from the same political party shall be permitted in the voting enclosure at any time, except that in addition one of the at-large observers from each party may also be in the voting enclosure. This right shall not extend to the chair of a political party during a primary unless that party is participating in the primary. In any election in which an unaffiliated candidate is named on the ballot, the candidate or the candidate's campaign manager shall have the right to appoint two observers for each voting place consistent with the provisions specified herein. Persons appointed as observers must be registered voters of the county for which appointed and must have good moral character. No person who is a candidate on the ballot in a primary or election may serve as an observer or runner in that primary or election. Observers shall take no oath of office.

(b) Individuals authorized to appoint observers must submit in writing to the chief judge of each precinct a signed list of the observers appointed for that precinct, except that the list of at-large observers authorized in subsection (a) of this section shall be submitted to the county director of elections. Individuals authorized to appoint observers must, prior to 10:00 A.M. on the fifth day prior to any primary or general election, submit in writing to the chair of the county board of elections two signed copies of a list of observers appointed by them, designating the precinct or at-large status for which each observer is appointed. Before the opening of the voting place on the day of a primary or general election, the chair shall deliver one copy of the list to the chief judge for each affected precinct, except that the list of at-large observers shall be provided by the county director of elections to the chief judge. The chair shall retain the other copy. The chair, or the chief judge and judges for each affected precinct, may for good cause reject any appointee and require that another be appointed. The names of any persons appointed in place of those persons rejected shall be furnished in writing to the chief judge of each affected precinct no later than the time for opening the voting place on the day of any primary or general election, either by the chair of the county board of elections or the person making the substitute appointment.

If party chairs appoint observers at one-stop sites under G.S. 163-227.2, those party chairs shall provide a list of the observers appointed before 10:00 A.M. on the fifth day before the observer is to observe. At-large observers may serve at any one-stop site.

(c) An observer shall do no electioneering at the voting place, and shall in no manner impede the voting process or interfere or communicate with or observe any voter in casting a ballot, but, subject to these restrictions, the chief judge and judges of elections shall permit the observer to make such observation and take such notes as the observer may desire.

(d) Whether or not the observer attends to the polls for the requisite time provided by this section, each observer shall be entitled to obtain at times specified by the State Board of Elections, but not less than three times during election day with the spacing not less than one hour apart, a list of the persons who have voted in the precinct so far in that election day. Counties that use an "authorization to vote document" instead of poll books may comply with the requirement in the previous sentence by permitting each observer to inspect election records so that the observer may create a list of persons who have voted in the precinct so far that election day; each observer shall be entitled to make the inspection at times specified by the State Board of Elections, but not less than three times during election day with the spacing not less than one hour apart.

Instead of having an observer receive the voting list, the county party chair may send a runner to do so, even if an observer has not been appointed for that precinct. The runner may be the precinct party chair or any person named by the county party chair. Each county party chair using runners in an election shall provide to the county board of elections before 10:00 A.M. on the fifth day before election day a list of the runners to be used. That party chair must notify the chair of the county board of elections or the board chair's designee of the names of all runners to be used in each precinct before the runner goes to the precinct. The runner may receive a voter list from the precinct on the same schedule as an observer. Whether obtained by observer or runner, each party is entitled to only one voter list at each of the scheduled times. No runner may enter the voting enclosure except when necessary to announce that runner's presence and to receive the list. The runner must leave immediately after being provided with the list. (1929, c. 164, s. 36; 1953, c. 843; 1955, c. 800; c. 871, s. 7; 1959, c. 616, s. 2; 1963, c. 303, s. 1; 1967, c. 775, s. 1; 1973, c. 793, ss. 14, 94; 1977, c. 453; 1991, c. 727, s. 3; 1993 (Reg. Sess., 1994), c. 762, s. 19; 1995 (Reg. Sess., 1996), c. 688, s. 1; c. 734, s. 4.1; 2005-428, s. 1(a); 2007-391, s. 22; 2008-187, s. 33(a); 2013-381, s. 11.1.)

§ 163-46. Compensation of precinct officials and assistants.

The precinct chief judge shall be paid the state minimum wage for his services on the day of a primary, special or general election. Judges of election shall each be paid the state minimum wage for their services on the day of a primary, special or general election. Assistants, appointed pursuant to G.S. 163-42, shall each be paid the state minimum wage for their services on the day of a primary, special or general election. Ballot counters appointed pursuant to G.S. 163-43 shall be paid a minimum of five dollars ($5.00) for their services on the day of a primary, general or special election. If an election official is being paid an hourly wage or daily fee on an election day and the official is performing additional election duties away from the assigned precinct voting place, the official shall not be entitled to any additional monies for those services, except for reimbursable expenses in performing the services.

If the county board of elections requests the presence of a chief judge or judge at the county canvass, the chief judge shall be paid the sum of twenty dollars ($20.00) per day and judges shall be paid the sum of fifteen dollars ($15.00) per day. If the county board of elections requests a precinct official, including chief judge or judge, to personally deliver official ballots or other official materials to the county board of elections, the precinct official shall be paid the sum of twenty dollars ($20.00) per day and judges shall be paid the sum of fifteen dollars ($15.00) per day.

The chairman of the county board of elections, along with the director of elections, shall conduct an instructional meeting prior to each primary and general election which shall be attended by each chief judge and judge of election, unless excused by the chairman, and such precinct election officials shall be paid the sum of fifteen dollars ($15.00) for attending the instructional meetings required by this section.

In its discretion, the board of county commissioners of any county may provide funds with which the county board of elections may pay chief judges, judges, assistants, and ballot counters in addition to the amounts specified in this section. Observers shall be paid no compensation for their services.

A person appointed to serve as chief judge, or judge of election when a previously appointed chief judge or judge fails to appear at the voting place or leaves his post on the day of an election or primary shall be paid the same compensation as the chief judge or judge appointed prior to that date.

For the purpose of this section, the phrase "the State minimum wage," means the amount set by G.S. 95-25.3(a). For the purpose of this section, no other provision of Article 2A of Chapter 95 of the General Statutes shall apply. (1901, c. 89, s. 42; Rev., s. 4311; C.S., s. 5932; 1927, c. 260, s. 2; 1931, c. 254, s. 16;

1933, c. 165, s. 3; 1935, c. 421, s. 1; 1939, c. 264, s. 1; 1941, c. 304, s. 1; 1945, c. 758, s. 3; 1947, c. 505, s. 11; 1951, c. 1009, s. 1; 1953, c. 843; 1955, c. 800; 1957, c. 182, s. 2; 1963, c. 303, s. 1; 1967, c. 775, s. 1; 1969, c. 24; 1971, c. 604; 1973, c. 793, ss. 15, 16, 94; 1977, c. 626, s. 1; 1979, c. 403; 1981, c. 796, ss. 1, 2; 1993 (Reg. Sess., 1994), c. 762, s. 20; 1995, c. 243, s. 1; 2001-398, s. 5; 2003-278, s. 3.)

§ 163-47. Powers and duties of chief judges and judges of election.

(a) The chief judges and judges of election shall conduct the primaries and elections within their respective precincts fairly and impartially, and they shall enforce peace and good order in and about the place of registration and voting. On the day of each primary and general and special election, the precinct chief judge and judges shall remain at the voting place from the time fixed by law for the commencement of their duties there until they have completed all those duties, and they shall not separate nor shall any one of them leave the voting place except for unavoidable necessity.

(b) On the day of an election or primary, the chief judge shall have charge of the registration list for the purpose of passing on the registration of persons who present themselves at the polls to vote.

(c) The chief judge and judges shall hear challenges of the right of registered voters to vote as provided by law.

(d) The chief judge and judges shall count the votes cast in their precincts and make such returns of the same as is provided by law.

(e) The chief judge and judges shall make such an accounting to the chairman of the county board of elections for ballots and for election supplies as is required by law.

(f) The chief judge and judges of election shall act by a majority vote on all matters not assigned specifically by law to the chief judge or to a judge. (1901, c. 89, s. 41; Rev., s. 4312; C.S., s. 5933; 1933, c. 165, s. 3; 1939, c. 263, s. 31/2; 1947, c. 505, s. 3; 1967, c. 775, s. 1; 1973, c. 793, s. 17; 1993 (Reg. Sess., 1994), c. 762, s. 4.)

§ 163-48. Maintenance of order at place of registration and voting.

The chief judge and judges of election shall enforce peace and good order in and about the place of registration and voting. They shall especially keep open and unobstructed the place at which voters or persons seeking to register or vote have access to the place of registration and voting. They shall prevent and stop improper practices and attempts to obstruct, intimidate, or interfere with any person in registering or voting. They shall protect challenger and witnesses against molestation and violence in the performance of their duties, and they may eject from the place of registration or voting any challenger or witness for violation of any provisions of the election laws. They shall prevent riots, violence, tumult, or disorder.

In the discharge of the duties prescribed in the preceding paragraph of this section, the chief judge and judges may call upon the sheriff, the police, or other peace officers to aid them in enforcing the law. They may order the arrest of any person violating any provision of the election laws, but such arrest shall not prevent the person arrested from registering or voting if he is entitled to do so. The sheriff, police officers, and other officers of the peace shall immediately obey and aid in the enforcement of any lawful order made by the precinct election officials in the enforcement of the election laws. The chief judge and judges of election of any precinct, or any two of such election officials, shall have the authority to deputize any person or persons as police officers to aid in maintaining order at the place of registration or voting. (1901, c. 89, s. 72; Rev., s. 4376; C.S., s. 5977; 1955, c. 871, s. 4; 1967, c. 775, s. 1; 1993 (Reg. Sess., 1994), c. 762, s. 21.)

§§ 163-49 through 163-53. Reserved for future codification purposes.

SUBCHAPTER III. QUALIFYING TO VOTE.

Article 6.

Qualifications of Voters.

§ 163-54. Registration a prerequisite to voting.

Only such persons as are legally registered shall be entitled to vote in any primary or election held under this Chapter. (1901, c. 89, s. 12; Rev., s. 4317; C. S., s. 5938; 1967, c. 775, s. 1.)

§ 163-55. Qualifications to vote; exclusion from electoral franchise.

(a) Residence Period for State Elections. - Every person born in the United States, and every person who has been naturalized, and who shall have resided in the State of North Carolina and in the precinct in which the person offers to vote for 30 days next preceding an election, shall, if otherwise qualified as prescribed in this Chapter, be qualified to vote in the precinct in which the person resides. Removal from one precinct to another in this State shall not operate to deprive any person of the right to vote in the precinct from which the person has removed until 30 days after the person's removal.

Except as provided in this Chapter, the following classes of persons shall not be allowed to vote in this State:

(1) Persons under 18 years of age.

(2) Any person adjudged guilty of a felony against this State or the United States, or adjudged guilty of a felony in another state that also would be a felony if it had been committed in this State, unless that person shall be first restored to the rights of citizenship in the manner prescribed by law.

(b) Precincts. - For purposes of qualification to vote in an election, a person's residence in a precinct shall be determined in accordance with G.S. 163-57. Qualification to vote in referenda shall be treated the same as qualification for elections to fill offices.

(c) Elections. - For purposes of the 30-day residence requirement to vote in an election in subsection (a) of this section, the term "election" means the day of the primary, second primary, general election, special election, or referendum. (19th amendt. U.S. Const.; amendt. State Const., 1920; 1901, c. 89, ss. 14, 15; Rev., ss. 4315, 4316; C.S., ss. 5936, 5937; Ex. Sess. 1920, c. 18, s. 1; 1933, c. 165, s. 4; 1945, c. 758, s. 7; 1955, c. 871, s. 2; 1967, c. 775, s. 1; 1971, c. 1231, s. 1; 1973, c. 793, s. 18; 2005-2, s. 2; 2008-150, s. 5(a); 2009-541, s. 5; 2013-381, s. 49.1.)

§ 163-56. Repealed by Session Laws 1973, c. 793, s. 19.

§ 163-57. Residence defined for registration and voting.

All election officials in determining the residence of a person offering to register or vote, shall be governed by the following rules, so far as they may apply:

(1) That place shall be considered the residence of a person in which that person's habitation is fixed, and to which, whenever that person is absent, that person has the intention of returning.

    a. In the event that a person's habitation is divided by a State, county, municipal, precinct, ward, or other election district, then the location of the bedroom or usual sleeping area for that person with respect to the location of the boundary line at issue shall be controlling as the residency of that person.

    b. If the person disputes the determination of residency, the person may request a hearing before the county board of elections making the determination of residency. The procedures for notice of hearing and the conduct of the hearing shall be as provided in G.S. 163-86. The presentation of an accurate and current determination of a person's residence and the boundary line at issue by map or other means available shall constitute prima facie evidence of the geographic location of the residence of that person.

    c. In the event that a person's residence is not a traditional residence associated with real property, then the location of the usual sleeping area for that person shall be controlling as to the residency of that person. Residence shall be broadly construed to provide all persons with the opportunity to register and to vote, including stating a mailing address different from residence address.

(2) A person shall not be considered to have lost that person's residence if that person leaves home and goes into another state, county, municipality, precinct, ward, or other election district of this State, for temporary purposes only, with the intention of returning.

(3) A person shall not be considered to have gained a residence in any county, municipality, precinct, ward, or other election district of this State, into which that person comes for temporary purposes only, without the intention of

making that county, municipality, precinct, ward, or other election district a permanent place of abode.

(4) If a person removes to another state or county, municipality, precinct, ward, or other election district within this State, with the intention of making that state, county, municipality, precinct, ward, or other election district a permanent residence, that person shall be considered to have lost residence in the state, county, municipality, precinct, ward, or other election district from which that person has removed.

(5) If a person removes to another state or county, municipality, precinct, ward, or other election district within this State, with the intention of remaining there an indefinite time and making that state, county, municipality, precinct, ward, or other election district that person's place of residence, that person shall be considered to have lost that person's place of residence in this State, county, municipality, precinct, ward, or other election district from which that person has removed, notwithstanding that person may entertain an intention to return at some future time.

(6) If a person goes into another state, county, municipality, precinct, ward, or other election district, or into the District of Columbia, and while there exercises the right of a citizen by voting in an election, that person shall be considered to have lost residence in that State, county, municipality, precinct, ward, or other election district from which that person removed.

(7) School teachers who remove to a county, municipality, precinct, ward, or other election district in this State for the purpose of teaching in the schools of that county temporarily and with the intention or expectation of returning during vacation periods to live where their parents or other relatives reside in this State and who do not have the intention of becoming residents of the county, municipality, precinct, ward, or other election district to which they have moved to teach, for purposes of registration and voting shall be considered residents of the county, municipality, precinct, ward, or other election district in which their parents or other relatives reside.

(8) If a person removes to the District of Columbia or other federal territory to engage in the government service, that person shall not be considered to have lost residence in this State during the period of such service unless that person votes in the place to which the person removed, and the place at which that person resided at the time of that person's removal shall be considered and held to be the place of residence.

(9) If a person removes to a county, municipality, precinct, ward, or other election district to engage in the service of the State government, that person shall not be considered to have lost residence in the county, municipality, precinct, ward, or other election district from which that person removed, unless that person votes in the place to which the person removed, and the place at which that person resided at the time of that person's removal shall be considered and held to be the place of residence.

(9a) The establishment of a secondary residence by an elected official outside the district of the elected official shall not constitute prima facie evidence of a change of residence.

(10) For the purpose of voting a spouse shall be eligible to establish a separate domicile.

(11) So long as a student intends to make the student's home in the community where the student is physically present for the purpose of attending school while the student is attending school and has no intent to return to the student's former home after graduation, the student may claim the college community as the student's domicile. The student need not also intend to stay in the college community beyond graduation in order to establish domicile there. This subdivision is intended to codify the case law. (19th amendt. U.S. Const.; amendt. State Const., 1920; 1901, c. 89, s. 15; Rev., s. 4316; C.S., s. 5937; Ex. Sess. 1920, c. 18, s. 1; 1933, c. 165, s. 4; 1945, c. 758, s. 7; 1955, c. 871, s. 2; 1967, c. 775, s. 1; 1981, c. 184; 1991, c. 727, s. 5.1; 1993 (Reg. Sess., 1994), c. 762, s. 22; 2001-316, s. 1; 2005-428, s. 3(b); 2006-262, s. 2.1.)

§ 163-58: Repealed by Session Laws 1985, c. 563, s. 3.

§ 163-59. Right to participate or vote in party primary.

No person shall be entitled to vote or otherwise participate in the primary election of any political party unless that person complies with all of the following:

(1) Is a registered voter.

(2) Has declared and has had recorded on the registration book or record the fact that the voter affiliates with the political party in whose primary the voter proposes to vote or participate.

(3) Is in good faith a member of that party.

Notwithstanding the previous paragraph, any unaffiliated voter who is authorized under G.S. 163-119 may also vote in the primary if the voter is otherwise eligible to vote in that primary except for subdivisions (2) and (3) of the previous paragraph.

Any person who will become qualified by age to register and vote in the general election for which the primary is held, even though not so qualified by the date of the primary, shall be entitled to register for the primary and general election prior to the primary and then to vote in the primary after being registered. Such person may register not earlier than 60 days nor later than the last day for making application to register under G.S. 163-82.6(c) prior to the primary. In addition, persons who will become qualified by age to register and vote in the general election for which the primary is held, who do not register during the special period may register to vote after such period as if they were qualified on the basis of age, but until they are qualified by age to vote, they may vote only in primary elections. (1915, c. 101, s. 5; 1917, c. 218; C.S., s. 6027; 1959, c. 1203, s. 6; 1967, c. 775, s. 1; 1971, c. 1166, s. 4; 1973, c. 793, s. 20; 1981, c. 33, s. 1; 1983, c. 324, s. 3; 1987, c. 408, s. 4; c. 457, s. 1; 1991 (Reg. Sess., 1992), c. 1032, s. 5; 1993 (Reg. Sess., 1994), c. 762, s. 23; 2007-391, s. 28; 2008-187, s. 33(a); 2009-541, s. 6; 2013-381, s. 16.2.)

§§ 163-60 through 163-64. Reserved for future codification purposes.

Article 7.

Registration of Voters.

§§ 163-65 through 163-82: Repealed by Session Laws 1993 (Reg. Sess., 1994), c. 762, s. 1.

Article 7A.

Registration of Voters.

§ 163-82.1. General principles of voter registration.

(a) Prerequisite to Voting. - No person shall be permitted to vote who has not been registered under the provisions of this Article or registered as previously provided by law.

(b) County Board's Duty to Register. - A county board of elections shall register, in accordance with this Article, every person qualified to vote in that county who makes an application in accordance with this Article.

(c) Permanent Registration. - Every person registered to vote by a county board of elections in accordance with this Article shall remain registered until:

(1) The registrant requests in writing to the county board of elections to be removed from the list of registered voters; or

(2) The registrant becomes disqualified through death, conviction of a felony, or removal out of the county; or

(3) The county board of elections determines, through the procedure outlined in G.S. 163-82.14, that it can no longer confirm where the voter resides.

(d) Repealed by Session Laws 2013-381, s. 12.1(a), effective September 1, 2013. (1953, c. 843; 1955, c. 800; 1963, c. 303, s. 1; 1965, c. 1116, s. 1; 1967, c. 775, s. 1; 1973, c. 793, s. 25; 1975, c. 395; 1981, c. 39, s. 1; c. 87, s. 1; c. 308, s. 1; 1985, c. 211, ss. 1, 2; 1993 (Reg. Sess., 1994), c. 762, s. 2; 2009-541, s. 7(a); 2013-381, s. 12.1(a).)

§ 163-82.2. Chief State Election Official.

The Executive Director of the State Board of Elections is the "Chief State Election Official" of North Carolina for purposes of P.L. 103-31, The National Voter Registration Act of 1993, subsequently referred to in this Article as the "National Voter Registration Act". As such the Executive Director is responsible for coordination of State responsibilities under the National Voter Registration Act. (1993 (Reg. Sess., 1994), c. 762, s. 2; 2001-319, s. 11.)

§ 163-82.3. Voter registration application forms.

(a) Form Developed by State Board of Elections. - The State Board of Elections shall develop an application form for voter registration. Any person may use the form to apply to do any of the following:

(1) Register to vote.

(2) Change party affiliation or unaffiliated status.

(3) Report a change of address within a county.

(4) Report a change of name.

(5) Repealed by Session Laws 2013-381, s. 12.1(b), effective September 1, 2013.

The county board of elections for the county where the applicant resides shall accept the form as application for any of those purposes if the form is submitted as set out in G.S. 163-82.3.

(b) Interstate Form. - The county board of elections where an applicant resides shall accept as application for any of the purposes set out in subsection (a) of this section the interstate registration form designed by the Federal Election Commission pursuant to section 9 of the National Voter Registration Act, if the interstate form is submitted in accordance with G.S. 163-82.6.

(c) Agency Application Form. - The county board of elections where an applicant resides shall accept as application for any of the purposes set out in subsection (a) of this section a form developed pursuant to G.S. 163-82.19 or G.S. 163-82.20. (1991 (Reg. Sess., 1992), c. 1044, s. 18(a); 1993, c. 74, s. 1; 1993 (Reg. Sess., 1994), c. 762, s. 2; 2009-541, s. 8(a); 2013-381, s. 12.1(b).)

§ 163-82.4. Contents of application form.

(a) Information Requested of Applicant. - The form required by G.S. 163-82.3(a) shall request the applicant's:

(1) Name,

(2) Date of birth,

(3) Residence address,

(4) County of residence,

(5) Date of application,

(6) Gender,

(7) Race,

(7a) Ethnicity,

(8) Political party affiliation, if any, in accordance with subsection (c) of this section,

(9) Telephone number (to assist the county board of elections in contacting the voter if needed in processing the application),

(10) Drivers license number or, if the applicant does not have a drivers license number, the last four digits of the applicant's social security number,

and any other information the State Board finds is necessary to enable officials of the county where the person resides to satisfactorily process the application. The form shall require the applicant to state whether currently registered to vote anywhere, and at what address, so that any prior registration can be cancelled. The portions of the form concerning race and ethnicity shall include as a choice any category shown by the most recent decennial federal census to compose at least one percent (1%) of the total population of North Carolina. The county board shall make a diligent effort to complete for the registration records any information requested on the form that the applicant does not complete, but no application shall be denied because an applicant does not state race, ethnicity, gender, or telephone number. The application shall conspicuously state that provision of the applicant's telephone number is optional. If the county board maintains voter records on computer, the free list provided under this subsection shall include telephone numbers if the county board enters the telephone number into its computer records of voters.

(a1)   No Drivers License or Social Security Number Issued. - The State Board shall assign a unique identifier number to an applicant for voter registration if the applicant has not been issued either a current and valid drivers license or a social security number. That unique identifier number shall serve to identify that applicant for voter registration purposes.

(b)   Notice of Requirements, Attestation, Notice of Penalty, and Notice of Confidentiality. - The form required by G.S. 163-82.3(a) shall contain, in uniform type, the following:

(1)   A statement that specifies each eligibility requirement (including citizenship) and an attestation that the applicant meets each such requirement, with a requirement for the signature of the applicant, under penalty of a Class I felony under G.S. 163-275(13).

(2)   A statement that, if the applicant declines to register to vote, the fact that the applicant has declined to register will remain confidential and will be used only for voter registration purposes.

(3)   A statement that, if the applicant does register to vote, the office at which the applicant submits a voter registration application will remain confidential and will be used only for voter registration purposes.

(c)   Party Affiliation or Unaffiliated Status. - The application form described in G.S. 163-82.3(a) shall provide a place for the applicant to state a preference to be affiliated with one of the political parties in G.S. 163-96, or a preference to be an "unaffiliated" voter. Every person who applies to register shall state his preference. If the applicant fails to declare a preference for a party or for unaffiliated status, that person shall be listed as "unaffiliated", except that if the person is already registered to vote in the county and that person's registration already contains a party affiliation, the county board shall not change the registrant's status to "unaffiliated" unless the registrant clearly indicates a desire in accordance with G.S. 163-82.17 for such a change. An unaffiliated registrant shall not be eligible to vote in any political party primary, except as provided in G.S. 163-119, but may vote in any other primary or general election. The application form shall so state.

(d) Citizenship and Age Questions. - Voter registration application forms shall include all of the following:

(1) The following question and statement:

a. "Are you a citizen of the United States of America?" and boxes for the applicant to check to indicate whether the applicant is or is not a citizen of the United States.

b. "If you checked 'no' in response to this question, do not submit this form.

(2) The following question and statement:

a. "Will you be 18 years of age on or before election day?" and boxes for the applicant to check to indicate whether the applicant will be 18 years of age or older on election day.

b. Repealed by Session Laws 2013-381, s. 12.1(c), effective September 1, 2013.

c. "If you checked 'no' in response to this question, do not submit this form.

(3) Repealed by Session Laws 2009-541, s. 9(a), effective January 1, 2010.

(e) Correcting Registration Forms. - If the voter fails to complete any required item on the voter registration form but provides enough information on the form to enable the county board of elections to identify and contact the voter, the voter shall be notified of the omission and given the opportunity to complete the form at least by 5:00 P.M. on the day before the county canvass as set in G.S. 163-182.5(b). If the voter corrects that omission within that time and is determined by the county board of elections to be eligible to vote, the board shall permit the voter to vote. If the information is not corrected by election day, the voter shall be allowed to vote a provisional official ballot. If the correct information is provided to the county board of elections by at least 5:00 P.M. on the day before the county canvass, the board shall count any portion of the provisional official ballot that the voter is eligible to vote. (1901, c. 89, s. 12; Rev., s. 4319; C.S., s. 5940; Ex. Sess. 1920, c. 93; 1933, c. 165, s. 5; 1951, c. 984, s. 1; 1953, c. 843; 1955, c. 800; c. 871, s. 2; 1957, c. 784, s. 2; 1963, c. 303, s. 1; 1967, c. 775, s. 1; 1971, c. 1166, s. 6; 1973, c. 793, s. 27; c. 1223, s. 3; 1975, c. 234, s. 2; 1979, c. 135, s. 1; c. 539, ss. 1-3; c. 797, ss. 1, 2; 1981, c. 222; c. 308, s. 2; 1991 (Reg. Sess., 1992), c. 1044, s. 18(a); 1993, c. 74, s. 1;

1993 (Reg. Sess., 1994), c. 762, s. 2; 1999-424, s. 7(c), (d); 1999-453, s. 8(a); 2003-226, s. 9; 2004-127, s. 4; 2005-428, s. 15; 2007-391, s. 20; 2008-187, s. 33(a); 2009-541, s. 9(a); 2013-381, s. 12.1(c).)

§ 163-82.5. Distribution of application forms.

The State Board of Elections shall make the forms described in G.S. 163-82.3 available for distribution through governmental and private entities, with particular emphasis on making them available for organized voter registration drives. (1991 (Reg. Sess., 1992), c. 1044, s. 18(a); 1993, c. 74, s. 1; 1993 (Reg. Sess., 1994), c. 762, s. 2.)

§ 163-82.6. Acceptance of application forms.

(a) How the Form May Be Submitted. - The county board of elections shall accept any form described in G.S. 163-82.3 if the applicant submits the form by mail, facsimile transmission, transmission of a scanned document, or in person. The applicant may delegate the submission of the form to another person. Any person who communicates to an applicant acceptance of that delegation shall deliver that form so that it is received by the appropriate county board of elections in time to satisfy the registration deadline in subdivision (1) or (2) of subsection (c) of this section for the next election. It shall be a Class 2 misdemeanor for any person to communicate to the applicant acceptance of that delegation and then fail to make a good faith effort to deliver the form so that it is received by the county board of elections in time to satisfy the registration deadline in subdivision (1) or (2) of subsection (c) of this section for the next election. It shall be an affirmative defense to a charge of failing to make a good faith effort to deliver a delegated form by the registration deadline that the delegatee informed the applicant that the form would not likely be delivered in time for the applicant to vote in the next election. It shall be a Class 2 misdemeanor for any person to sell or attempt to sell a completed voter registration form or to condition its delivery upon payment.

(a1) Misdemeanors. - It shall be a Class 2 misdemeanor for any person to do any of the following:

(1) To communicate to the applicant acceptance of the delegation described in subsection (a) of this section and then fail to make a good faith effort to deliver the form so that it is received by the county board of elections in

time to satisfy the registration deadline in subdivision (1) or (2) of subsection (c) of this section for the next election. It shall be an affirmative defense to a charge of failing to make a good faith effort to deliver a delegated form by the registration deadline that the delegatee informed the applicant that the form would not likely be delivered in time for the applicant to vote in the next election.

(2) To sell or attempt to sell a completed voter registration form or to condition its delivery upon payment.

(3) To change a person's information on a voter registration form prior to its delivery to a county board of elections.

(4) To coerce a person into marking a party affiliation other than the party affiliation the person desires.

(5) To offer a person a voter registration form that has a party affiliation premarked unless the person receiving the form has requested the premarking.

(b) Signature. - The form shall be valid only if signed by the applicant. An electronically captured signature, including signatures on applications generated by computer programs of third-party groups, shall not be valid on a voter registration form, except as provided in Article 21A of this Chapter. Notwithstanding the provisions of this subsection, an electronically captured image of the signature of a voter on an electronic voter registration form offered by a State agency shall be considered a valid signature for all purposes for which a signature on a paper voter registration form is used.

(c) Registration Deadlines for a Primary or Election. - In order to be valid for a primary or election, the form:

(1) If submitted by mail, must be postmarked at least 25 days before the primary or election, except that any mailed application on which the postmark is missing or unclear is validly submitted if received in the mail not later than 20 days before the primary or election,

(2) If submitted in person, by facsimile transmission, or by transmission of a scanned document, must be received by the county board of elections by a time established by that board, but no earlier than 5:00 P.M., on the twenty-fifth day before the primary or election,

(3) If submitted through a delegatee who violates the duty set forth in subsection (a) of this section, must be signed by the applicant and given to the delegatee not later than 25 days before the primary or election, except as provided in subsection (d) of this section.

(c1) If the application is submitted by facsimile transmission or transmission of a scanned document, a permanent copy of the completed, signed form shall be delivered to the county board no later than 20 days before the election.

(d) Instances When Person May Register and Vote on Primary or Election Day. - If a person has become qualified to register and vote between the twenty-fifth day before a primary or election and primary or election day, then that person may apply to register on primary or election day by submitting an application form described in G.S. 163-82.3(a) or (b) to:

(1) A member of the county board of elections;

(2) The county director of elections; or

(3) The chief judge or a judge of the precinct in which the person is eligible to vote,

and, if the application is approved, that person may vote the same day. The official in subdivisions (1) through (3) of this subsection to whom the application is submitted shall decide whether the applicant is eligible to vote. The applicant shall present to the official written or documentary evidence that the applicant is the person he represents himself to be. The official, if in doubt as to the right of the applicant to register, may require other evidence satisfactory to that official as to the applicant's qualifications. If the official determines that the person is eligible, the person shall be permitted to vote in the primary or election and the county board shall add the person's name to the list of registered voters. If the official denies the application, the person shall be permitted to vote a challenged ballot under the provisions of G.S. 163-88.1, and may appeal the denial to the full county board of elections. The State Board of Elections shall promulgate rules for the county boards of elections to follow in hearing appeals for denial of primary or election day applications to register. No person shall be permitted to register on the day of a second primary unless he shall have become qualified to register and vote between the date of the first primary and the date of the succeeding second primary.

(e) For purposes of subsection (d) of this section, persons who "become qualified to register and vote" during a time period:

(1) Include those who during that time period are naturalized as citizens of the United States or who are restored to citizenship after a conviction of a felony; but

(2) Do not include persons who reach the age of 18 during that time period, if those persons were eligible to register while 17 years old during an earlier period.

(f) The county board of elections shall forward by electronic means any application submitted for the purpose of preregistration to the State Board of Elections. No later than 60 days prior to the first election in which the applicant will be legally entitled to vote, the State Board of Elections shall notify the appropriate county board of elections to verify the qualifications and address of the applicant in accordance with G.S. 163-82.7. (1901, c. 89, ss. 18, 21; Rev., ss. 4322, 4323; C.S., ss. 5946, 5947; 1923, c. 111, s. 3; 1933, c. 165, s. 5; 1947, c. 475; 1953, c. 843; 1955, c. 800; 1957, c. 784, ss., 3, 4; 1961, c. 382; 1963, c. 303, ss. 1, 2; 1967, c. 761, s. 3; c. 775, s. 1; 1969, c. 750, ss. 1, 2; 1977, c. 626, s. 1; 1979, c. 539, s. 5; c. 766, s., 2; 1981, c. 33, s. 2; 1981 (Reg. Sess., 1982), c. 1265, s. 6; 1983, c. 553; 1985, c. 260, s. 1; 1991, c. 363, s. 1; 1991 (Reg. Sess., 1992), c. 1032, s. 1; 1991 (Reg. Sess., 1992), c. 1044, s. 18(a); 1993, c. 74, s. 1; 1993 (Reg. Sess., 1994), c. 762, s. 2; 1995, c. 243, s. 1; 1997-456, s. 27; 1999-426, s. 1(a), (b); 2001-315, s. 1; 2001-319, s. 6(a); 2003-226, s. 4; 2004-127, s. 9(a); 2007-253, s. 2; 2007-391, s. 16(a); 2008-150, s. 5(d), (e); 2009-541, s. 10(a); 2013-381, ss. 13.1, 16.3.)

§ 163-82.6A. Address and name changes at one-stop sites.

(a) through (d) Repealed by Session Laws 2013-381, s. 16.1, effective January 1, 2014.

(e) Change of Registration at One-Stop Voting Site. - A person who is already registered to vote in the county may update the information in the registration record in accordance with procedures prescribed by the State Board of Elections, but an individual's party affiliation may not be changed during the one-stop voting period before any first or second partisan primary in which the individual is eligible to vote.

(f) Repealed by Session Laws 2013-381, s. 16.1, effective January 1, 2014. (2007-253, s. 1; 2009-541, s. 11; 2013-381, ss. 16.1, 16.1A.)

§ 163-82.7. Verification of qualifications and address of applicant; denial or approval of application.

(a) Tentative Determination of Qualification. - When a county board of elections receives an application for registration submitted pursuant to G.S. 163-82.6, the board either:

(1) Shall make a determination that the applicant is not qualified to vote at the address given, or

(2) Shall make a tentative determination that the applicant is qualified to vote at the address given, subject to the mail verification notice procedure outlined in subsection (c) of this section

within a reasonable time after receiving the application.

(b) Denial of Registration. - If the county board of elections makes a determination pursuant to subsection (a) of this section that the applicant is not qualified to vote at the address given, the board shall send, by certified mail, a notice of denial of registration. The notice of denial shall contain the date on which registration was denied, and shall be mailed within two business days after denial. The notice of denial shall inform the applicant of alternatives that the applicant may pursue to exercise the franchise. If the applicant disagrees with the denial, the applicant may appeal the decision under G.S. 163-82.18.

(c) Verification of Address by Mail. - If the county board of elections tentatively determines that the applicant is qualified to vote at the address given, then the county board shall send a notice to the applicant, by nonforwardable mail, at the address the applicant provides on the application form. The notice shall state that the county will register the applicant to vote if the Postal Service does not return the notice as undeliverable to the county board. The notice shall also inform the applicant of the precinct and voting place to which the applicant will be assigned if registered.

(d) Approval of Application. - If the Postal Service does not return the notice as undeliverable, the county board shall register the applicant to vote.

(e) Second Notice if First Notice Is Returned as Undeliverable. - If the Postal Service returns the notice as undeliverable, the county board shall send a second notice by nonforwardable mail to the same address to which the first was sent. If the second notice is not returned as undeliverable, the county board shall register the applicant to vote.

(f) Denial of Application Based on Lack of Verification of Address. - If the Postal Service returns as undeliverable the notice sent by nonforwardable mail pursuant to subsection (e) of this section, the county board shall deny the application. The county board need not try to notify the applicant further.

(g) Voting When Verification Process Is Incomplete. - In cases where an election occurs before the process of verification outlined in this section has had time to be completed, the county board of elections shall be guided by the following rules:

(1) If the county board has made a tentative determination that an applicant is qualified to vote under subsection (a) of this section, then that person shall not be denied the right to vote in person in an election unless the Postal Service has returned as undeliverable two notices to the applicant: one mailed pursuant to subsection (c) of this section and one mailed pursuant to subsection (e) of this section. This subdivision does not preclude a challenge to the voter's qualifications under Article 8 of this Chapter.

(2) If the Postal Service has returned as undeliverable a notice sent within 25 days before the election to the applicant under subsection (c) of this section, then the applicant may vote only in person in that first election and may not vote by absentee ballot except in person under G.S. 163-227.2. The county board of elections shall establish a procedure at the voting site for:

a. Obtaining the correct address of any person described in this subdivision who appears to vote in person; and

b. Assuring that the person votes in the proper place and in the proper contests.

If a notice mailed under subsection (c) or subsection (e) of this section is returned as undeliverable after a person has already voted by absentee ballot, then that person's ballot may be challenged in accordance with G.S. 163-89.

(3) If a notice sent pursuant to subsection (c) or (e) of this section is returned by the Postal Service as undeliverable after a person has already voted in an election, then the county board shall treat the person as a registered voter but shall send a confirmation mailing pursuant to G.S. 163-82.14(d)(2) and remove or retain the person on the registration records in accordance with that subdivision. (1991 (Reg. Sess., 1992), c. 1044, s. 18(a); 1993, c. 74, s. 1; 1993 (Reg. Sess., 1994), c. 762, s. 2; 1999-455, s. 16.)

§ 163-82.7A. (Effective January 1, 2016 - see note) Declaration of religious objection to photograph.

(a) At the time of approval of the application to register to vote, a voter with a sincerely held religious objection to being photographed may execute a declaration before an election official to that effect to be incorporated as part of the official record of voter registration.

(b) At any time after the voter has registered to vote that the voter has determined the voter has a sincerely held religious objection to being photographed, that voter may execute a declaration before an election official to be incorporated as part of the official record of that voter's voter registration.

(c) At any time after a voter has executed a declaration before an election official under this section and that voter no longer has a sincerely held religious objection to being photographed, that voter may request the cancellation of the declaration in writing to the county board.

(d) All declarations under subsections (a) and (b) of this section shall include a statement by the voter that the voter has a sincerely held religious objection to being photographed and a requirement for the signature of the voter, which includes a notice that a false or fraudulent declaration is a Class I felony pursuant to G.S. 163-275(13).

(e) The State Board shall adopt rules to establish a standard form for the administration of this section. (2013-381, s. 2.3.)

§ 163-82.8. Voter registration cards.

(a) Authority to Issue Card. - With the approval of the board of county commissioners, the county board of elections may issue to each voter in the county a voter registration card, or may issue cards to all voters registered after January 1, 1995.

(b)   Content and Format of Card. - At a minimum, the voter registration card shall:

(1)   List the voter's name, address, and voting place;

(2)   Contain the address and telephone number of the county board of elections, along with blanks to report a change of address within the county, change of name, and change of party affiliation; and

(3)   Be wallet size.

No voter registration card may be issued by a county board of elections unless the State Board of Elections has approved the format of the card.

(c)   Ways County Board and Registrant May Use Card. - If the county board of elections issues voter registration cards, the county board may use that card as a notice of tentative approval of the voter's application pursuant to G.S. 163-82.7(c), provided that the mailing contains the statements and information required in that subsection. The county board may also satisfy the requirements of G.S. 163-82.15(b), 163-82.16(b), or 163-82.17(b) by sending the registrant a replacement of the voter registration card to verify change of address, change of name, or change of party affiliation. A registrant may use the card to report a change of address, change of name, or change of party affiliation, satisfying G.S. 163-82.15, 163-82.16, or 163-82.17.

(d)   Card as Evidence of Registration. - A voter registration card shall be evidence of registration but shall not preclude a challenge as permitted by law.

(e)   Display of Card May Not Be Required to Vote. - No county board of elections may require that a voter registration card be displayed in order to vote. (1901, c. 89, ss. 18, 21; Rev., ss. 4322, 4323; C.S., ss. 5946, 5947; 1923, c. 111, s. 3; 1933, c. 165, s. 5; 1947, c. 475; 1953, c. 843; 1955, c. 800; 1957, c. 784, ss. 3, 4; 1961, c. 382; 1963, c. 303, ss. 1, 2; 1967, c. 761, s. 3; c. 775, s. 1; 1969, c. 750, ss. 1, 2; 1977, c. 626, s. 1; 1979, c. 539, s. 5; c. 766, s. 2; 1981, c. 33, s. 2; 1981 (Reg. Sess., 1982), c. 1265, s. 6; 1983, c. 553; 1985, c. 260, s. 1; 1991, c. 363, s. 1; 1991 (Reg. Sess., 1992), c. 1032, s. 1; 1993 (Reg. Sess., 1994), c. 762, s. 2.)

§ 163-82.9. Cancellation of prior registration.

If an applicant indicates on an application form described in G.S. 163-82.3 a current registration to vote in any other county, municipality, or state, the county board of elections, upon registering the person to vote, shall send a notice to the appropriate officials in the other county, municipality, or state and shall ask them to cancel the person's voter registration there. If an applicant completes an application form described in G.S. 163-82.3 except that the applicant neglects to complete the portion of the form that authorizes cancellation of previous registration in another county, the State Board of Elections shall notify the county board of elections in the previous county of the new registration, and the board in the previous county shall cancel the registration. The State Board of Elections shall adopt rules to prevent disenfranchisement in the implementation of this section. Those rules shall include adequate notice to the person whose previous registration is to be cancelled. (1973, c. 793, s. 28; c. 1223, s. 4; 1977, c. 265, s. 3; 1983, c. 411, ss. 1, 2; 1993 (Reg. Sess., 1994), c. 762, s. 2; 1995, c. 509, s. 115; 2005-428, s. 9.)

§ 163-82.10. Official record of voter registration.

(a) Official Record. - The State voter registration system is the official voter registration list for the conduct of all elections in the State. The State Board of Elections and the county board of elections may keep copies of voter registration data, including voter registration applications, in any medium and format expressly approved by the Department of Cultural Resources pursuant to standards and conditions established by the Department and mutually agreed to by the Department and the State Board of Elections. A completed and signed registration application form, if available, described in G.S. 163-82.3, once approved by the county board of elections, becomes backup to the official registration record of the voter. Full or partial social security numbers, dates of birth, the identity of the public agency at which the voter registered under G.S. 163-82.20, any electronic mail address submitted under Article 21A of this Chapter, and drivers license numbers that may be generated in the voter registration process, by either the State Board of Elections or a county board of elections, are confidential and shall not be considered public records and subject to disclosure to the general public under Chapter 132 of the General Statutes. Cumulative data based on those items of information may be publicly disclosed as long as information about any individual cannot be discerned from the disclosed data. Disclosure of information in violation of this subsection shall not give rise to a civil cause of action. This limitation of liability does not apply to the disclosure of information in violation of this subsection as a result of gross negligence, wanton conduct, or intentional wrongdoing that would otherwise be actionable. The signature of the voter, either on the paper application or an electronically captured image of it, may be viewed by the public but may not be copied or traced except by election officials for election administration purposes. Any such copy or tracing is not a public record.

(a1) Paperless, Instant Electronic Transfer. - The application described in G.S. 163-82.3 may be either a paper hard copy or an electronic document.

(b) Access to Registration Records. - Upon request by that person, the county board of elections shall provide to any person a list of the registered voters of the county or of any precinct or precincts in the county. The county board may furnish selective lists according to party affiliation, gender, race, date of registration, precinct name, precinct identification code, congressional district, senate district, representative district, and, where applicable, county commissioner district, city governing board district, fire district, soil and water conservation district, and voter history including primary, general, and special districts, or any other reasonable category. No list produced under this section shall contain a voter's date of birth. However, lists may be produced according to voters' ages. Both the following shall apply to all counties:

(1) The county board of elections shall make the voter registration information available to the public on electronic or magnetic medium. For purposes of this section, "electronic or magnetic medium" means any of the media in use by the State Board of Elections at the time of the request.

(2) Information requested on electronic or magnetic medium shall contain the following: voter name, county voter identification number, residential address, mailing address, sex, race, age but not date of birth, party affiliation, precinct name, precinct identification code, congressional district, senate district, representative district, and, where applicable, county commissioner district, city governing board district, fire district, soil and water conservation district, and any other district information available, and voter history including primary, general, and special districts, or any other reasonable category.

The county board shall require each person to whom a list is furnished to reimburse the board for the actual cost incurred in preparing it, except as provided in subsection (c) of this section. Actual cost for the purpose of this section shall not include the cost of any equipment or any imputed overhead expenses. When furnishing information under this subsection to a purchaser on a magnetic medium provided by the county board or the purchaser, the county board may impose a service charge of up to twenty-five dollars ($25.00).

(c) Free Lists. - A county board shall provide, upon written request, one free list of all the registered voters in the county to the State chair of each political party and to the county chair of each political party once in every odd-numbered year, once during the first six calendar months of every even-numbered year, and once during the latter six calendar months of every even-numbered year. Each free list shall include the name, address, gender, age but not date of birth, race, political affiliation, voting history, precinct, precinct name, precinct identification code, congressional district, senate district, representative district, and, where applicable, county commissioner district, city governing board district, fire district, soil and water conservation district, and voter history including primary, general, and special districts of each registered voter. All free lists shall be provided as soon as practicable on one of any electronic or magnetic media, but no later than 30 days after written request. Each State party chair shall provide the information on the media received from the county boards or a copy of the media containing the data itself to candidates of that party who request the data in writing. As used in this section, "political party" means a political party as defined in G.S. 163-96.

(d) Exception for Address of Certain Registered Voters. - Notwithstanding subsections (b) and (c) of this section, if a registered voter submits to the county board of elections a copy of a protective order without attachments, if any, issued to that person under G.S. 50B-3 or a lawful order of any court of competent jurisdiction restricting the access or contact of one or more persons with a registered voter or a current and valid Address Confidentiality Program authorization card issued pursuant to the provisions of Chapter 15C of the General Statutes, accompanied by a signed statement that the voter has good reason to believe that the physical safety of the voter or a member of the voter's family residing with the voter would be jeopardized if the voter's address were open to public inspection, that voter's address is a public record but shall be kept confidential as long as the protective order remains in effect or the voter remains a certified program participant in the Address Confidentiality Program. That voter's name, precinct, and the other data contained in that voter's registration record shall remain a public record. That voter's signed statement submitted under this subsection is a public record but shall be kept confidential as long as the protective order remains in effect or the voter remains a certified program participant in the Address Confidentiality Program. It is the responsibility of the voter to provide the county board with a copy of the valid protective order in effect or a current and valid Address Confidentiality Program authorization card issued pursuant to the provisions of Chapter 15C of the General Statutes. The voter's actual address shall be used for any election-related purpose by any board of elections. That voter's address shall be available for inspection by a law enforcement agency or by a person identified in a court order, if inspection of the address by that person is directed by that court order. It shall not be a violation of this section if the address of a voter who is participating in the Address Confidentiality Program is discovered by a member of the public in public records disclosed by a county board of elections prior to December 1, 2001. Addresses required to be kept confidential by this section shall not be made available to the jury commission under the provisions of G.S. 9-2. (1901, c. 89, s. 83; Rev., s. 4382; C.S., s. 6016; 1931, c. 80; 1939, c. 263, s. 31/2; 1949, c. 916, ss. 6, 7; 1953, c. 843; 1955, c. 800; 1959, c. 883; 1963, c. 303, s. 1; 1965, c. 1116, s. 1; 1967, c. 775, s. 1; 1973, c. 793, ss. 22, 25; 1975, c. 12; c. 395; 1979, 2nd Sess., c. 1242; 1981, c. 39, s. 1; c. 87, s.1; c. 308, s. 1; c. 656; 1983, c. 218, ss. 1, 2; 1985, c. 211, ss. 1, 2; c. 472, s. 1; 1993 (Reg. Sess., 1994), c. 762, s. 2; 1995 (Reg. Sess., 1996), c. 688, s. 2; 2001-396, s. 1; 2002-171, s. 8; 2003-226, ss. 2, 3; 2003-278, s. 6; 2004-127, s. 17(c); 2005-428, s. 10(a), (b); 2007-391, s. 19; 2008-187, s. 33(a); 2009-541, s. 12; 2011-182, s. 9.)

§ 163-82.10A. Permanent voter registration numbers.

The statewide voter registration system shall assign to each voter a unique registration number. That number shall be permanent for that voter and shall not be changed or reassigned by the county board of elections. (2001-319, s. 8.1(a); 2003-226, s. 10.)

§ 163-82.10B. Confidentiality of date of birth.

Boards of elections shall keep confidential the date of birth of every voter-registration applicant and registered voter, except in the following situations:

(1) When a voter has filed notice of candidacy for elective office under G.S. 163-106, 163-122, 163-123, or 163-294.2, or 163-323, has been nominated as a candidate under G.S. 163-98 or G.S. 163-114, or has otherwise formally become a candidate for elective office. The exception of this subdivision does not extend to an individual who meets the definition of "candidate" only by beginning a tentative candidacy by receiving funds or making payments or

giving consent to someone else to receive funds or transfer something of value for the purpose of exploring a candidacy.

(2)   When a voter is serving in an elective office.

(3)   When a voter has been challenged pursuant to Article 8 of this Chapter.

(4)   When a voter-registration applicant or registered voter expressly authorizes in writing the disclosure of that individual's date of birth.

(5)   When requested by a county jury commission established pursuant to G.S. 9-1 for purposes of preparing the master jury list in that county pursuant to G.S. 9-2.

The disclosure of an individual's age does not constitute disclosure of date of birth in violation of this section.

The county board of elections shall give precinct officials access to a voter's date of birth where necessary for election administration, consistent with the duty to keep dates of birth confidential.

Disclosure of a date of birth in violation of this section shall not give rise to a civil cause of action. This limitation of liability does not apply to the disclosure of a date of birth in violation of this subsection as a result of gross negligence, wanton conduct, or intentional wrongdoing that would otherwise be actionable. (2004-127, s. 17(a); 2013-166, s. 1.)

§ 163-82.11. Establishment of statewide computerized voter registration.

(a)   Statewide System as Official List. - The State Board of Elections shall develop and implement a statewide computerized voter registration system to facilitate voter registration and to provide a central database containing voter registration information for each county. The system shall serve as the single system for storing and managing the official list of registered voters in the State. The system shall serve as the official voter registration list for the conduct of all elections in the State. The system shall encompass both software development and purchasing of the necessary hardware for the central and distributed-network systems.

(b) Uses of Statewide System. - The State Board of Elections shall develop and implement the system so that each county board of elections can do all the following:

(1) Verify that an applicant to register in its county is not also registered in another county.

(2) Be notified automatically that a registered voter in its county has registered to vote in another county.

(3) Receive automatically data about a person who has applied to vote at a drivers license office or at another public agency that is authorized to accept voter registration applications.

(c) Compliance With Federal Law. - The State Board of Elections shall update the statewide computerized voter registration list and database to meet the requirements of section 303(a) of the Help America Vote Act of 2002 and to reflect changes when citizenship rights are restored under G.S. 13-1.

(d) Role of County and State Boards of Elections. - Each county board of elections shall be responsible for registering voters within its county according to law. Each county board of elections shall maintain its records by using the statewide computerized voter registration system in accordance with rules promulgated by the State Board of Elections. Each county board of elections shall enter through the computer system all additions, deletions, and changes in its list of registered voters promptly to the statewide computer system.

(e) Cooperation on List for Jury Commission. - The State Board of Elections shall assist the Division of Motor Vehicles in providing to the county jury commission of each county, as required by G.S. 20-43.4, a list of all registered voters in the county and all persons in the county with drivers license records. The list of registered voters provided by the State Board of Elections shall not include any registered voter who has been inactive for eight years or more. (1993 (Reg. Sess., 1994), c. 762, s. 2; 2003-226, s. 6; 2007-512, s. 4.)

§ 163-82.12. Promulgation of guidelines relating to computerized voter registration.

The State Board of Elections shall make all guidelines necessary to administer the statewide voter registration system established by this Article. All county boards of elections shall follow these guidelines and cooperate with the State Board of Elections in implementing guidelines. These guidelines shall include provisions for all of the following:

(1) Establishing, developing, and maintaining a computerized central voter registration file.

(2) Linking the central file through a network with computerized voter registration files in each of the counties.

(3) Interacting with the computerized drivers license records of the Division of Motor Vehicles and with the computerized records of other public agencies authorized to accept voter registration applications.

(4) Protecting and securing the data.

(5) Converting current voter registration records in the counties in computer files that can be used on the statewide computerized registration system.

(6) Enabling the statewide system to determine whether the voter identification information provided by an individual is valid.

(7) Enabling the statewide system to interact electronically with the Division of Motor Vehicles system to validate identification information.

(8) Enabling the Division of Motor Vehicles to provide real-time interface for the validation of the drivers license number and last four digits of the social security number.

(8b) Notifying voter-registration applicants whose drivers license or last four digits of social security number does not result in a validation, attempting to resolve the discrepancy, initiating investigations under G.S. 163-33(3) or challenges under Article 8 of this Chapter where warranted, and notifying any voters of the requirement under G.S. 163-166.12(b2) to present identification when voting.

(9) Enabling the statewide system to assign a unique identifier to each legally registered voter in the State.

(10) Enabling the State Board of Elections to assist the Division of Motor Vehicles in providing to the jury commission of each county, as required by G.S.

20-43.4, a list of all registered voters in the county and all persons in the county with drivers license records.

These guidelines shall not be considered to be rules subject to Article 2A of Chapter 150B of the General Statutes. However, the State Board shall publish in the North Carolina Register the guidelines and any changes to them after adoption, with that publication noted as information helpful to the public under G.S. 150B-21.17(a)(6). Copies of those guidelines shall be made available to the public upon request or otherwise by the State Board. (1993 (Reg. Sess., 1994), c. 762, s. 2; 2003-226, s. 7(a); 2007-391, s. 21(b); 2008-187, s. 33(a); 2013-410, s. 14(a).)

§ 163-82.13. Access to statewide voter registration file.

(a)   Free Copy for Political Parties. - Beginning January 1, 1996, the State Board of Elections shall make available free of charge, upon written request, one magnetic copy of the statewide computerized voter registration file to the chairman of each political party as defined in G.S. 163-96 as soon as practicable after the close of registration before every statewide primary and election. The file made available to the political party chairmen shall contain the name, address, gender, age but not date of birth, race, voting history, political affiliation, and precinct of every registered voter in the State. If a county board enters telephone numbers into its computer lists of registered voters, then the free list provided under this subsection shall include telephone numbers.

(b)   Copies for Sale to Others. - Beginning January 1, 1996, the State Board of Elections shall sell, upon written request, to other public and private organizations and persons magnetic copies of the statewide computerized voter registration file. The State Board of Elections may sell selective lists of registered voters according to county, congressional or legislative district, party affiliation, gender, age but not date of birth, race, date of registration, or any other reasonable category, or a combination of categories. The State Board of Elections shall require all persons to whom any list is furnished under this subsection to reimburse the board for the actual cost incurred in preparing it.(1993 (Reg. Sess., 1994), c. 762, s. 2; 2004-127, s. 17(d).)

§ 163-82.14. List maintenance.

(a) Uniform Program. - The State Board of Elections shall adopt a uniform program that makes a diligent effort not less than twice each year:

(1) To remove the names of ineligible voters from the official lists of eligible voters, and

(2) To update the addresses and other necessary data of persons who remain on the official lists of eligible voters.

That program shall be nondiscriminatory and shall comply with the provisions of the Voting Rights Act of 1965, as amended, and with the provisions of the National Voter Registration Act. The State Board of Elections, in addition to the methods set forth in this section, may use other methods toward the ends set forth in subdivisions (1) and (2) of this subsection, including address-updating services provided by the Postal Service, and entering into data sharing agreements with other states to cross-check information on voter registration and voting records. Any data sharing agreement shall require the other state or states to comply with G.S. 163-82.10 and G.S. 163-82.10B. Each county board of elections shall conduct systematic efforts to remove names from its list of registered voters in accordance with this section and with the program adopted by the State Board. The county boards of elections shall complete their list maintenance mailing program by April 15 of every odd-numbered year, unless the State Board of Elections approves a different date for the county.

(b) Death. - The Department of Health and Human Services shall furnish free of charge to the State Board of Elections every month, in a format prescribed by the State Board of Elections, the names of deceased persons who were residents of the State. The State Board of Elections shall distribute every month to each county board of elections the names on that list of deceased persons who were residents of that county. The Department of Health and Human Services shall base each list upon information supplied by death certifications it received during the preceding month. Upon the receipt of those names, each county board of elections shall remove from its voter registration records any person the list shows to be dead. Each county board of elections shall also remove from its voter registration records a person identified as deceased by a signed statement of a near relative or personal representative of the estate of the deceased voter. The county board need not send any notice to the address of the person so removed.

(c) Conviction of a Felony. -

(1) Report of Conviction Within the State. - The State Board of Elections, on or before the fifteenth day of every month, shall report to the county board of elections of that county the name, county of residence, and residence address if available, of each individual against whom a final judgment of conviction of a felony has been entered in that county in the preceding calendar month.

(2) Report of Federal Conviction. - The Executive Director of the State Board of Elections, upon receipt of a notice of conviction sent by a United States Attorney pursuant to section 8(g) of the National Voter Registration Act, shall notify the appropriate county boards of elections of the conviction.

(3) County Board's Duty Upon Receiving Report of Conviction. - When a county board of elections receives a notice pursuant to subdivision (1) or (2) of this subsection relating to a resident of that county and that person is registered to vote in that county, the board shall, after giving 30 days' written notice to the voter at his registration address, and if the voter makes no objection, remove the person's name from its registration records. If the voter notifies the county board of elections of his objection to the removal within 30 days of the notice, the chairman of the board of elections shall enter a challenge under G.S. 163-85(c)(5), and the notice the county board received pursuant to this subsection shall be prima facie evidence for the preliminary hearing that the registrant was convicted of a felony.

(d) Change of Address. - A county board of elections shall conduct a systematic program to remove from its list of registered voters those who have moved out of the county, and to update the registration records of persons who have moved within the county. The county board shall remove a person from its list if the registrant:

(1) Gives confirmation in writing of a change of address for voting purposes out of the county. "Confirmation in writing" for purposes of this subdivision shall include:

a. A report to the county board from the Department of Transportation or from a voter registration agency listed in G.S. 163-82.20 that the voter has reported a change of address for voting purposes outside the county;

b. A notice of cancellation received under G.S. 163-82.9; or

c. A notice of cancellation received from an election jurisdiction outside the State.

(2) Fails to respond to a confirmation mailing sent by the county board in accordance with this subdivision and does not vote or appear to vote in an election beginning on the date of the notice and ending on the day after the date of the second general election for the United States House of Representatives that occurs after the date of the notice. A county board sends a confirmation notice in accordance with this subdivision if the notice:

a. Is a postage prepaid and preaddressed return card, sent by forwardable mail, on which the registrant may state current address;

b. Contains or is accompanied by a notice to the effect that if the registrant did not change residence but remained in the county, the registrant should return the card not later than the deadline for registration by mail in G.S. 163-82.6(c)(1); and

c. Contains or is accompanied by information as to how the registrant may continue to be eligible to vote if the registrant has moved outside the county.

A county board shall send a confirmation mailing in accordance with this subdivision to every registrant after every congressional election if the county board has not confirmed the registrant's address by another means.

(3) Any registrant who is removed from the list of registered voters pursuant to this subsection shall be reinstated if the voter appears to vote and gives oral or written affirmation that the voter has not moved out of the county but has maintained residence continuously within the county. That person shall be allowed to vote as provided in G.S. 163-82.15(f). (1953, c. 843; 1955, c. 800; 1963, c. 303, s. 1; 1965, c. 1116, s. 1; 1967, c. 775, s. 1; 1973, c. 793, ss. 25, 28; c. 1223, s. 4; 1975, c. 395; 1977, c. 265, s. 3; 1981, c. 39, s. 1; c. 87, s. 1; c. 308, s. 1; 1983, c. 411, ss. 1, 2; 1985, c. 211, ss. 1, 2; 1987, c. 691, s. 1; 1993 (Reg. Sess., 1994), c. 762, s. 2; 1997-443, s. 11A.117; 1999-453, s. 7(a), (b); 2001-319, ss. 8(a), 11; 2005-428, s. 14; 2007-391, ss. 18, 32; 2008-187, s. 33(a); 2013-381, ss. 18.1, 39.1(b).)

§ 163-82.15. Change of address within the county.

(a) Registrant's Duty to Report. - No registered voter shall be required to re-register upon moving from one precinct to another within the same county. Instead, a registrant shall notify the county board of the change of address by the close of registration for an election as set out in G.S. 163-82.6(c). In addition to any other method allowed by G.S. 163-82.6, the form may be submitted by electronic facsimile, under the same deadlines as if it had been submitted in person. The registrant shall make the notification by means of a voter registration form as described in G.S. 163-82.3, or by another written notice, signed by the registrant, that includes the registrant's full name, former residence address, new residence address, and the registrant's attestation that the registrant moved at least 30 days before the next primary or election from the old to the new address.

(b) Verification of New Address by Mail. - When a county board of elections receives a notice that a registrant in that county has changed residence within the same county, the county board shall send a notice, by nonforwardable mail, to the registrant at the new address. The notice shall inform the registrant of any new precinct and voting place that will result from the change of address, and it shall state whether the registrant shall vote at the new voting place during the upcoming election or at a later election. If the Postal Service returns the county board's notice to the registrant as undeliverable, the county board shall either:

(1) Send a second notice by nonforwardable mail to the new address and, if it is returned as undeliverable, send to the registrant's old address a confirmation notice as described in G.S. 163-82.14(d)(2); or

(2) Send to the registrant's old address a confirmation notice as described in G.S. 163-82.14(d)(2) without first sending a second nonforwardable notice to the new address.

In either case, if the registrant does not respond to the confirmation notice as described in G.S. 163-82.14(d)(2), then the county board shall proceed with the removal of the registrant from the list of voters in accordance with G.S. 163-82.14(d).

(c) Board's Duty to Make Change. - If the county board confirms the registrant's new address in accordance with subsection (b) of this section, the county board shall as soon as practical change the record to reflect the new address.

(d) Unreported Move Within the Same Precinct. - A registrant who has moved from one address to another within the same precinct shall, notwithstanding failure to notify the county board of the change of address before an election, be permitted to vote at the voting place of that precinct upon oral or written affirmation by the registrant of the change of address before a precinct official at that voting place.

(e) Unreported Move to Another Precinct Within the County. - If a registrant has moved from an address in one precinct to an address in another precinct within the same county more than 30 days before an election and has failed to notify the county board of the change of address before the close of registration for that election, the county board shall permit that person to vote in that election. The county board shall permit the registrant described in this subsection to vote at the registrant's new precinct, upon the registrant's written affirmation of the new address, or, if the registrant prefers, at a central location in the county to be chosen by the county board. If the registrant appears at the old precinct, the precinct officials there shall send the registrant to the new precinct or, if the registrant prefers, to the central location, according to rules which shall be prescribed by the State Board of Elections. At the new precinct, the registrant shall be processed by a precinct transfer assistant, according to rules which shall be prescribed by the State Board of Elections. Any voter subject to this subsection may instead vote a provisional ballot according to the provisions of G.S. 163-166.11.

(f) When Registrant Disputes Registration Records. - If the registration records indicate that the registrant has moved outside the precinct, but the registrant denies having moved from the address within the precinct previously shown on the records, the registrant shall be permitted to vote at the voting place for the precinct where the registrant claims to reside, if the registrant gives oral or written affirmation before a precinct official at that voting place.

(g) Precinct Transfer Assistants. - The county board of elections shall either designate a board employee or appoint other persons to serve as precinct transfer assistants to receive the election-day transfers of the voters described in subsection (e) of this section. In addition, board members and employees may perform the duties of precinct transfer assistants. The State Board of Elections shall promulgate uniform rules to carry out the provisions of this section, and shall define in those rules the duties of the precinct transfer assistant. (1979, c. 135, s. 2; 1983, c. 392, s. 2; 1984, Ex. Sess., c. 3, ss. 1, 2; 1987, c. 549, s. 1; 1989, c. 427; 1991, c. 12, s. 1; 1991 (Reg. Sess., 1992), c. 1032, s. 3; 1993 (Reg. Sess., 1994), c. 762, s. 2; 2001-314, s. 1; 2005-2, s. 3; 2006-262, s. 2.)

§ 163-82.15A. Administrative change of registration when county line is adjusted.

When a boundary between counties is established by legislation or under G.S. 153A-18, the Executive Director shall direct the county boards of elections involved to administratively change the voter registration of any voter whose county of residence is altered by the establishment of the boundary. The voter shall not be required to submit a new application to register, and the provisions of G.S. 163-57 shall apply to the determination of residency. The Executive Director shall prescribe a method of notifying the voter of the change of county registration, the correct precinct, and other relevant information. (2005-428, s. 3(a).)

§ 163-82.16. Change of name.

(a) Registrant's Duty to Report. - If the name of a registrant is changed in accordance with G.S. 48-1-104, G.S. 50-12, or Chapter 101 of the General Statutes, or if a married registrant assumes the last name of the registrant's spouse, the registrant shall not be required to re-register, but shall report the change of name to the county board not later than the last day for applying to register to vote for an election in G.S. 163-82.6. The registrant shall report the change on a form described in G.S. 163-82.3 or on a voter registration card described in G.S. 163-82.8 or in another written statement that is signed, contains the registrant's full names, old and new, and the registrant's current residence address.

(b) Verification of New Name by Mail. - When a county board of elections receives a notice of name change from a registrant in that county, the county board shall send a notice, by nonforwardable mail, to the registrant's residence address. The notice shall state that the registrant's records will be changed to reflect the new name if the registrant does not respond that the name change is incorrect. If the Postal Service returns the county board's notice to the registrant as undeliverable, the county board shall send to the registrant's residence address a confirmation notice as described in G.S. 163-82.14(d)(2).

If the registrant does not respond to the confirmation notice as described in G.S. 163-82.14(d)(2), then the county board shall proceed with the removal of the registrant from the list of voters in accordance with G.S. 163-82.14(d).

(c) Board's Duty to Make Change. - If the county board confirms the registrant's address in accordance with subsection (b) of this section and the registrant does not deny making the application for the name change, the county board shall as soon as practical change the record of the registrant's name to conform to that stated in the application.

(d) Unreported Name Change. - A registrant who has not reported a name change in accordance with subsection (a) of this section shall be permitted to vote if the registrant reports the name change to the chief judge at the voting place, or to the county board along with the voter's application for an absentee ballot. (1979, c. 480; 1981, c. 33, s. 3; 1989 (Reg. Sess., 1990), c. 991, s. 3; 1991 (Reg. Sess., 1992), c. 1032, s. 2; 1993 (Reg. Sess., 1994), c. 762, s. 2; 1995, c. 457, s. 9.)

§ 163-82.17. Change of party affiliation.

(a) Registrant's Duty to Report. - Any registrant who desires to have the record of his party affiliation or unaffiliated status changed on the registration list shall, no later than the last day for making application to register under G.S. 163-82.6 before the election, indicate the change on an application form as described in G.S. 163-82.3 or on a voter registration card described in G.S. 163-82.8. No registrant shall be permitted to change party affiliation or unaffiliated status for a primary, second primary, or special or general election after the deadline for registration applications for that election as set out in G.S. 163-82.6.

(b) Verification of Affiliation Change by Mail. - When a county board of elections receives a notice of change of party affiliation or unaffiliated status from a registrant in that county, the county board shall send a notice, by nonforwardable mail, to the registrant's residence address. The notice shall state that the registrant's records will be changed to reflect the change of status if the registrant does not respond by stating that he does not desire a change in status. The notice shall also inform the registrant of the time that the change of affiliation status will occur, and shall explain the provisions of subsection (d) of this section. If the Postal Service returns the county board's notice to the registrant as undeliverable, the county board shall send to the registrant's residence address a confirmation notice as described in G.S. 163-82.14(d)(2). If the registrant does not respond to the confirmation notice as described in G.S. 163-82.14(d)(2), then the county board shall proceed with the removal of the registrant from the list of voters in accordance with G.S. 163-82.14(d).

(c) Board's Duty to Make Change. - If the county board confirms the registrant's address in accordance with subsection (b) of this section and the registrant does not deny making the application to change affiliated or unaffiliated status, the county board of elections shall as soon as practical change the record of the registrant's party affiliation, or unaffiliated status, to conform to that stated in the application. Thereafter the voter shall be considered registered and qualified to vote in accordance with the change, except as provided in subsection (d) of this section.

(d) Deadline to Change Status Before Primary. - If a registrant applies to change party affiliation or unaffiliated status later than the last day for applying to register under G.S. 163-82.6 before a primary, the registrant shall not be entitled to vote in the primary of a party in which the registrant's status on that last day did not entitle the registrant to vote.

(e) Authority of County Board or Director to Make Correction. - If at any time the chairman or director of elections of the county board of elections is satisfied that an error has been made in designating the party affiliation of any voter on the registration records, then the chairman or director of elections of the county board of elections shall make the necessary correction after receiving from the voter a sworn statement as to the error and the correct status. (1939, c. 263, s. 6; 1949, c. 916, ss. 4, 8; 1953, c. 843; 1955, c. 800; c. 871, s. 3; 1957, c. 784, s. 5; 1963, c. 303, s. 1; 1967, c. 775, s. 1; 1973, c. 793, ss. 30, 31; c. 1223, s. 5; 1975, c. 234, s. 2; 1977, c. 130, s. 1; c. 626, s. 1; 1981, c. 33, s. 4; c. 219, s. 4; 1983, c. 576, s. 4; 1987, c. 408, ss. 1, 6; 1989, c. 635, s. 2; 1991 (Reg. Sess., 1992), c. 1032, s. 4; 1993 (Reg. Sess., 1994), c. 762, s. 2; 1995, c. 243, s. 1.)

§ 163-82.18. Appeal from denial of registration.

(a) Right to Appeal. - Any applicant who receives notice of denial of registration pursuant to G.S. 163-82.7 may appeal the denial within five days after receipt of the notice of denial. The county board of elections shall promptly set a date for a public hearing. The notice of appeal shall be in writing and shall be signed by the appealing party, shall include the appealing party's name, date of birth, address, and reasons for the appeal.

(b) Hearing Before County Board of Elections. - The county board of elections shall set a date and time for a public hearing and shall notify the appealing party. Every person appealing to the county board of elections from denial of registration shall be entitled to a prompt and fair hearing on the question of the denied applicant's right and qualifications to register as a voter. All cases on appeal to a county board of elections shall be heard de novo.

Two members of the county board of elections shall constitute a quorum for the purpose of hearing appeals on questions of registration. The decision of a majority of the members of the board shall be the decision of the board. The board shall be authorized to subpoena witnesses and to compel their attendance and testimony under oath, and it is further authorized to subpoena papers and documents relevant to any matters pending before the board.

If at the hearing the board shall find that the person appealing from a denial of registration meets all requirements of law for registration as a voter in the county, the board shall enter an order directing that the appellant be registered and assign the appellant to the appropriate precinct. Not later than five days after an appeal is heard before the county board of elections, the board shall give written notice of its decision to the appealing party.

(c) Appeal to Superior Court. - Any person aggrieved by a final decision of a county board of elections denying registration may at any time within 10 days from the date on which he receives notice of the decision appeal to the superior court of the county in which the board is located. Upon such an appeal, the appealing party shall be the plaintiff and the county board of elections shall be the defendant, and the matter shall be heard de novo in the superior court in the manner in which other civil actions are tried and disposed of in that court.

If the decision of the court is that the order of the county board of elections shall be set aside, then the court shall enter its order so providing and adjudging that the plaintiff is entitled to be registered as a qualified voter in the precinct in which he originally made application to register, and in such case the plaintiff's name shall be entered in the registration book of that precinct. The court shall not order the registration of any person in a precinct in which he did not apply to register prior to the proceeding in court.

From the judgment of the superior court an appeal may be taken to the appellate division in the same manner as other appeals are taken from judgments of that court in civil actions. (1957, c. 287, dd. 2-4; 1967, c. 775, s. 1; 1969, c. 44, s. 82; 1981, c. 542, ss. 1, 2; 1993 (Reg. Sess., 1994), c. 762, s. 2.)

§ 163-82.19. Voter registration at drivers license offices; coordination on data interface.

(a) Voter Registration at Drivers License Offices. - The Division of Motor Vehicles shall, pursuant to the rules adopted by the State Board of Elections, modify its forms so that any eligible person who applies for original issuance, renewal or correction of a drivers license, or special identification card issued under G.S. 20-37.7 may, on a part of the form, complete an application to register to vote, or to update the voter's registration if the voter has changed his or her address or moved from one precinct to another or from one county to another. The person taking the application shall ask if the applicant is a citizen of the United States. If the applicant states that the applicant is not a citizen of the United States, or declines to answer the question, the person taking the application shall inform the applicant that it is a felony for a person who is not a citizen of the United States to apply to register to vote. Any person who willfully and knowingly and with fraudulent intent gives false information on the application is guilty of a Class I felony. The application shall state in clear language the penalty for violation of this section. The necessary forms shall be prescribed by the State Board of Elections. The form must ask for the previous voter registration address of the voter, if any. If a previous address is listed, and it is not in the county of residence of the applicant, the appropriate county board of elections shall treat the application as an authorization to cancel the previous registration and also process it as such under the procedures of G.S. 163-82.9. If a previous address is listed and that address is in the county where the voter applies to register, the application shall be processed as if it had been submitted under G.S. 163-82.9.

Registration shall become effective as provided in G.S. 163-82.7. Applications to register to vote accepted at a drivers license office under this section until the deadline established in G.S. 163-82.6(c)(2) shall be treated as timely made for an election, and no person who completes an application at that drivers license office shall be denied the vote in that election for failure to apply earlier than that deadline.

All applications shall be forwarded by the Department of Transportation to the appropriate board of elections not later than five business days after the date of acceptance, according to rules which shall be promulgated by the State Board of Elections. Those rules shall provide for a paperless, instant, electronic transfer of applications to the appropriate board of elections.

(b) Coordination on Data Interface. - The Department of Transportation jointly with the State Board of Elections shall develop and operate a computerized interface to match information in the database of the statewide voter registration system with the drivers license information in the Division of Motor Vehicles to the extent required to enable the State Board of Elections and the Department of Transportation to verify the accuracy of the information provided on applications for voter registration, whether the applications were received at drivers license offices or elsewhere. The Department of Transportation and the State Board shall implement the provisions of this subsection so as to comply with section 303 of the Help America Vote Act of 2002. The Department of Transportation shall enter into an agreement with the Commissioner of Social Security so as to comply with section 303 of the Help America Vote Act of 2002. (1983, c. 854, s. 1; 1991 (Reg. Sess., 1992), c. 1044, s. 19(a); 1993, c. 74, s. 2; 1993 (Reg. Sess., 1994), c. 762, s. 2; 1998-149, s. 11.1; 2001-319, s. 7(a); 2003-226, s. 7(b); 2009-541, s. 13(a); 2013-381, s. 12.1(e).)

§ 163-82.20. Voter registration at other public agencies.

(a) Voter Registration Agencies. - Every office in this State which accepts:

(1) Applications for a program of public assistance under Article 2 of Chapter 108A of the General Statutes or under Article 13 of Chapter 130A of the General Statutes;

(2) Applications for State-funded State or local government programs primarily engaged in providing services to persons with disabilities, with such office designated by the State Board of Elections; or

(3) Claims for benefits under Chapter 96 of the General Statutes, the Employment Security Law, is designated as a voter registration agency for purposes of this section.

(b) Duties of Voter Registration Agencies. - A voter registration agency described in subsection (a) of this section shall, unless the applicant declines, in writing, to register to vote:

(1) Distribute with each application for service or assistance, and with each recertification, renewal, or change of address relating to such service or assistance:

a. The voter registration application form described in G.S. 163-82.3(a) or (b); or

b. The voter registration agency's own form, if it is substantially equivalent to the form described in G.S. 163-82.3(a) or (b) and has been approved by the State Board of Elections, provided that the agency's own form may be a detachable part of the agency's paper application or may be a paperless computer process, as long as the applicant is required to sign an attestation as part of the application to register.

(2) Provide a form that contains the elements required by section 7(a)(6)(B) of the National Voter Registration Act; and

(3) Provide to each applicant who does not decline to register to vote the same degree of assistance with regard to the completion of the registration application as is provided by the office with regard to the completion of its own forms.

(c) Provided that voter registration agencies designated under subdivision (a)(3) of this section shall only be required to provide the services set out in this subsection to applicants for new claims, reopened claims, and changes of address under Chapter 96 of the General Statutes, the Employment Security Law.

(d) Home Registration for Disabled. - If a voter registration agency provides services to a person with disability at the person's home, the voter registration agency shall provide the services described in subsection (b) of this section at the person's home.

(e) Prohibitions. - Any person providing any service under subsection (b) of this section shall not:

(1) Seek to influence an applicant's political preference or party registration, except that this shall not be construed to prevent the notice provided by G.S. 163-82.4(c) to be given if the applicant refuses to declare his party affiliation;

(2) Display any such political preference or party allegiance;

(3) Make any statement to an applicant or take any action the purpose or effect of which is to discourage the applicant from registering to vote; or

(4) Make any statement to an applicant or take any action the purpose or effect of which is to lead the applicant to believe that a decision to register or not to register has any bearing on the availability of services or benefits.

(f) Confidentiality of Declination to Register. - No information relating to a declination to register to vote in connection with an application made at a voter registration agency may be used for any purpose other than voter registration.

(g) Transmittal From Agency to Board of Elections. - Any voter registration application completed at a voter registration agency shall be accepted by that agency in lieu of the applicant's mailing the application. Any such application so received shall be transmitted to the appropriate board of elections not later than five business days after acceptance, according to rules which shall be promulgated by the State Board of Elections.

(h) Twenty-Five-Day Deadline for an Election. - Applications to register accepted by a voter registration agency shall entitle a registrant to vote in any primary, general, or special election unless the registrant shall have made application later than the twenty-fifth calendar day immediately preceding such primary, general, or special election, provided that nothing shall prohibit voter registration agencies from continuing to accept applications during that period.

(i) Ineligible Applications Prohibited. - No person shall make application to register to vote under this section if that person is ineligible on account of age, citizenship, lack of residence for the period of time provided by law, or because of conviction of a felony. (1993 (Reg. Sess., 1994), c. 762, s. 2; 1995, c. 507, s. 25.10(c); 1995 (Reg. Sess., 1996), c. 608, s. 1; 2009-541, s. 14(a); 2013-381, s. 12.1(f).)

§ 163-82.20A. Voter registration upon restoration of citizenship.

The State Board of Elections, the Division of Adult Correction of the Department of Public Safety, and the Administrative Office of the Courts shall jointly develop and implement educational programs and procedures for persons to apply to register to vote at the time they are restored to citizenship and all filings required have been completed under Chapter 13 of the General Statutes. Those procedures shall be designed to do both of the following:

(1) Inform the person that the restoration of rights removes the person's disqualification from voting, but that in order to vote the person must register to vote.

(2) Provide an opportunity to that person to register to vote.

At a minimum, the program shall include a written notice to the person whose citizenship has been restored, informing that person that the person may now register to vote, with a voter registration form enclosed with the notice. (2007-391, s. 26(a); 2011-145, s. 19.1(h).)

§ 163-82.21. Voter registration at military recruitment offices.

The Executive Director, jointly with the Department of Defense, shall develop and implement procedures for persons to apply to register to vote at recruitment offices of the Armed Forces of the United States in compliance with section 7(c) of the National Voter Registration Act. (1993 (Reg. Sess., 1994), c. 762, s. 2; 2001-319, s. 11; 2011-183, s. 111.)

§ 163-82.22. Voter registration at public libraries and public agencies.

(a) Every library covered by G.S. 153A-272 shall make available to the public the application forms described in G.S. 163-82.3, and shall keep a sufficient supply of the forms so that they are always available. Every library covered by G.S. 153A-272 shall designate at least one employee to assist voter registration applicants in completing the form during all times that the library is open.

(b) If approved by the State Board of Elections, the county board of elections, and the county board of commissioners, a county may offer voter registration in accordance with this section through the following additional public offices:

(1) Senior centers or facilities operated by the county.

(2) Parks and recreation services operated by the county. (1975, c. 234, s. 1; 1977, c. 626, s. 1; 1983, c. 588, ss. 2, 3; c. 707; 1991 (Reg. Sess., 1992), c. 973, ss. 1, 2; c. 1044, s. 19(b); 1993, c. 74, s. 2; 1993 (Reg. Sess., 1994), c. 762, s. 2; 2013-381, s. 5.1.)

§ 163-82.23. Voter registration at public high schools.

Every public high school shall make available to its students and others who are eligible to register to vote the application forms described in G.S. 163-82.3, and shall keep a sufficient supply of the forms so that they are always available. A local board of education may, but is not required to, designate high school employees to assist in completing the forms. Only employees who volunteer for this duty may be designated by boards of education. (1975, c. 234, s. 1; 1977, c. 626, s. 1; 1983, c. 588, ss. 2, 3; c. 707; 1991 (Reg. Sess., 1992), c. 973, ss. 1, 2; c. 1044, s. 19(b); 1993, c. 74, s. 2; 1993 (Reg. Sess., 1994), c. 762, s. 2; 2009-541, s. 15(a); 2013-381, s. 12.1(d).)

§ 163-82.24. Statewide training and certification for election officials.

(a) Training. - The State Board of Elections shall conduct training programs in election law and procedures. Every county elections director shall receive training conducted by the State Board at least as often as required in the following schedule:

(1) Once during each odd-numbered year before the municipal election held in the county;

(2) Once during each even-numbered year before the first partisan primary; and

(3) Once during each even-numbered year after the partisan primaries but before the general election.

Every member of a county board of elections shall receive training conducted by the State Board at least once during the six months after the member's initial appointment and at least once again during the first two years of the member's service. The State Board of Elections shall promulgate rules for the training of precinct officials, which shall be followed by the county boards of elections.

(b) Certification. - The State Board of Elections shall conduct a program for certification of election officials. The program shall include training in election law and procedures. Before issuing certification to an election official, the State Board shall administer an examination designed to determine the proficiency of the official in election law and procedures. The State Board shall set adequate standards for the passage of the examination. (1993 (Reg. Sess., 1994), c. 762, s. 2; 1995, c. 243, s. 1; 2001-319, s. 2(a).)

§ 163-82.25: Repealed by Session Laws 2013-381, s. 19.1, effective January 1, 2014. (1991 (Reg. Sess., 1992), c. 1044, s. 19(e); 1993 (Reg. Sess., 1994), c. 762, s. 2; 2009-541, s. 16(a); repealed by 2013-381, s. 19.1, effective January 1, 2014.)

§ 163-82.26. Rule-making authority.

The State Board of Elections shall promulgate rules necessary to implement the provisions of this Article. (1993 (Reg. Sess., 1994), c. 762, s. 2.)

§ 163-82.27. Help America Vote Act of 2002.

As used in this Chapter, the term "Help America Vote Act of 2002" means the Help America Vote Act of 2002, Public Law 107-252, 116 Stat. 1666 (2002), codified at 42 U.S.C. §§ 15481-15485. Citations to titles and sections of the Help America Vote Act of 2002 are as they appear in the Public Law. The State Board shall have the authority to adopt rules and guidelines to implement the minimum requirements of the Help America Vote Act of 2002. (2003-226, s. 21.)

§ 163-82.28. The HAVA Election Fund.

There is established a special fund to be known as the Election Fund. All funds received for implementation of the Help America Vote Act of 2002, Public Law 107-252, shall be deposited in that fund. The State Board of Elections shall use funds in the Election Fund only to implement HAVA. (2003-12, s. 1; 2005-276, s. 23A.2(a); 2005-323, s. 7; 2006-264, s. 76(d).)

§ 163-83. Reserved for future codification purposes.

Article 8.

Challenges.

§ 163-84. Time for challenge other than on day of primary or election.

The registration records of each county shall be open to inspection by any registered voter of the State, including any chief judge or judge of elections, during the normal business hours of the county board of elections on the days when the board's office is open. At those times the right of any person to register, remain registered, or vote shall be subject to objection and challenge. (1901, c. 89, s. 19; Rev., s. 4339; C.S., s. 5972; 1929, c. 164, s. 36; 1953, c. 843; 1955, c. 800; c. 871, s. 7; 1959, c. 616, s. 2; 1963, c. 303, s. 1; 1967, c. 775, s. 1; 1973, c. 793, s. 33; 1993 (Reg. Sess., 1994), c. 762, s. 24; 2013-381, s. 20.1.)

§ 163-85. Challenge procedure other than on day of primary or election.

(a) Right to Challenge; When Challenge May Be Made. - Any registered voter of the county may challenge the right of any person to register, remain registered or vote in such county. No such challenge may be made after the twenty-fifth day before each primary, general, or special election.

(b) Challenges Shall Be Made to the County Board of Elections. - Each challenge shall be made separately, in writing, under oath and on forms prescribed by the State Board of Elections, and shall specify the reasons why the challenged voter is not entitled to register, remain registered, or vote. When a challenge is made, the board of elections shall cause the word "challenged" to be written in pencil on the registration records of the voter challenged. The challenge shall be signed by the challenger and shall set forth the challenger's address.

(c) Grounds for Challenge. - Such challenge may be made only for one or more of the following reasons:

(1) That a person is not a resident of the State of North Carolina, or

(2) That a person is not a resident of the county in which the person is registered, provided that no such challenge may be made if the person removed his residency and the period of removal has been less than 30 days, or

(3) That a person is not a resident of the precinct in which the person is registered, provided that no such challenge may be made if the person removed his residency and the period of removal has been less than 30 days, or

(4) That a person is not 18 years of age, or if the challenge is made within 60 days before a primary, that the person will not be 18 years of age by the next general election, or

(5) That a person has been adjudged guilty of a felony and is ineligible to vote under G.S. 163-55(2), or

(6), (7) Repealed by Session Laws 1985, c. 563, ss. 11.1, 11.2.

(7a) That a person is dead, or

(8) That a person is not a citizen of the United States, or

(9) With respect to municipal registration only, that a person is not a resident of the municipality in which the person is registered, or

(10) That the person is not who he or she represents himself or herself to be.

(d) Preliminary Hearing. - When a challenge is made, the county board of election shall schedule a preliminary hearing on the challenge, and shall take such testimony under oath and receive such other evidence proffered by the challenger as may be offered. The burden of proof shall be on the challenger, and if no testimony is presented, the board shall dismiss the challenge. If the challenger presents evidence and if the board finds that probable cause exists that the person challenged is not qualified to vote, then the board shall schedule a hearing on the challenge.

(e) Prima Facie Evidence That Voter No Longer Resides in Precinct. - The presentation of a letter mailed by returnable first-class mail to the voter at the address listed on the voter registration card and returned because the person does not live at the address shall constitute prima facie evidence that the person no longer resides in the precinct. (1901, c. 89, s. 19; Rev., s. 4339; C.S., s. 5972; 1953, c. 843; 1955, c. 800; 1963, c. 303, s. 1; 1967, c. 775, s. 1; 1973, c. 793, s. 34; 1979, c. 357, s. 1; 1985, c. 563, ss. 11-11.2, 11.5; c. 589, s. 60; 1993 (Reg. Sess., 1994), c. 762, s. 25; 2009-526, s. 1.2; 2009-541, s. 16.1(a); 2009-550, s. 11; 2010-96, s. 18.)

§ 163-86. Hearing on challenge.

(a) A challenge made under G.S. 163-85 shall be heard and decided before the date of the next primary or election, except that if the board finds that because of the number of challenges, it cannot hold all hearings before the date of the election, it may order the challenges to be heard and decided at the next time the challenged person appears and seeks to vote, as if the challenge had been filed under G.S. 163-87. Unless the hearing is ordered held under G.S. 163-87, it shall be heard and decided by the board of elections.

(b) At least 10 days prior to the hearing scheduled under G.S. 163-86(c), the board of elections shall mail by first-class mail, a written notice of the challenge to the challenged voter, to the address of the voter listed in the registration records of the county. The notice shall state succinctly the grounds asserted, and shall state the time and place of the hearing. If the hearing is to be held at the polls, the notice shall state that fact and shall list the date of the next scheduled election, the location of the voter's polling place, and the time the polls will be open. A copy of the notice shall be sent to the person making the challenge and to the chairman of each political party in the county.

(c) At the time and place set for the hearing on a challenge entered prior to the date of a primary or election, the county board of elections shall explain to the challenged registrant the qualifications for registration and voting in this State. The board chairman, or in his absence the board secretary, shall then administer the following oath to the challenged registrant:

"You swear (or affirm) that the statements and information you shall give in this hearing with respect to your identity and qualifications to be registered and to vote shall be the truth, the whole truth, and nothing but the truth, so help you, God."

After swearing the challenged registrant, the board shall examine him as to his qualifications to be registered and to vote. If the challenged registrant insists that he is qualified, the board shall tender to him the following oath or affirmation:

"You do solemnly swear (or affirm) that you are a citizen of the United States; that you are at least 18 years of age or will become 18 by the date of the next general election; that you have or will have resided in this State and in the precinct for which registered for 30 days by the date of the next primary or election; that you are not disqualified from voting by the Constitution or the laws of this State; that your name is ____, and that in such name you were duly registered as a voter of ____ precinct; and that you are the person you represent yourself to be, so help you, God."

If the challenged registrant refuses to take the tendered oath, or submit to the board the affidavit required by subsection (d), below, the challenge shall be sustained. If the challenged registrant takes the tendered oath, the board may, nevertheless, sustain the challenge if it finds the challenged registrant is not a legal voter.

The board, in conducting hearings on challenges, shall have authority to subpoena any witnesses it may deem appropriate, and administer the necessary oaths or affirmations to all witnesses brought before it to testify to the qualifications of the persons challenged.

(d) Appearance by Challenged Registrant. - The challenged registrant shall appear in person at the challenge hearing. If he is unable to appear in person, he may be represented by another person and must tender to the county board of elections an affidavit that he is a citizen of the United States, is at least 18 years of age or will become 18 by the date of the next general election, has or will have resided in this State and in the precinct for which registered for 30 days by the date of the next primary or election, is not disqualified from voting by the Constitution or laws of this State, is named ____ and was duly registered as a voter of ____ precinct in such name, and is the person represented to be by the affidavit. (1901, c. 89, s. 22; Rev., s. 4340; C.S., s. 5973; 1955, c. 871, s. 2; 1967, c. 775, s. 1; 1971, c. 1231, s. 1; 1973, c. 793, s. 35; 1979, c. 357, s. 2; 2008-150, s. 5(b).)

§ 163-87. (Effective until January 1, 2016) Challenges allowed on day of primary or election.

On the day of a primary or election, at the time a registered voter offers to vote, any other registered voter of the county may exercise the right of challenge, and when he does so may enter the voting enclosure to make the challenge, but he shall retire therefrom as soon as the challenge is heard.

On the day of a primary or election, any other registered voter of the county may challenge a person for one or more of the following reasons:

(1) One or more of the reasons listed in G.S. 163-85(c).

(2) That the person has already voted in that primary or election.

(3) Repealed by Session Laws 2009-541, s. 16.1(b), effective August 28, 2009.

(4) If the challenge is made with respect to voting in a partisan primary, that the person is a registered voter of another political party.

The chief judge, judge, or assistant appointed under G.S. 163-41 or 163-42 may enter challenges under this section against voters in the precinct for which appointed regardless of the place of residence of the chief judge, judge, or assistant.

If a person is challenged under this subsection, and the challenge is sustained under G.S. 163-85(c)(3), the voter may still transfer his registration under G.S. 163-82.15(e) if eligible under that section, and the registration shall not be cancelled under G.S. 163-90.2(a) if the transfer is made. A person who has transferred his registration under G.S. 163-82.15(e) may be challenged at the precinct to which the registration is being transferred. (1915, c. 101, s. 11; 1917, c. 218; C.S., s. 6031; 1921, c. 181, s. 6; 1923, c. 111, s. 14; 1929, c. 164, s. 36; 1953, c. 843; 1955, c. 800; c. 871, s. 7; 1959, c. 616, s. 2; c. 1203, s. 7; 1963, c. 303, s. 1; 1967, c. 775, s. 1; 1985, c. 563, ss. 11.4, 14; 1987, c. 408, s. 7; 1993 (Reg. Sess., 1994), c. 762, s. 26; 1995 (Reg. Sess., 1996), c. 734, s. 4; 2006-262, s. 3(a); 2009-541, s. 16.1(b); 2013-381, s. 20.2.)

§ 163-87. (Effective January 1, 2016) Challenges allowed on day of primary or election.

On the day of a primary or election, at the time a registered voter offers to vote, any other registered voter of the county may exercise the right of challenge, and when the voter does so may enter the voting enclosure to make the challenge, but the voter shall retire therefrom as soon as the challenge is heard.

On the day of a primary or election, any other registered voter of the county may challenge a person for one or more of the following reasons:

(1) One or more of the reasons listed in G.S. 163-85(c).

(2) That the person has already voted in that primary or election.

(3) Repealed by Session Laws 2009-541, s. 16.1(b), effective August 28, 2009.

(4) If the challenge is made with respect to voting in a partisan primary, that the person is a registered voter of another political party.

(5) Except as provided in G.S. 163-166.13(d) and G.S. 163-166.14, the voter does not present photo identification in accordance with G.S. 163-166.13.

The chief judge, judge, or assistant appointed under G.S. 163-41 or 163-42 may enter challenges under this section against voters in the precinct for which appointed regardless of the place of residence of the chief judge, judge, or assistant.

If a person is challenged under this subsection, and the challenge is sustained under G.S. 163-85(c)(3), the voter may still transfer that voter's registration under G.S. 163-82.15(e) if eligible under that section, and the registration shall not be cancelled under G.S. 163-90.2(a) if the transfer is made. A person who has transferred that voter's registration under G.S. 163-82.15(e) may be challenged at the precinct to which the registration is being transferred. (1915, c. 101, s. 11; 1917, c. 218; C.S., s. 6031; 1921, c. 181, s. 6; 1923, c. 111, s. 14; 1929, c. 164, s. 36; 1953, c. 843; 1955, c. 800; c. 871, s. 7; 1959, c. 616, s. 2; c. 1203, s. 7; 1963, c. 303, s. 1; 1967, c. 775, s. 1; 1985, c. 563, ss. 11.4, 14; 1987, c. 408, s. 7; 1993 (Reg. Sess., 1994), c. 762, s. 26; 1995 (Reg. Sess., 1996), c. 734, s. 4; 2006-262, s. 3(a); 2009-541, s. 16.1(b); 2013-381, ss. 2.9, 20.2.)

§ 163-88. Hearing on challenge made on day of primary or election.

A challenge entered on the day of a primary or election shall be heard and decided by the chief judge and judges of election of the precinct in which the challenged registrant is registered before the polls are closed on the day the challenge is made. When the challenge is heard the precinct officials conducting the hearing shall explain to the challenged registrant the qualifications for registration and voting in this State, and shall examine him as to his qualifications to be registered and to vote. If the challenged registrant insists that he is qualified, and if, by sworn testimony, he shall prove his identity with the person in whose name he offers to vote and his continued residence in the precinct since he was registered, one of the judges of election or the chief judge shall tender to him the following oath or affirmation, omitting the portions in brackets if the challenge is heard on the day of an election other than a primary:

"You do solemnly swear (or affirm) that you are a citizen of the United States; that you are at least 18 years of age [or will become 18 by the date of the next general election]; that you have [or will have] resided in this State and in the precinct for which registered for 30 days [by the date of the next general election]; that you are not disqualified from voting by the Constitution and laws of this State; that your name is_____, and that in such name you were duly registered as a voter of this precinct; that you are the person you represent yourself to be; [that you are affiliated with the _____ party]; and that you have not voted in this [primary] election at this or any other voting place. So help you, God."

If the challenged registrant refuses to take the tendered oath, the challenge shall be sustained, and the precinct officials conducting the hearing shall mark the registration records to reflect their decision, and they shall erase the challenged registrant's name from the pollbook if it has been entered therein. If the challenged registrant takes the tendered oath, the precinct officials conducting the hearing may, nevertheless, sustain the challenge unless they are satisfied that the challenged registrant is a legal voter. If they are satisfied that he is a legal voter, they shall overrule the challenge and permit him to vote. Whenever any person's vote is received after having taken the oath prescribed in this section, the chief judge or one of the judges of election shall write on the registration record and on the pollbook opposite the registrant's name the word "sworn."

Precinct election officials conducting hearings on challenges on the day of a primary or election shall have authority to administer the necessary oaths or affirmations to all witnesses brought before them to testify to the qualifications of the person challenged.

A letter or postal card mailed by returnable mail and returned by the United States Postal Service purportedly because the person no longer lives at that address or because a forwarding order has expired shall not be admissible evidence in a challenge heard under this section which was made under G.S. 163-87. (1901, c. 89, s. 22; Rev., s. 4340; C.S., s. 5973; 1955, c. 871, s. 2; 1967, c. 775, s. 1; 1971, c. 1231, s. 1; 1973, c. 1223, s. 6; 1985, c. 380, ss. 1, 1.1; 1993 (Reg. Sess., 1994), c. 762, s. 27.)

§ 163-88.1. Request for challenged ballot.

(a) If the decision of the chief judge and judges pursuant to G.S. 163-88 is to sustain the challenge, the challenged voter may request a challenged ballot by submitting an application to the chief judge, such application shall include as part thereof an affidavit that such person possesses all the qualifications for voting and is entitled to vote at the election. The form of such affidavit shall be prescribed by the State Board of Elections and shall be available at the polls.

(b) Any person requesting a challenged ballot shall have the letter "C" entered at the appropriate place on the voter's permanent registration record. The voter's name shall be entered on a separate page in the pollbook entitled "Challenged Ballot," and serially numbered. The challenged ballot shall be the same type of ballot used for absentee voters, and the chief judge shall write across the top of the ballot "Challenged Ballot #____," and shall insert the same serial number as entered in the pollbook. The chief judge shall deliver to such voter a challenged ballot together with an envelope marked "Challenged Ballot" and serially numbered. The challenged voter shall forthwith mark the ballot in the presence of the chief judge in such manner that the chief judge shall not know how the ballot is marked. He shall then fold the ballot in the presence of the chief judge so as to conceal the markings and deposit and seal it in the serially numbered envelope. He shall then deliver such envelope to the chief judge. The chief judge shall retain all such envelopes in an envelope provided by the county board of elections, which he shall seal immediately after the polls close, and deliver to the board chairman at the canvass.

(c) The chairman of the county board of elections shall preserve such ballots in the sealed envelopes for a period of six months after the election. However, in the case of a contested election, either party to such action may request the court to order that the sealed envelopes containing challenged ballots be delivered to the board of elections by the chairman. If so ordered, the board of elections shall then convene and consider each challenged ballot and rule as to which ballots shall be counted. In such consideration, the board may take such further evidence as it deems necessary, and shall have the power of subpoena. If any ballots are ordered to be counted, they shall be added to the vote totals. (1979, c. 357, s. 3; 1993 (Reg. Sess., 1994), c. 762, s. 28.)

§ 163-89. Procedures for challenging absentee ballots.

(a) Time for Challenge. - The absentee ballot of any voter may be challenged on the day of any statewide primary or general election or county bond election beginning no earlier than noon and ending no later than 5:00 P.M., or by the chief judge at the time of closing of the polls as provided in G.S. 163-232 and G.S. 163-251(b). The absentee ballot of any voter received by the county board of elections pursuant to G.S. 163-231(b)(ii) or (iii) may be challenged no earlier than noon on the day following the election and no later than 5:00 p.m. on the next business day following the deadline for receipt of such absentee ballots.

(b) Who May Challenge. - Any registered voter of the same precinct as the absentee voter may challenge that voter's absentee ballot.

(c) Form and Nature of Challenge. - Each challenged absentee ballot shall be challenged separately. The burden of proof shall be on the challenger. Each challenge shall be made in writing and, if they are available, shall be made on forms prescribed by the State Board of Elections. Each challenge shall specify the reasons why the ballot does not comply with the provisions of this Article or why the absentee voter is not legally entitled to vote in the particular primary or election. The challenge shall be signed by the challenger.

(d) To Whom Challenge Addressed; to Whom Challenge Delivered. - Each challenge shall be addressed to the county board of elections. It may be filed with the board at its offices or with the chief judge of the precinct in which the challenger and absentee voter are registered. If it is delivered to the chief judge, the chief judge shall personally deliver the challenge to the chairman of the county board of elections on the day of the county canvass.

(e) Hearing Procedure. - All challenges filed under this section shall be heard by the county board of elections on the day set for the canvass of the returns. All members of the board shall attend the canvass and all members shall be present for the hearing of challenges to absentee ballots.

Before the board hears a challenge to an absentee ballot, the chairman shall mark the word "challenged" after the voter's name in the register of absentee ballot applications and ballots issued and in the pollbook of absentee voters.

The board then shall hear the challenger's reasons for the challenge, and it shall make its decision without opening the container-return envelope or removing the ballots from it.

The board shall have authority to administer the necessary oaths or affirmations to all witnesses brought before it to testify to the qualifications of the voter challenged or to the validity or invalidity of the ballot.

If the challenge is sustained, the chairman shall mark the word "sustained" after the word "challenged" following the voter's name in the register of absentee ballot applications and ballots issued and in the pollbook of absentee voters; the voter's ballots shall not be counted; and the container-return envelope shall not be opened but shall be marked "Challenge Sustained." All envelopes so marked shall be preserved intact by the chairman for a period of six months from canvass day or longer if any contest then is pending concerning the validity of any absentee ballot.

If the challenge is overruled, the absentee ballots shall be removed from the container-return envelopes and counted by the board of elections, and the board shall adjust the appropriate abstracts of returns to show that the ballots have been counted and tallied in the manner provided for unchallenged absentee ballots.

If the challenge was delivered to the board by the chief judge of the precinct and was sustained, the board shall reopen the appropriate ballot boxes, remove such ballots, determine how those ballots were voted, deduct such ballots from the returns, and adjust the appropriate abstracts of returns.

Any voter whose ballots have been challenged may, either personally or through an authorized representative, appear before the board at the hearing on the challenge and present evidence as to the validity of the ballot. (1939, c. 159, ss. 8, 9; 1945, c. 758, s. 8; 1953, c. 1114; 1963, c. 547, s. 8; 1965, c. 871; 1967, c. 775, s. 1; 1973, c. 536, s. 4; 1993 (Reg. Sess., 1994), c. 762, s. 29; 2009-537, s. 8(c).)

§ 163-90. Challenge as felon; answer not to be used on prosecution.

If any registered voter is challenged as having been convicted of any crime which excludes him from the right of suffrage, he shall be required to answer any question in relation to the alleged conviction, but his answers to such questions shall not be used against him in any criminal prosecution. (1901, c. 89, s. 71; Rev., s. 3388; C.S., s. 5974; 1967, c. 775, s. 1.)

§ 163-90.1. Burden of proof.

(a)   Challenges shall not be made indiscriminately and may only be made if the challenger knows, suspects or reasonably believes such a person not to be qualified and entitled to vote.

(b)   No challenge shall be sustained unless the challenge is substantiated by affirmative proof. In the absence of such proof, the presumption shall be that the voter is properly registered or affiliated. (1979, c. 357, s. 4.)

§ 163-90.2. Action when challenge sustained, overruled, or dismissed.

(a)   When any challenge is sustained for any cause listed under G.S. 163-85(c), the board shall cancel or correct the voter registration of the voter. The board shall maintain such record for at least six months and during the pendency of any appeal. The challenged ballot shall be counted for any ballot items for which the challenged voter is eligible to vote, as if it were a provisional official ballot under the provisions of G.S. 163-166.11(4).

(b)   Repealed by Session Laws 2006-252, s. 3(b), effective August 27, 2006.

(c)   When any challenge made under G.S. 163-85 is overruled or dismissed, the board shall erase the word "challenged" which appears on the person's registration records.

(d)   A decision by a county board of elections on any challenge made under the provisions of this Article shall be appealable to the Superior Court of the county in which the offices of that board are located within 10 days. Only those persons against whom a challenge is sustained or persons who have made a challenge which is overruled shall have standing to file such appeal. (1979, c. 357, s. 4; 1987 (Reg. Sess., 1988), c. 1028, s. 11; 2006-262, s. 3(b).)

§ 163-90.3. Making false affidavit perjury.

Any person who shall knowingly make any false affidavit or shall knowingly swear or affirm falsely to any matter or thing required by the terms of this Article to be sworn or affirmed shall be guilty of a Class I felony. (1979, c. 357, s. 4; 1987, c. 565, s. 2.)

Article 8A.

HAVA Administrative Complaint Procedure.

§ 163-91. Complaint procedure.

(a) The State Board of Elections shall establish a complaint procedure as required by section 402 of Title IV of the Help America Vote Act of 2002 for the resolution of complaints alleging violations of Title III of that Act.

(b) With respect to the adoption of the complaint procedure under this section, the State Board of Elections is exempt from the requirements of Article 2A of Chapter 150B of the General Statutes. Prior to adoption or amendment of the complaint procedure under this section, the State Board of Elections shall complete all of the following:

(1) Publish the proposed plan in the North Carolina Register at least 30 days prior to the adoption of the final complaint procedure.

(2) Accept oral and written comments on the proposed complaint procedure.

(3) Hold at least one public hearing on the proposed complaint procedure.

(c) Hearings and final determinations of complaints filed under the procedure adopted pursuant to this section are not subject to Articles 3 and 4 of Chapter 150B of the General Statutes. (2003-226, s. 17(a).)

§§ 163-92 through 163-95. Reserved for future codification purposes.

SUBCHAPTER IV. POLITICAL PARTIES.

Article 9.

Political Party Definition.

§ 163-96. "Political party" defined; creation of new party.

(a) Definition. - A political party within the meaning of the election laws of this State shall be either:

(1) Any group of voters which, at the last preceding general State election, polled for its candidate for Governor, or for presidential electors, at least two percent (2%) of the entire vote cast in the State for Governor or for presidential electors; or

(2) Any group of voters which shall have filed with the State Board of Elections petitions for the formulation of a new political party which are signed by registered and qualified voters in this State equal in number to two percent (2%) of the total number of voters who voted in the most recent general election for Governor. Also the petition must be signed by at least 200 registered voters from each of four congressional districts in North Carolina. To be effective, the petitioners must file their petitions with the State Board of Elections before 12:00 noon on the first day of June preceding the day on which is to be held the first general State election in which the new political party desires to participate. The State Board of Elections shall forthwith determine the sufficiency of petitions filed with it and shall immediately communicate its determination to the State chairman of the proposed new political party.

(b) Petitions for New Political Party. - Petitions for the creation of a new political party shall contain on the heading of each page of the petition in bold print or all in capital letters the words: "THE UNDERSIGNED REGISTERED VOTERS IN ____ COUNTY HEREBY PETITION FOR THE FORMATION OF A NEW POLITICAL PARTY TO BE NAMED ____ AND WHOSE STATE CHAIRMAN IS ____, RESIDING AT ____ AND WHO CAN BE REACHED BY TELEPHONE AT ____."

All printing required to appear on the heading of the petition shall be in type no smaller than 10 point or in all capital letters, double spaced typewriter size. In addition to the form of the petition, the organizers and petition circulators shall inform the signers of the general purpose and intent of the new party.

The petitions must specify the name selected for the proposed political party. The State Board of Elections shall reject petitions for the formation of a new party if the name chosen contains any word that appears in the name of any existing political party recognized in this State or if, in the Board's opinion, the name is so similar to that of an existing political party recognized in this State as to confuse or mislead the voters at an election.

The petitions must state the name and address of the State chairman of the proposed new political party.

(b1)   Each petition shall be presented to the chairman of the board of elections of the county in which the signatures were obtained, and it shall be the chairman's duty:

(1)   To examine the signatures on the petition and place a check mark on the petition by the name of each signer who is qualified and registered to vote in his county.

(2)   To attach to the petition his signed certificate

a.   Stating that the signatures on the petition have been checked against the registration records and

b.   Indicating the number found qualified and registered to vote in his county.

(3)   To return each petition, together with the certificate required by the preceding subdivision, to the person who presented it to him for checking.

The group of petitioners shall submit the petitions to the chairman of the county board of elections in the county in which the signatures were obtained no later than 5:00 P.M. on the fifteenth day preceding the date the petitions are due to be filed with the State Board of Elections as provided in subsection (a)(2) of this section. Provided the petitions are timely submitted, the chairman of the county board of elections shall proceed to examine and verify the signatures under the provisions of this subsection. Verification shall be completed within two weeks from the date such petitions are presented.

(c)   Repealed by Session Laws 1983, c. 576, s. 3. (1901, c. 89, s. 85; Rev., s. 4292; 1915, c. 101, s. 31; 1917, c. 218; C.S., ss. 5913, 6052; 1933, c. 165, ss. 1, 17; 1949, c. 671, ss. 1, 2; 1967, c. 775, s. 1; 1975, c. 179; 1979, c. 411, s. 3; 1981, c. 219, ss. 1-3; 1983, c. 576, ss. 1-3; 1997-456, s. 27; 1999-424, s. 5(a); 2004-127, s. 14; 2006-234, s. 1.)

§ 163-97. Termination of status as political party.

When any political party fails to meet the test set forth in G.S. 163-96(a)(1), it shall cease to be a political party within the meaning of the primary and general election laws and all other provisions of this Chapter. (1901, c. 89, s. 85; Rev., s. 4292; C.S., s. 5913; 1933, c. 165, s. 1; 1949, c. 671, s. 1; 1967, c. 775, s. 1; 2006-234, s. 2.)

§ 163-97.1. Voters affiliated with expired political party.

The State Board of Elections shall be authorized to promulgate appropriate procedures to order the county boards of elections to change the registration affiliation of all voters who are recorded on the voter registration books as being affiliated with a political party which has lost its legal status as provided in G.S. 163-97. The State Board of Elections shall not implement the authority contained in this section earlier than 90 days following the certification of the election in which the political party failed to continue its legal status as provided in G.S. 163-97. All voters affiliated with such expired political party shall be changed to "unaffiliated designation" by the State Board's order and all such registrants shall be entitled to declare a political party affiliation as provided in G.S. 163-82.17. (1975, c. 789; 1977, c. 408, s. 1; 2004-127, s. 10.)

§ 163-98. General election participation by new political party.

In the first general election following the date on which a new political party qualifies under the provisions of G.S. 163-96, it shall be entitled to have the names of its candidates for national, State, congressional, and local offices printed on the official ballots upon paying a filing fee equal to that provided for candidates for the office in G.S. 163-107 or upon complying with the alternative available to candidates for the office in G.S. 163-107.1.

For the first general election following the date on which it qualifies under G.S. 163-96, a new political party shall select its candidates by party convention. Following adjournment of the nominating convention, but not later than the first day of July prior to the general election, the president of the convention shall certify to the State Board of Elections the names of persons chosen in the convention as the new party's candidates in the ensuing general election. Any candidate nominated by a new party shall be affiliated with the party at the time of certification to the State Board of Elections. The requirement of affiliation with the party will be met if the candidate submits at or before the time of certification as a candidate an application to change party affiliation to that party. The State

Board of Elections shall print names thus certified on the appropriate ballots as the nominees of the new party. The State Board of Elections shall send to each county board of elections the list of any new party candidates so that the county board can add those names to the appropriate ballot. (1901, c. 89, s. 85; Rev., s. 4292; C.S., s. 5913; 1933, c. 165, s. 1; 1949, c. 671, s. 1; 1967, c. 775, s. 1; 1979, c. 411, s. 4; 2002-159, s. 55(b); 2006-234, s. 3; 2008-150, s. 10.1(a).)

§ 163-99. Use of schools and other public buildings for political meetings.

The governing authority having control over schools or other public buildings which have facilities for group meetings, or where polling places are located, is hereby authorized and directed to permit the use of such buildings without charge, except custodial and utility fees, by political parties, as defined in G.S. 163-96, for the express purpose of annual or biennial precinct meetings and county and district conventions. Provided, that the use of such buildings by political parties shall not be permitted at times when school is in session or which would interfere with normal school activities or functions normally carried on in such school buildings, and such use shall be subject to reasonable rules and regulations of the school boards and other governing authorities. (1975, c. 465; 1983, c. 519, ss. 1, 2.)

§§ 163-100 through 163-103. Reserved for future codification purposes.

SUBCHAPTER V. NOMINATION OF CANDIDATES.

Article 10.

Primary Elections.

§ 163-104. Primaries governed by general election laws; authority of State Board of Elections to modify time schedule.

Unless otherwise provided in this Chapter, primary elections shall be conducted as far as practicable in accordance with the general election laws of this State. All provisions of this Chapter and of other laws governing elections, not inconsistent with this Article and other provisions of law dealing specifically with primaries, shall apply as fully to primary elections and to the acts and things done thereunder as to general elections. Nevertheless, for purposes of primary elections the State Board of Elections may, by general rule, modify the general election law time schedule with regard to ascertaining, declaring, and reporting results.

All acts made criminal if committed in connection with a general election shall likewise be criminal, with the same punishment, when committed in a primary election held under the provisions of this Chapter. (1915, c. 101, s. 3; 1917, c. 218; C.S., s. 6020; 1967, c. 775, s. 1.)

§ 163-105. Payment of expense of conducting primary elections.

The expense of printing and distributing the poll and registration books, blanks, and ballots for those offices required by G.S. 163-109(b) to be furnished by the State, and the per diem and expenses of the State Board of Elections while engaged in the discharge of primary election duties imposed by law upon that Board, shall be paid by the State.

The expenses of printing and distributing the ballots for those offices required by G.S. 163-109(c) to be furnished by counties, and the per diem (or salary) and expenses of the county board of elections and the chief judges and judges of election, while engaged in the discharge of primary election duties imposed by law upon them, shall be paid by the counties. (1915, c. 101, s. 7; 1917, c. 218; C.S., s. 6026; 1927, c. 260, s. 21; 1933, c. 165, s. 14; 1967, c. 775, s. 1; 1985, c. 563, s. 1; 1993 (Reg. Sess., 1994), c. 762, s. 30.)

§ 163-106. Notices of candidacy; pledge; with whom filed; date for filing; withdrawal.

(a) Notice and Pledge. - No one shall be voted for in a primary election without having filed a notice of candidacy with the appropriate board of elections, State or county, as required by this section. To this end every candidate for selection as the nominee of a political party shall file with and place in the possession of the board of elections specified in subsection (c) of this section, a notice and pledge in the following form:

Date _____

I hereby file notice as a candidate for nomination as _____ in the _____ party primary election to be held on _____, _____ I affiliate with the _____ party, (and I certify that I am now registered on the registration records of the precinct in which I reside as an affiliate of the _____ party.)

I pledge that if I am defeated in the primary, I will not run for the same office as a write-in candidate in the next general election.

Signed _____

(Name of Candidate)

Witness:

_____

_____

(Title of witness)

Each candidate shall sign the notice of candidacy in the presence of the chairman or secretary of the board of elections, State or county, with which the candidate files. In the alternative, a candidate may have the candidate's signature on the notice of candidacy acknowledged and certified to by an officer authorized to take acknowledgments and administer oaths, in which case the candidate may mail or deliver by commercial courier service the candidate's notice of candidacy to the appropriate board of elections.

In signing the notice of candidacy the candidate shall use only that candidate's legal name and may use any nickname by which he is commonly known. A candidate may also, in lieu of that candidate's legal first name and legal middle initial or middle name (if any) sign a nickname, provided that the candidate appends to the notice of candidacy an affidavit that the candidate has been commonly known by that nickname for at least five years prior to the date of making the affidavit. The candidate shall also include with the affidavit the way that candidate's name (as permitted by law) should be listed on the ballot if another candidate with the same last name files a notice of candidacy for that office.

A notice of candidacy signed by an agent or any person other than the candidate shall be invalid.

Prior to the date on which candidates may commence filing, the State Board of Elections shall print and furnish, at State expense, to each county board of elections a sufficient number of the notice of candidacy forms prescribed by this subsection for use by candidates required to file with county boards of elections.

(a1) Disclosure of Felony Conviction. - At the same time the candidate files notice of candidacy under this section, the candidate shall file with the same office a statement answering the following question: "Have you ever been convicted of a felony?" The State Board of Elections shall adapt the notice of candidacy form to include the statement required by this subsection. The form shall make clear that a felony conviction need not be disclosed if the conviction was dismissed as a result of reversal on appeal or resulted in a pardon of innocence or expungement. The form shall require a candidate who answers "yes" to the question to provide the name of the offense, the date of conviction, the date of the restoration of citizenship rights, and the county and state of conviction. The form shall require the candidate to swear or affirm that the statements on the form are true, correct, and complete to the best of the candidate's knowledge or belief. The form shall be available as a public record in the office of the board of elections where the candidate files notice of candidacy and shall contain an explanation that a prior felony conviction does not preclude holding elective office if the candidate's rights of citizenship have been restored. This subsection shall also apply to individuals who become candidates for election by the people under G.S. 163-114, 163-122, 163-123, 163-98, 115C-37, 130A-50, Article 24 of Chapter 163 of the General Statutes, or any other statute or local act. Those individuals shall complete the question at the time the documents are filed initiating their candidacy. The State Board of Elections shall adapt those documents to include the statement required by this subsection. If an individual does not complete the statement required by this subsection, the board of elections accepting the filing shall notify the individual of the omission, and the individual shall have 48 hours after notice to complete the statement. If the individual does not complete the statement at the time of filing or within 48 hours after the notice, the individual's filing is not complete, the individual's name shall not appear on the ballot as a candidate, and votes for the individual shall not be counted. It is a Class I felony to complete the form knowing that information as to felony conviction or restoration of citizenship is untrue. This subsection shall not apply to candidates required by G.S. 138A-22(d) to file Statements of Economic Interest.

(b) Eligibility to File. - No person shall be permitted to file as a candidate in a primary if, at the time he offers to file notice of candidacy, he is registered on the appropriate registration book or record as an affiliate of a political party other than that in whose primary he is attempting to file. No person who has changed his political party affiliation or who has changed from unaffiliated status to party affiliation as permitted in G.S. 163-82.17, shall be permitted to file as a candidate in the primary of the party to which he changed unless he has been affiliated with the political party in which he seeks to be a candidate for at least 90 days prior to the filing date for the office for which he desires to file his notice of candidacy.

A person registered as "unaffiliated" shall be ineligible to file as a candidate in a party primary election.

(c) Time for Filing Notice of Candidacy. - Candidates seeking party primary nominations for the following offices shall file their notice of candidacy with the State Board of Elections no earlier than 12:00 noon on the second Monday in February and no later than 12:00 noon on the last business day in February preceding the primary:

Governor

Lieutenant Governor

All State executive officers

United States Senators

Members of the House of Representatives of the United States

District attorneys

Candidates seeking party primary nominations for the following offices shall file their notice of candidacy with the county board of elections no earlier than 12:00 noon on the second Monday in February and no later than 12:00 noon on the last business day in February preceding the primary:

State Senators

Members of the State House of Representatives

All county offices.

(d)   Notice of Candidacy for Certain Offices to Indicate Vacancy. - In any primary in which there are two vacancies for United States Senator from North Carolina, each candidate shall, at the time of filing notice of candidacy, file with the State Board of Elections a written statement designating the vacancy to which he seeks nomination. Votes cast for a candidate shall be effective only for his nomination to the vacancy for which he has given notice of candidacy as provided in this subsection.

(e)   Withdrawal of Notice of Candidacy. - Any person who has filed notice of candidacy for an office shall have the right to withdraw it at any time prior to the close of business on the third business day prior to the date on which the right to file for that office expires under the terms of subsection (c) of this section. If a candidate does not withdraw before the deadline, except as provided in G.S. 163-112, his name shall be printed on the primary ballot, any votes for him shall be counted, and he shall not be refunded his filing fee.

(f)   Candidates required to file their notice of candidacy with the State Board of Elections under subsection (c) of this section shall file along with their notice a certificate signed by the chairman of the board of elections or the director of elections of the county in which they are registered to vote, stating that the person is registered to vote in that county, stating the party with which the person is affiliated, and that the person has not changed his affiliation from another party or from unaffiliated within three months prior to the filing deadline under subsection (c) of this section. In issuing such certificate, the chairman or director shall check the registration records of the county to verify such information. During the period commencing 36 hours immediately preceding the filing deadline the State Board of Elections shall accept, on a conditional basis, the notice of candidacy of a candidate who has failed to secure the verification ordered herein subject to receipt of verification no later than three days following the filing deadline. The State Board of Elections shall prescribe the form for such certificate, and distribute it to each county board of elections no later than the last Monday in December of each odd-numbered year.

(g)   When any candidate files a notice of candidacy with a board of elections under subsection (c) of this section or under G.S. 163-291(2), the board of elections shall, immediately upon receipt of the notice of candidacy, inspect the registration records of the county, and cancel the notice of candidacy of any person who does not meet the constitutional or statutory qualifications for the office, including residency.

The board shall give notice of cancellation to any candidate whose notice of candidacy has been cancelled under this subsection by mail or by having the notice served on him by the sheriff, and to any other candidate filing for the same office. A candidate who has been adversely affected by a cancellation or another candidate for the same office affected by a substantiation under this subsection may request a hearing on the cancellation. If the candidate requests a hearing, the hearing shall be conducted in accordance with Article 11B of Chapter 163 of the General Statutes.

(h) No person may file a notice of candidacy for more than one office described in subsection (c) of this section for any one election. If a person has filed a notice of candidacy with a board of elections under this section for one office, then a notice of candidacy may not later be filed for any other office under this section when the election is on the same date unless the notice of candidacy for the first office is withdrawn under subsection (e) of this section; provided that this subsection shall not apply unless the deadline for filing notices of candidacy for both offices is the same. Notwithstanding this subsection, a person may file a notice of candidacy for a full term as United States Senator, and also file a notice of candidacy for the remainder of the unexpired term of that same seat in an election held under G.S. 163-12, and may file a notice of candidacy for a full term as a member of the United States House of Representatives, and also file a notice of candidacy for the remainder of the unexpired term in an election held under G.S. 163-13.

(i) Repealed by Session Laws 2001-403, s. 3, effective January 1, 2002. (1915, c. 101, ss. 6, 15; 1917, c. 218; C.S., ss. 6022, 6035; 1921, c. 217; 1923, c. 111, s. 13; C.S., s. 6055(a); 1927, c. 260, s. 19; 1929, c. 26, s. 1; 1933, c. 165, s. 12; 1937, c. 364; 1947, c. 505, s. 7; 1949, c. 672, s. 4; c. 932; 1951, c. 1009, s. 3; 1955, c. 755; c. 871, s. 1; 1959, c. 1203, s. 4; 1965, c. 262; 1967, c. 775, s. 1; c. 1063, s. 2; 1969, c. 44, s. 83; c. 1190, s. 56; 1971, cc. 189, 675, 798; 1973, c. 47, s. 2; c. 793, s. 36; c. 862; 1975, c. 844, s. 2; 1977, c. 265, ss. 4, 5; c. 408, s. 2; c. 661, ss. 2, 3; 1979, c. 24; c. 411, s. 5; 1981, c. 32, ss. 1, 2; 1983, c. 330, s. 1; 1985, c. 472, s. 2; c. 558, s. 1; c. 759, s. 6; 1985 (Reg. Sess., 1986), c. 957, s. 1; 1987, c. 509, s. 13; c. 738, s. 124; 1987 (Reg. Sess., 1988), c. 1028, s. 1; 1993 (Reg. Sess., 1994), c. 762, s. 31; 1995, c. 243, s. 1; 1996, 2nd Ex. Sess., c. 9, s. 8; 1999-456, s. 59; 2001-403, s. 3; 2001-466, s. 5.1(a); 2002-158, ss. 8, 9; 2002-159, s. 55(a); 2006-155, s. 2; 2007-369, s. 1; 2009-47, s. 1; 2013-381, s. 21.1.)

§ 163-107. Filing fees required of candidates in primary; refunds.

(a) Fee Schedule. - At the time of filing a notice of candidacy, each candidate shall pay to the board of elections with which he files under the provisions of G.S. 163-106 a filing fee for the office he seeks in the amount specified in the following tabulation:

Office Sought	Amount of Filing Fee
Governor annual salary of the office sought	One percent (1%) of the
Lieutenant Governor annual salary of the office sought	One percent (1%) of the
All State executive offices annual salary of the office sought	One percent (1%) of the
All District Attorneys of the General salary of	One percent (1%) of the annual
Court of Justice	the office sought
United States Senator annual salary of the office sought	One percent (1%) of the
Members of the United States House annual salary of	One percent (1%) of the
of Representatives	the office sought
State Senator annual salary of the office sought	One percent (1%) of the
Member of the State House of annual salary of	One percent (1%) of the
Representatives	the office sought

All county offices not compensated by fees annual salary of the office sought	One percent (1%) of the
All county offices compensated partly annual	One percent (1%) of the first
by salary and partly by fees (exclusive of fees)	salary to be received

The salary of any office that is the basis for calculating the filing fee is the starting salary for the office, rather than the salary received by the incumbent, if different. If no starting salary can be determined for the office, then the salary used for calculation is the salary of the incumbent, as of January 1 of the election year.

(b) Refund of Fees. - If any person who has filed a notice of candidacy and paid the filing fee prescribed in subsection (a) of this section, withdraws his notice of candidacy within the period prescribed in G.S. 163-106(e), he shall be entitled to have the fee he paid refunded. If the fee was paid to the State Board of Elections, the chairman of that board shall cause a warrant to be drawn on the Treasurer of the State for the refund payment. If the fee was paid to a county board of elections, the chairman of the Board shall certify to the county finance officer that the refund should be made, and the county finance officer shall make the refund in accordance with the provisions of the Local Government Budget and Fiscal Control Act. If any person who has filed a notice of candidacy and paid the filing fee prescribed in subsection (a) of this section dies prior to the date of the primary election provided by G.S. 163-1, the personal representative of the estate shall be entitled to have the fee refunded if application is made to the board of elections to which the fee was paid no later than one year after the date of death, and refund shall be made in the same manner as in withdrawal of notice of candidacy.

If any person files a notice of candidacy and pays a filing fee to a board of elections other than that with which he is required to file under the provisions of G.S. 163-106(e), he shall be entitled to have the fee refunded in the manner prescribed in this subsection if he requests the refund before the date on which the right to file for that office expires under the provisions of G.S. 163-106(e). (1915, c. 101, s. 4; 1917, c. 218; 1919, cc. 50, 139; C.S., ss. 6023, 6024; 1927, c. 260, s. 20; 1933, c. 165, s. 12; 1939, c. 264, s. 2; 1959, c. 1203, s. 5; 1967, c. 775, s. 1; 1969, c. 44, s. 84; 1973, c. 47, s. 2; c. 793, s. 37; 1977, c. 265, s. 6;

1983, c. 913, s. 56; 1995, c. 464, s. 1; 1996, 2nd Ex. Sess., c. 9, s. 9; 2001-403, s. 4; 2002-158, s. 10; 2005-428, s. 8.)

§ 163-107.1. Petition in lieu of payment of filing fee.

(a)   Any qualified voter who seeks nomination in the party primary of the political party with which he affiliates may, in lieu of payment of any filing fee required for the office he seeks, file a written petition requesting him to be a candidate for a specified office with the appropriate board of elections, State, county or municipal.

(b)   If the candidate is seeking the office of United States Senator, Governor, Lieutenant Governor, or any State executive officer, the petition must be signed by 10,000 registered voters who are members of the political party in whose primary the candidate desires to run, except that in the case of a political party as defined by G.S. 163-96(a)(2) which will be making nominations by primary election, the petition must be signed by five percent (5%) of the registered voters of the State who are affiliated with the same political party in whose primary the candidate desires to run, or in the alternative, the petition shall be signed by no less than 8,000 registered voters regardless of the voter's political party affiliation, whichever requirement is greater. The petition must be filed with the State Board of Elections not later than 12:00 noon on Monday preceding the filing deadline before the primary in which he seeks to run. The names on the petition shall be verified by the board of elections of the county where the signer is registered, and the petition must be presented to the county board of elections at least 15 days before the petition is due to be filed with the State Board of Elections. When a proper petition has been filed, the candidate's name shall be printed on the primary ballot.

(c)   County, Municipal and District Primaries. - If the candidate is seeking one of the offices set forth in G.S. 163-106(c) but which is not listed in subsection (b) of this section, or a municipal or any other office requiring a partisan primary which is not set forth in G.S. 163-106(c) or (d), he shall file a written petition with the appropriate board of elections no later than 12:00 noon on Monday preceding the filing deadline before the primary. The petition shall be signed by five percent (5%) of the registered voters of the election area in which the office will be voted for, who are affiliated with the same political party in whose primary the candidate desires to run, or in the alternative, the petition shall be signed by no less than 200 registered voters regardless of said voter's political party affiliation, whichever requirement is greater. The board of elections shall verify the names on the petition, and if the petition is found to be sufficient, the candidate's name shall be printed on the appropriate primary ballot. Petitions for candidates for member of the U.S. House of Representatives, District Attorney, and members of the State House of Representatives from multi-county districts or members of the State Senate from multi-county districts must be presented to the county board of elections for verification at least 15 days before the petition is due to be filed with the State Board of Elections, and such petition must be filed with the State Board of Elections no later than 12:00 noon on Monday preceding the filing deadline. The State Board of Elections may adopt rules to implement this section and to provide standard petition forms.

(d) Nonpartisan Primaries and Elections. - Any qualified voter who seeks to be a candidate in any nonpartisan primary or election may, in lieu of payment of the filing fee required, file a written petition signed by five percent (5%) of the registered voters in the election area in which the office will be voted for with the appropriate board of elections. Any qualified voter may sign the petition. The petition shall state the candidate's name, address and the office which he is seeking. The petition must be filed with the appropriate board of elections no later than 60 days prior to the filing deadline for the primary or election, and if found to be sufficient, the candidate's name shall be printed on the ballot. (1975, c. 853; 1977, c. 386; 1985, c. 563, s. 13; 1996, 2nd Ex. Sess., c. 9, s. 12; 2001-403, s. 7; 2002-158, s. 11; 2013-381, s. 22.1.)

§ 163-108. Certification of notices of candidacy.

(a) Within three days after the time for filing notices of candidacy with the State Board of Elections under the provisions of G.S. 163-106(c) has expired, the chairman or secretary of that Board shall certify to the Secretary of State the name, address, and party affiliation of each person who has filed with the State Board of Elections, indicating in each instance the office sought.

(b) No later than 10 days after the time for filing notices of candidacy under the provisions of G.S. 163-106(c) has expired, the chairman of the State Board of Elections shall certify to the chairman of the county board of elections in each county in the appropriate district the names of candidates for nomination to the following offices who have filed the required notice and pledge and paid the required filing fee to the State Board of Elections, so that their names may be printed on the official county ballots: Superior court judge, district court judge, and district attorney.

(c) In representative districts composed of more than one county and in multi-county senatorial districts the chairman or secretary of the county board of elections in each county shall, within three days after the time for filing notices of candidacy under the provisions of G.S. 163-106(c) has expired, certify to the State Board of Elections (i) the names of all candidates who have filed notice of candidacy in his county for member of the State Senate, or, if such is the fact, that no candidates have filed in his county for that office, and (ii) the names of all candidates who have filed notice of candidacy in his county for the office of member of the State House of Representatives or, if such is the fact, that no candidates have filed in his county for that office. The chairman of the county board of elections shall forward a copy of this report to the chairman of the board of elections of each of the other counties in the representative or senatorial district. Within 10 days after the time for filing notices of candidacy for those offices has expired the chairman or secretary of the State Board of Elections shall certify to the chairman of the county board of elections in each county of each multi-county representative or senatorial district the names of all candidates for the House of Representatives and Senate which must be printed on the county ballots.

(d) Within two days after he receives each of the letters of certification from the chairman of the State Board of Elections required by subsections (b) and (c) of this section, each county elections board chairman shall acknowledge receipt by letter addressed to the chairman of the State Board of Elections. (1915, c. 101, s. 8; 1917, c. 218; C.S., s. 6028; 1927, c. 260, s. 22; 1966, Ex. Sess., c. 5, s. 8; 1967, c. 775, s. 1; 1973, c. 793, s. 38; 1979, c. 797, s. 5; 1983, c. 331, s. 1.)

§ 163-108.1. Nomination of members of House of Representatives.

Chapter 826, Session Laws of 1957; Chapter 484, Session Laws of 1961; Chapter 621, Session Laws of 1959; Chapter 894, Session Laws of 1945; Chapter 442, Session Laws of 1955; Chapter 103, Public-Local Laws of 1941; Chapter 439, Session Laws of 1955; Chapter 238, Session Laws of 1959; and all other special and local acts providing for the nomination of candidates for the State House of Representatives by convention in any county, are modified and amended as follows: In the several representative districts of the State containing two or more counties, each political party shall nominate candidates for membership in the State House of Representatives according to the provisions of the statewide primary law, Article 19 [Article 10], Chapter 163 of the General Statutes of North Carolina, or by district convention of the party when so provided by law. In a county assigned to a multi-county representative district, no political party shall nominate candidates for the State House of Representatives by party convention for the single county. (1966, Ex. Sess., c. 5, s. 16.)

§ 163-109: Repealed by Session Laws 2002-159, s. 55.(j), effective January 1, 2003, and applicable to all primaries and elections held on or after that date.

§ 163-110. Candidates declared nominees without primary.

If a nominee for a single office is to be selected and only one candidate of a political party files for that office, or if nominees for two or more offices (constituting a group) are to be selected, and only the number of candidates equal to the number of the positions to be filled file for a political party for said offices, then the appropriate board of elections shall, upon the expiration of the filing period for said office, declare such persons as the nominees or nominee of that party, and the names shall not be printed on the primary ballot, but shall be printed on the general election ballot as candidate for that political party for that office. For the following offices, this declaration shall be made by the county board of elections with which the aspirant filed notice of candidacy: All county offices, State Senators in single-county senatorial districts, and members of the State House of Representatives in single-county representative districts. For all other offices, this declaration shall be made by the State Board of Elections. (1915, c. 101, ss. 13, 19; 1917, c. 218; C.S., ss. 6033, 6039; 1966, Ex. Sess., c. 5, ss. 9, 11; 1967, c. 775, s. 1; 1973, c. 793, s. 42; 1975, c. 19, s. 68; 1981, c. 220, ss. 1, 2.)

§ 163-111. Determination of primary results; second primaries.

(a) Nomination Determined by Substantial Plurality; Definition of Substantial Plurality. - Except as otherwise provided in this section, nominations in primary elections shall be determined by a substantial plurality of the votes cast. A substantial plurality within the meaning of this section shall be determined as follows:

(1) If a nominee for a single office is to be selected, and there is more than one person seeking nomination, the substantial plurality shall be ascertained by

multiplying the total vote cast for all aspirants by forty percent (40%). Any excess of the sum so ascertained shall be a substantial plurality, and the aspirant who obtains a substantial plurality shall be declared the nominee. If two candidates receive a substantial plurality, the candidate receiving the highest vote shall be declared the nominee.

(2)   If nominees for two or more offices (constituting a group) are to be selected, and there are more persons seeking nomination than there are offices, the substantial plurality shall be ascertained by dividing the total vote cast for all aspirants by the number of positions to be filled, and by multiplying the result by forty percent (40%). Any excess of the sum so ascertained shall be a substantial plurality, and the aspirants who obtain a substantial plurality shall be declared the nominees. If more candidates obtain a substantial plurality than there are positions to be filled, those having the highest vote (equal to the number of positions to be filled) shall be declared the nominees.

(b)   Right to Demand Second Primary. - If an insufficient number of aspirants receive a substantial plurality of the votes cast for a given office or group of offices in a primary, a second primary, subject to the conditions specified in this section, shall be held:

(1)   If a nominee for a single office is to be selected and no aspirant receives a substantial plurality of the votes cast, the aspirant receiving the highest number of votes shall be declared nominated by the appropriate board of elections unless the aspirant receiving the second highest number of votes shall request a second primary in accordance with the provisions of subsection (c) of this section. In the second primary only the two aspirants who received the highest and next highest number of votes shall be voted for.

(2)   If nominees for two or more offices (constituting a group) are to be selected and aspirants for some or all of the positions within the group do not receive a substantial plurality of the votes, those candidates equal in number to the positions remaining to be filled and having the highest number of votes shall be declared the nominees unless some one or all of the aspirants equal in number to the positions remaining to be filled and having the second highest number of votes shall request a second primary in accordance with the provisions of subsection (c) of this section. In the second primary to select nominees for the positions in the group remaining to be filled, the names of all those candidates receiving the highest number of votes and all those receiving the second highest number of votes and demanding a second primary shall be printed on the ballot.

(c) Procedure for Requesting Second Primary. -

(1) A candidate who is apparently entitled to demand a second primary, according to the unofficial results, for one of the offices listed below, and desiring to do so, shall file a request for a second primary in writing with the Executive Director of the State Board of Elections no later than 12:00 noon on the ninth day (including Saturdays and Sundays) following the date on which the primary was conducted, and such request shall be subject to the certification of the official results by the State Board of Elections. If the vote certification by the State Board of Elections determines that a candidate who was not originally thought to be eligible to call for a second primary is in fact eligible to call for a second primary, the Executive Director of the State Board of Elections shall immediately notify such candidate and permit him to exercise any options available to him within a 48-hour period following the notification:

Governor,

Lieutenant Governor,

All State executive officers,

District Attorneys of the General Court of Justice,

United States Senators,

Members of the United States House of Representatives,

State Senators in multi-county senatorial districts, and

Members of the State House of Representatives in multi-county representative districts.

(2) A candidate who is apparently entitled to demand a second primary, according to the unofficial results, for one of the offices listed below and desiring to do so, shall file a request for a second primary in writing with the chairman or director of the county board of elections no later than 12:00 noon on the ninth day (including Saturdays and Sundays) following the date on which the primary was conducted, and such request shall be subject to the certification of the official results by the county board of elections:

State Senators in single-county senatorial districts,

Members of the State House of Representatives in single-county representative districts, and

All county officers.

(3) Immediately upon receipt of a request for a second primary the appropriate board of elections, State or county, shall notify all candidates entitled to participate in the second primary, by telephone followed by written notice, that a second primary has been requested and of the date of the second primary.

(d) Tie Votes; How Determined. -

(1) In the event of a tie for the highest number of votes in a first primary between two candidates for party nomination for a single county, or single-county legislative district office, the board of elections of the county in which the two candidates were voted for shall conduct a recount and declare the results. If the recount shows a tie vote, a second primary shall be held on the date prescribed in subsection (e) of this section between the two candidates having an equal vote, unless one of the aspirants, within three days after the result of the recount has been officially declared, files a written notice of withdrawal with the board of elections with which he filed notice of candidacy. Should that be done, the remaining aspirant shall be declared the nominee. In the event of a tie for the highest number of votes in a first primary among more than two candidates for party nomination for one of the offices mentioned in this subdivision, no recount shall be held, but all of the tied candidates shall be entered in a second primary.

(2) In the event of a tie for the highest number of votes in a first primary between two candidates for a State office, for United States Senator, or for any district office (including State Senator in a multi-county senatorial district and member of the State House of Representatives in a multi-county representative district), no recount shall be held solely by reason of the tie, but the two candidates having an equal vote shall be entered in a second primary to be held on the date prescribed in subsection (e) of this section, unless one of the two candidates files a written notice of withdrawal with the State Board of Elections within three days after the result of the first primary has been officially declared and published. Should that be done, the remaining aspirant shall be declared the nominee. In the event of a tie for the highest number of votes in a first primary among more than two candidates for party nomination for one of the

offices mentioned in this subdivision, no recount shall be held, but all of the tied candidates shall be entered in a second primary.

(3) In the event one candidate receives the highest number of votes cast in a first primary, but short of a substantial plurality, and two or more of the other candidates receive the second highest number of votes cast in an equal number, the proper board of elections shall declare the candidate having the highest vote to be the party nominee, unless all but one of the tied candidates give written notice of withdrawal to the proper board of elections within three days after the result of the first primary has been officially declared. If all but one of the tied candidates withdraw within the prescribed three-day period, and the remaining candidate demands a second primary in accordance with the provisions of subsection (c) of this section, a second primary shall be held between the candidate who received the highest vote and the remaining candidate who received the second highest vote.

(e) Date of Second Primary; Procedures. - If a second primary is required under the provisions of this section, the appropriate board of elections, State or county, shall order that it be held 10 weeks after the first primary if any of the offices for which a second primary is required are for a candidate for the office of United States Senate or member of the United States House of Representatives. Otherwise, the second primary shall be held seven weeks after the first primary.

There shall be no registration of voters between the dates of the first and second primaries. Persons whose qualifications to register and vote mature after the day of the first primary and before the day of the second primary may register on the day of the second primary and, when thus registered, shall be entitled to vote in the second primary. The second primary is a continuation of the first primary and any voter who files a proper and timely written affirmation of change of address within the county under the provisions of G.S. 163-82.15, in the first primary may vote in the second primary without having to refile that written affirmation if the voter is otherwise qualified to vote in the second primary. Subject to this provision for registration, the second primary shall be held under the laws, rules, and regulations provided for the first primary.

(f) No Third Primary Permitted. - In no case shall there be a third primary. The candidates receiving the highest number of votes in the second primary shall be nominated. If in a second primary there is a tie for the highest number of votes between two candidates, the proper party executive committee shall select the party nominee for the office in accordance with the provisions of G.S.

163-114. (1915, c. 101, s. 24; 1917, c. 179, s. 2; c. 218; C.S., s. 6045; 1927, c. 260, s. 23; 1931, c. 254, s. 17; 1959, c. 1055; 1961, c. 383; 1966, Ex. Sess., c. 5, s. 13; 1967, c. 775, s. 1; 1969, c. 44, s. 85; 1973, c. 47, s. 2; c. 793, ss. 43, 44; 1975, c. 844, s. 3; 1977, c. 265, s. 9; 1981, c. 645, ss. 1, 2; 1989, c. 549; 1995, c. 243, s. 1; 1996, 2nd Ex. Sess., c. 9, s. 10; 1999-424, s. 7(e); 2001-319, s. 11; 2001-403, s. 5; 2002-158, s. 12; 2003-278, s. 10(d); 2006-192, s. 2; 2011-182, s. 4.)

§ 163-112. Death of candidate before primary; vacancy in single office.

(a) Death of One of Two Candidates within 30 Days after the Filing Period Closes. - If at the time the filing period closes, only two persons have filed notice of candidacy for nomination by a political party to a single office, and one of the candidates dies within 30 days after the filing period closes, then the proper board of elections shall, upon notice of the death, reopen the filing period for that party contest, for an additional three days. Should no candidate file during the three days, the board of elections shall certify the remaining candidate as the nominee of his party as provided in G.S. 163-110.

(b) Death of One of More Than Two Candidates within 30 Days after the Filing Period Closes. - If at the close of the filing period more than two candidates have filed for a single-seat office, and within 30 days after the filing period closes the board of elections receives notice of a candidate's death, the board shall immediately open the filing period for that party contest, for three additional days in order for candidates to file for that office. The name of the deceased candidate shall not be printed on the ballot.

In the event a candidate's death occurs more than 30 days after the closing of the original filing period, the names of the remaining candidates shall be printed on the ballot. If the ballots have been printed at the time death occurs, the ballots shall not be reprinted and any votes cast for a deceased candidate shall not be counted or considered for any purpose. In the event the death of a candidate or candidates leaves only one candidate, then such candidate shall be certified as the party's nominee for that office.

(c) Vacancy in Group Offices within 30 Days after the Filing Period Closes. - If at the time the filing period closes more persons have filed notice of candidacy for nomination by a political party to an office constituting a group than there are positions to be filled, and a candidate or candidates die within 30 days after the filing period closes, and there remains only the number of candidates equal to or fewer than the number of positions to be filled, the appropriate board of elections shall reopen the filing period for that party contest, for three days for that office. Should no persons file during the three-day period, then those candidates already filed shall be certified as the party nominees for that office.

(d)   Vacancy in Group Offices More Than 30 Days after the Filing Period Closes. - In the event a candidate or candidates death occurs more than 30 days after the original filing period closes for an office constituting a group, then regardless of the number of candidates filed for nomination, the board of elections shall be governed as follows:

(1)   If the ballots have not been printed at the time the board of elections receives notice of the death, the deceased candidate's name shall not be printed on the ballot.

(2)   If the ballots have been printed at the time the board of elections receives notice of the death, the ballots shall not be reprinted but votes cast for the deceased candidate shall not be counted for any purpose.

(3)   In the event the death of a candidate or candidates results in the number of candidates being equal to or less than the number of positions to be filled for that office, then the remaining candidates shall be certified as the party nominees for that office and no primary shall be held for that office.

(4)   If death or disqualification of candidates results in the number of candidates being less than the number of positions to be filled for that office, then the appropriate party executive committee shall, in accordance with G.S. 163-114, make nominations of persons equal to the number of positions to be filled and no primary shall be held and those names shall be printed on the general election ballot.(1959, c. 1054; 1967, c. 775, s. 1; 1981, c. 434; 1993, c. 553, s. 60; 2001-466, s. 1(f); 2003-278, s. 4; 2003-434, 1st Ex. Sess., s. 5(e); 2004-127, s. 13.)

§ 163-113. Nominee's right to withdraw as candidate.

A person who has been declared the nominee of a political party for a specified office under the provisions of G.S. 163-182.15 or G.S. 163-110, shall not be permitted to resign as a candidate unless, prior to the first day on which military and overseas absentee ballots are transmitted to voters under Article 21A of this Chapter, that [the] person submits to the board of elections which certified the nomination a written request that person be permitted to withdraw. (1929, c. 164, s. 8; 1967, c. 775, s. 1; 2001-398, s. 6; 2013-381, s. 23.1.)

§ 163-114. Filling vacancies among party nominees occurring after nomination and before election.

If any person nominated as a candidate of a political party for one of the offices listed below (either in a primary or convention or by virtue of having no opposition in a primary) dies, resigns, or for any reason becomes ineligible or disqualified before the date of the ensuing general election, the vacancy shall be filled by appointment according to the following instructions:

Position	
President	Vacancy is to be filled by appointment of
Vice President	national executive committee of political party in which vacancy occurs
Presidential elector or alternate elector	Vacancy is to be filled by appointment of
Any elective State office	State executive committee of political party in which vacancy occurs
United States Senator	
A district office, including:	Appropriate district executive committee of political party in which vacancy occurs
Member of the United States House	

of Representatives

District Attorney

State Senator in a multi-county

senatorial district

Member of State House of

Representatives in a multi-county

representative district

State Senator in a single-county political	County executive committee of
senatorial district	party in which vacancy occurs,
Member of State House of State	provided, in the case of the
Representatives in a single-county Representative in a	Senator or State
representative district all the	single-county district where not
Any elective county office then in	county is located in that district,
the	voting, only those members of
who reside	county executive committee
	within the district shall vote

302

The party executive making a nomination in accordance with the provisions of this section shall certify the name of its nominee to the chairman of the board of elections, State or county, that has jurisdiction over the ballot item under G.S. 163-182.4. If at the time a nomination is made under this section the general election ballots have already been printed, the provisions of G.S.163-165.3(c) shall apply. If a vacancy occurs in a nomination of a political party and that vacancy arises from a cause other than death and the vacancy in nomination occurs more than 120 days before the general election, the vacancy in nomination may be filled under this section only if the appropriate executive committee certifies the name of the nominee in accordance with this paragraph at least 75 days before the general election.

In a county not all of which is located in one congressional district, in choosing the congressional district executive committee member or members from that area of the county, only the county convention delegates or county executive committee members who reside within the area of the county which is within the congressional district may vote.

In a county which is partly in a multi-county senatorial district or which is partly in a multi-county House of Representatives district, in choosing that county's member or members of the senatorial district executive committee or House of Representatives district executive committee for the multi-county district, only the county convention delegates or county executive committee members who reside within the area of the county which is within that multi-county district may vote.

An individual whose name appeared on the ballot in a primary election preliminary to the general election shall not be eligible to be nominated to fill a vacancy in the nomination of another party for the same office in the same year. (1929, c. 164, s. 19; 1967, c. 775, s. 1; 1973, c. 793, s. 45; 1981 (Reg. Sess., 1982), c. 1265, ss. 4, 5; 1987, c. 509, s. 10; c. 526; c. 738, s. 124; 1987 (Reg. Sess., 1988), c. 1037, s. 126.1; 1991, c. 727, s. 8; 1996, 2nd Ex. Sess., c. 9, s. 13; 2001-353, s. 1; 2001-403, s. 8; 2001-460, s. 4; 2003-142, s. 1; 2006-234, s. 6.)

§ 163-115. Special provisions for obtaining nominations when vacancies occur in certain offices.

(a) If a vacancy occurs in the office of the clerk of superior court, otherwise than by expiration of the term, or if the people fail to elect, the vacancy shall be filled as provided in Sec. 9(3) of Article IV of the North Carolina Constitution. If the vacancy occurs after the time for filing notice of candidacy in the primary has expired in a year when a regular election is not being held to elect a clerk of the superior court by expiration of term, then the county executive committee of each political party shall nominate a candidate whose name shall appear on the general election ballot. The candidate elected in the general election shall serve the unexpired portion of the term of the person causing the vacancy.

(b) In the event a special election is called to fill a vacancy in the State's delegation in the United States House of Representatives, the provisions of G.S. 163-13 shall apply.

(c) If a vacancy occurs in an elective State or district office (other than member of the United States House of Representatives) during the period opening 10 days before the filing period for the office ends and closing 30 days before the ensuing general election, a nomination shall be made by the proper executive committee of each political party as provided in G.S. 163-114, and the names of the nominees shall be printed on the general election ballots.

(d) If a vacancy occurs on a county board of commissioners and G.S. 153A-27 or G.S. 153A-27.1 requires that a person shall be elected to the seat vacated for the remainder of the unexpired term, and the vacancy occurs:

(1) Beginning on the tenth day before the filing period ends under G.S. 163-106(c), a nomination shall be made by the county executive committee of each political party and the names of the nominees shall be printed on the general election ballots.

(2) Prior to the tenth day before the filing period ends under G.S. 163-106(c), nominations shall be made by primary election as provided by this Article.

(e) If a vacancy occurs in the office of United States Senator, and the vacancy occurs:

(1) Beginning on the tenth day before the filing period ends under G.S. 163-106(c), a nomination shall be made by the State executive committee of each political party and the names of the nominees shall be printed on the general election ballots.

(2) Prior to the tenth day before the filing period ends under G.S. 163-106(c), nominations shall be made by primary election as provided by this Article. (1915, c. 101, s. 33; 1917, c. 179, s. 3; c. 218; C.S., s. 6053; 1923, c. 111, s. 16; 1955, c. 574; 1957, c. 1242; 1966, Ex. Sess., c. 5, s. 14; 1967, c. 775, s. 1; 1973, c. 793, s. 46; 1985, c. 563, ss. 7, 7.1; c. 759, s. 1; 1997-456, s. 27.)

§§ 163-116 through 163-118. Repealed by Session Laws 1973, c. 793, ss. 47-49.

§ 163-119. Voting by unaffiliated voter in party primary.

If a political party has, by action of its State Executive Committee reported to the State Board of Elections by resolution delivered no later than the first day of December preceding a primary, provided that unaffiliated voters may vote in the primary of that party, an unaffiliated voter may vote in the primary of that party by announcing that intention under G.S. 163-166.7(a). For a party to withdraw its permission, it must do so by action of its State Executive Committee, similarly reported to the State Board of Elections no later than the first day of December preceding the primary where the withdrawal is to become effective. (1993 (Reg. Sess., 1994), c. 762, s. 7; 2002-159, s. 21(a).)

§ 163-120. Reserved for future codification purposes.

§ 163-121. Reserved for future codification purposes.

Vision Books Order Form

Fax Orders: 1-980-299-5965

Phone Orders: 1-704-898-0770

E-mail Orders: www.visionbooks.org

Mail Orders: Vision Books, LLC
P.O. Box 42406
Charlotte, NC 28215

Shipp To:
Name_____
Address_____
City_____State_____Zip_____
Phone_____Fax_____
Email_____@_____

Bill To: We can bill a third party on your behalf.
Name_____
Address_____
City_____State_____Zip_____
Phone____(_____)_____Fax_____
Email_____@_____

Pamphlet Number ($15.00 Each)	Qty	Total Cost
_____	_____	_____
_____	_____	_____
_____	_____	_____
_____	_____	_____
_____	_____	_____
_____	_____	_____
_____	_____	_____
_____	_____	_____
<u>Full Volume Set 1-92</u>	<u>92 Pamphlets</u>	<u>1,380.00</u>

Free Shipping & Handling on Full Volume Orders
Add $1.00 Shipping & Handling Per Pamphlet $_____

Total Cost $_____

Thank you for your support. Management!

DID YOU ENJOY THIS BOOK?

Vision Books, LLC would like to hear from you! If you or someone you know has been fasely imprisoned, we would like to hear your story. If the 'North Carolina Criminal Law and Procedure' has had an effect in your life or if you have suggestions, we would like to hear from you. Send your letters to:

Vision Books, LLC
Attn: Staff Writers
P.O. Box 42406
Charlotte, NC 28215
Email: staff@visionbooks.org

Order Additional Copies:

Fax Orders:	1-980-299-5965
Phone Orders:	1-704-898-0770
E-mail Orders:	www.visionbooks.org
Mail Orders:	Vision Books, LLC P.O. Box 42406 Charlotte, NC 28215

www.ingramcontent.com/pod-product-compliance
Lightning Source LLC
Chambersburg PA
CBHW051627170526
45167CB00001B/91